BLACK GHOST OF EMPIRE

THE LONG DEATH OF SLAVERY
AND THE FAILURE OF EMANCIPATION

KRIS MANJAPRA

SCRIBNER
New York   London   Toronto   Sydney   New Delhi

Scribner

An Imprint of Simon & Schuster, Inc.
1230 Avenue of the Americas
New York, NY 10020

First Scribner trade paperback edition February 2023

SCRIBNER and design are registered trademarks of The Gale Group, Inc., used under license by
Simon & Schuster, Inc., the publisher of this work.

For information about special discounts for bulk purchases, please contact
Simon & Schuster Special Sales at 1-866-506-1949 or business@simonandschuster.com.

The Simon & Schuster Speakers Bureau can bring authors to your live event. For more information
or to book an event, contact the Simon & Schuster Speakers Bureau at
1-866-248-3049 or visit our website at www.simonspeakers.com.

Interior design by Wendy Blum

Manufactured in the United States of America

1   3   5   7   9   10   8   6   4   2

Library of Congress Cataloging-in-Publication Data

Names: Manjapra, Kris, 1978– author.
Title: Black ghost of empire : the long death of slavery and the failure of emancipation / Kris Manjapra.
Description: New York : Scribner, 2022. | Includes bibliographical references and index.
Identifiers: LCCN 2021059433 | ISBN 9781982123475 (hardcover) | ISBN 9781982123505 (ebook)
Subjects: LCSH: Liberty—Case studies. | Race relations—Case studies. | Slavery—Political aspects. | BISAC:
HISTORY / African American & Black | HISTORY /United States / General
Classification: LCC HM1266 .M38 2022 | DDC 306.3/620973—dc23/eng/20220104

LC record available at https://lccn.loc.gov/2021059433

ISBN 978-1-9821-2347-5
ISBN 978-1-9821-2349-9 (pbk)
ISBN 978-1-9821-2350-5 (ebook)

To Jeanile and Laurenna,
my mothers

and that was Emancipation—

jubilation, O jubilation—
vanishing swiftly
as the sea's lace dries in the sun,

but that was not History

—Derek Walcott,
"The Sea Is History" (1979)

CONTENTS

CONTENTS

NOTE ON TERMINOLOGY

I use the terms *black people* and *African people* interchangeably. When I refer to African people, I mean people of the global African diaspora, whether located in the continent of Africa or in countries around the world. Black people, in my usage, also refers to the global presence of Africans. The machinations of slavery and colonialism have sought to divide and separate African communities over more than five hundred years. The interchangeable use of *black* and *African* in this book points to the shared experience that persists through the divisions.

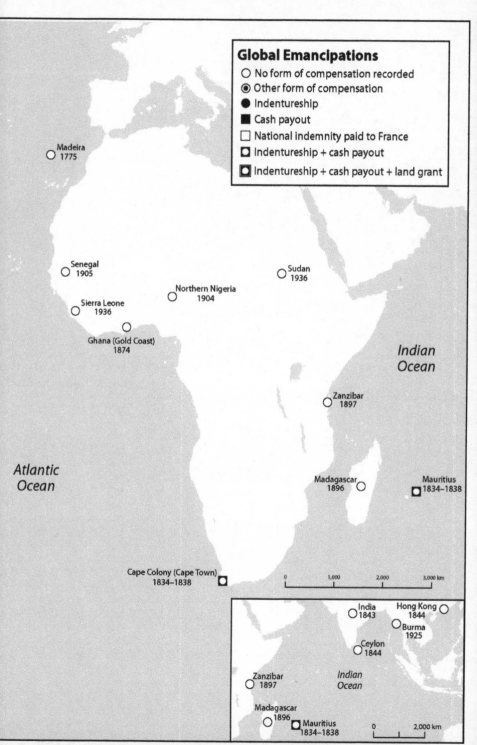

Map design by Patrick Florance & Carolyn Talmadge, Research Technology, TTS, Tufts University.

BLACK
GHOST
OF
EMPIRE

INTRODUCTION

EMANCIPATION AND THE VOID

The Bahamas, place of my birth, is a Caribbean nation-state of some seven hundred islands and cays extending like vertebrae along the southern rim of the Sargasso Sea. Andros Island, the largest of the chain, is surrounded by tidal flats, coral reefs, karst formations, and lime muds along its rubble coasts. Atlantic waters undulate and crash at its shores, but they also penetrate into its pine-covered and craggy interior, burrowing deep cylindrical holes into the carbonate bedrock of the landscape. The island itself is pockmarked and eaten through by the alien sea. The last time I visited Andros, I was seeking to fill a void—a hole—in my family history. The island taught me something important about the presence inside voids, and my relationship to them.

The void is the most succinct encapsulation of Atlantic slavery and its ongoing afterlife. Five hundred years of racial slavery designated African-descended peoples as devoid of human value. It stripped them of their personal and family names, obliterated their kinship ties, and assigned them a market price as atomized pieces of human property. Slavery swallowed millions of Africans into the bellies of ships, enumerated and inventoried them, transported them across the seas, and spat them out into slave markets across the Americas and Europe. It was an incalculably traumatic system of genocide, tearing families apart and alienating people from their own sense of themselves; forcing them to reconstruct life, joy, and family again and again. Slavery constituted a centuries-long war against African peoples. And the emancipations—the acts meant to end slavery—only extended the war forward in time.

Voids are complex because they are nothing at all, and yet everything at once. Inside the void, black people reconstituted life, kin, and community amid the terrorization and destruction of slavery and the plantation regime. They created new art and meaning in and beyond the hole of the ship and the void of the slave price. The enslaved rebelled and fled, tended to their ancestors, and fed and nourished their children. They saved money, organized political movements and strikes, and constructed communities of mutual care and succor. They loved. They celebrated and rejoiced and made space for their own liberation from within slavery's trap.

I began my trip on the northern Andros coast of the Bahamas in a town where my ancestors participated in the establishment of a free black village in the aftermath of Britain's abolition of maritime trafficking in enslaved people in 1807. "Free villages" sprang up across many of the British Caribbean islands, especially after Britain's abolition of plantation slavery in 1838, as black people remade their communities in the wake of slavery. At the village of Mastik Point, Alexander Bain, a mixed-race son of a large-scale white slave-owner, established one of many "Bain towns," in which he apportioned plots of land to the freed people, some of whom were rescued directly from slave ships. The freed people used the land to build small homes, keep subsistence plots, and anchor their fishing boats. In the postslavery period, the people of Mastik Point were buffeted by the currents of oppression and reenslavement that continued after, and because of, emancipation. Illegal trafficking in abducted people from Africa to the Bahamas continued all the way up until the 1880s, more than seventy years after the British abolition of the slave trade. Throughout the late nineteenth century, the Bahamian coast served as an important port for global human trafficking. Portuguese and Spanish ships, alongside ships from Baltimore and Boston, moored themselves along these shoals as a first point of entry into the slave markets of the Caribbean. From the Bahamian carapace, slaving vessels sailed farther on to the Mississippi Cotton Kingdom, to the sugar island of Cuba, and to the coffee plantations of Brazil.[1]

The rumor in my family is that my great-great-great-grandmother, Laurenna Woodside, survived the horror of a slave ship chartered from Luanda, Angola, sometime in the 1880s. The story is full of voids, as I don't know where in western or central Africa she was kidnapped from, or how she ended up in Mastik Point to make a life with other people descended from African captives. She married a black seaman named Ezekiel. Laurenna died at age nineteen after giving birth to her second child. I came to Andros because these meager details beckoned me. I consulted birth and marriage registries. I met with distant family members and traveled between villages along the northern coast. And what I encountered was not historical detail, but historical void. None of the elder villagers I met remembered Laurenna because she had passed away a generation before the oldest among them was born. My family's history of slavery traces, in its gaps, the obliteration of kinship ties committed by the weapon of slave ships.

Before I departed Andros, a friend took me to one of the island's blue holes. These are deep columns of water that descend into the limestone bedrock. Some even connect through subterranean caves directly out to the ocean. Standing at the edge of this blue hole, I noticed the pool's darkness and stillness making the surface into a perfect mirror for the surrounding pine trees and the intense blue sky. It looked like a portal, or a channel, into the unknown and the submarine. On the edge of that geological enigma, I reflected on how my encounter with the void of my family's history had some relationship with the experience of peering into this blue hole. When it comes to histories that arise from the trauma of Atlantic slavery, voids and negations indicate both absence *and* some other, obscure submerged presence that calls to be known. As I walked around the pool, I felt compelled to tend to something, cross over into something, attune myself to what could not be seen but was present nonetheless. It struck me that this was, in a way, like our relationship to history itself—history filled with assorted unknowns and unclaimed experiences that call out from the voids.[2]

THE GHOST LINE

W. E .B. Du Bois, the Pan-Africanist philosopher, proposed in 1900 that "the problem of the twentieth century is the problem of the color-line."[3] The struggles for human rights and civil rights, and their intersections with the battle for gender rights and environmental rights, continue to be life-and-death issues of our times. In addition to the color line, the problem of the twenty-first century, I believe, is also the problem of the *ghost line*. This ghost line separates the history of Man from the history of his voids. Societies draw veils to divide the realm of the seen and remembered from the realm of the systemically erased and disavowed. If the color line creates racial divides to oppress and dispossess, the ghost line creates existential divides between being and nothingness; between those said to be present and those designated as society's present-absences.[4]

To ghost someone is to ignore them, to see through them, and to look past them. To ghostline a people's history is to systematically ignore the meaning of their collective experience, generation after generation, century after century.[5] Ghostlining, as distinct from colorlining or from redlining, is the cunning practice, adopted by whole societies, of "unseeing" the plundered parts, and "unhearing" their historical demands for reparative justice.[6]

The ghosts in our social order are the misrecognized, the disavowed, and the ignored historical presences among us. "Ghostly matter" is actively produced from social trauma and denial.[7] Because of slavery and colonialism, certain human groups have been made into "[phantoms] in other people's eyes."[8] As Ralph Ellison diagnosed in *Invisible Man*, ghosted people are made into the "personification of the Negative," and into the "amorphous thing." They are told "you don't exist," and that their history is not substantial enough to remember and to call *human* history.[9] Ghostlined experience is its own kind of trap, which affects everything to do with daily life, including access to food, housing, education, civic protections, and the vote. The political line between the remembered and the disavowed causes ills for everyone involved: victims, perpetrators, and beneficiaries.

EMANCIPATIONS BY COMPARISON

Historians have focused, understandably, on the narratives of the abolition of slavery—on a story of endings. Highly respected historical schools, perhaps most associated with the work of Seymour Drescher, highlight the efforts of white abolitionists across the Atlantic, and the antislavery campaigns they waged. In Drescher's view, European and Euro-American abolitionist sentiment and political commitment, from the late 1700s to the early 1900s, represent "global achievements," providing the architecture for present-day ideas of human rights.[10] This view, however, obscures that when white societies actually began *implementing* their antislavery ideas, they did so in ways that prolonged and extended the captivity and oppression of black people around the world. The politicians, administrators, and social elites who implemented emancipation established a historical manual for how to breach human rights. They withdrew justice from the historical victims and appeased the perpetrators. If anything, the very way we think of "the human," and who counts as human, has emerged as a centuries-long struggle because of the way abolitions were carried out.

The laws and policies that, together, we call "emancipation" transformed abolitionist ideas into abolition as a social fact. As we will see, the emancipation processes across many societies—in the form of laws, policies, and institutions—aggravated slavery's historical trauma and extended white supremacist rule and antiblackness. Emancipations conserved and then reactivated the racial caste system of slavery, putting it to new uses that still structure the disequilibrium of life chances in our present societies.

When history writing focuses only on abolition—and the "ending" of slavery—the half is not told. Histories that tell us the hurt is over, that abolitionist achievements endure, disregard the reality of ongoing racial oppressions. What happened after slavery ended, in the legal and procedural aftermaths called "emancipation," and in the rebellious self-liberations of black communities, matters for the work of reparative justice. Reparative justice demands ways of retelling the past that detect the voices previously consigned to the archival void; and of rewriting history in ways that matter to those voices and that make those voices matter to us.

Emancipations provided a failed pathway to justice, just as they were designed to do. This failure was not accidental, but systematic.[11] It was not the result of faulty implementation, but of careful planning and international coordination among European and American states over many generations. As we shall see, the governments and political elites in charge of emancipation processes around the world in the eighteenth and nineteenth centuries designed laws and policies to incarcerate, deport, indebt, and imperil the freedom of African peoples. Ideas about property rights, the sources of economic value, the bounds of democracy and citizenship, and the supposed divisions of civilization shaped these emancipation processes.

Emancipation, from the Latin *emancipatio*, means "to let free from his hand." Embedded in the etymology of the word, and its roots in ancient Roman law, is the legitimation of a supposed authority of some kinds of people to trade or sell ownership rights (*mancipatio*) in other kinds of people.[12] Under Roman law, *emancipatio* referred to the act by which a paterfamilias (a property-owning male householder) could *voluntarily* give up his power (*potestas*) over other human beings in his household, including children and slaves. Emancipation was, thus, legally construed as the voluntary grant of an owner, not as the righteous vindication of the captives.

Emancipation, as a procedure of ancient Roman law and reinvented as a legal and political instrument across Europe and the Americas in the eighteenth and nineteenth centuries, honored and upheld the authority of enslavers, while erasing the humanity of those subjected to slavery. No wonder emancipations never required slave-owning society to make amends with the enslaved. Even as the formal institution of slavery was abolished, the rights of erstwhile slave-owners and the broader structure of racial domination was preserved. Emancipations ensured the compensation and gratification of slave-owners and their beneficiaries and disregarded any responsibility to the enslaved. Governments empowered perpetrators to shape the postslavery future with their own hands.[13]

To make this point concrete, consider this selected comparative list of emancipations. Notice the variety of ways these emancipations upheld the supposed original right by some people to possess and dominate other people based on ideas of racial difference. Governments across Europe and the Americas designed decades-long projects to pay reparations to enslavers and oppressors.

Location	End of Slavery Declared	Reparations Package for Enslavers
Pennsylvania	1780	• Captive labor of Africans continues for sixty-seven years, until 1847
British empire	1833	• Captive labor of Africans continues for five years, until 1838 • £20 million (approx. $200 billion today) paid in cash and stocks to enslavers
French empire	1848	• The French state pays 6 million francs (approx. $27 billion today) to enslavers in its plantation colonies
Cuba	1879	• Captive labor of Africans continues for seven years, until 1886 • 120,000,000 pesos (approx. $2.4 billion today) were to be paid to enslavers

Across Europe, the Americas, and some plantation colonies in the Indian Ocean such as Mauritius and Réunion, European and American governments engineered intergenerational systems of reparations for plantation elites and investors. French slave-owners and their families, expelled from Haiti, received government support for one hundred years after the Haitian revolution. American slave-owners and their descendants, from the time of the first emancipations in the 1780s to the dawning of Jim Crow in the 1880s and beyond, distorted laws, voting rights, and civic policies and expanded prison systems. British slave-owners and their heirs received lucrative state-funded reparations bankrolled by British taxpayers for 180 years until 2015. On the other hand, the emancipated African people of the Caribbean states were deprived of education, health care, the right to land and livelihood, the vote, and the foundations for independent economies. Additionally, European states confiscated the lands and destroyed the sovereignties of African states in heightened fashion after 1875 using the alibi of emancipation, as they imposed an order of imperialist rule and underdevelopment, the consequences of which extend into our present day.

The language of emancipation during the nineteenth century referred to black people as various kinds of postslavery property, calling them "cargo" and "contraband." European and American states designated emancipated persons not as "citizens" but as "freed people." Across many parts of the Americas, the descendants of freed people did not receive the franchise until the latter twentieth century, and laws and policies and social norms still target them today. The established order developed new carceral institutions, such as indentureship, sharecropping, and convict leasing, to force generations of black people to pay the oppressors with their labor long after the "final" emancipation date. The process of emancipations belonged to the slave-owners and to the established political interests aligned with them.

This book pursues a comparative perspective on emancipation processes across the globe. We explore five types of emancipation across the Americas, Europe, and Africa, which reverberated across Asia, too. We begin with the *gradual emancipations*, in New England, the American mid-Atlantic, and, later, in the Spanish Americas that made black people pay for their freedom. We turn to the *retroactive emancipation* that tried to contain the revolution in Haiti. We explore the British empire's *compensated emancipation*, which allowed slave-owners to enrich themselves enormously, not only with continued forced labor but also with huge cash payouts from public coffers. The British empire's compensated emancipation set a new standard for reparations to slave-owners that many other governments would follow. We consider the *war emancipation*, forged on the battlefields of the American Civil War, and the ongoing dirty war against black people in the United States that follows in its wake. And we conclude with the emancipations that provided pretexts for massive colonial occupations across Africa. Each chapter considers a specific example of emancipation as well as an explanation of how historical injustice continued, without rectification or amends. Each chapter flows in chronological order, showing how different emancipation processes borrowed from each other and circulated across the global expanse.

Black communities practiced self-emancipation, insurgency, and many large and small forms of liberation in counter-response to state-led emancipation processes. Black people demanded freedom beyond the limits, sentences, and time schedules of what was handed to them by emancipators.[14] They insisted on self-determination, the right to land and its bounty, and freedom to experience joy and protection in their communities, rooted in their old and new traditions. Self-liberating African peoples demanded the creation of good relationships and reciprocity with other peoples on earth. And, as we shall see, from the very beginning of abolitionism, black people did not stop insisting on the proper amends for the historical injustices of slavery and emancipation.

Black memory speaks, beckons, and demands reckoning.[15] Black people, experiencing historical plunder—the "history that hurts"—do not acquiesce into an assigned void.[16] They have spent centuries making livelihoods behind the veil of the ghost line, creating pleasures and insurgencies in the dark.

So, the history of slavery and emancipation is not a story of endings, but of unendings. Ghosts announce the unended. They unsettle, frighten, and haunt. And who would not agree that our twenty-first century is haunted by its accumulating past? Ghosts trouble postslavery societies in our consciences, our memories, and our social disorders, in order to disturb us and ask for redress. This haunting beckons us to remake good relations from within the ongoing aftermath of historical trauma. The ghosts in our history demand reparative action—diverse practices of reparations, restitution, and redress—by all of us standing on the ground of slavery and by the ruling order built upon it. Through reparative action, based in the will to truth and peace, not the will to power, we can all help one another become more human or, perhaps, more than the humankind we have known. That is the future history beyond the vanishing point. Something has to end for something new to begin.

CHAPTER 1

MAKING AFRICANS PAY, GRADUALLY, IN THE AMERICAN NORTH

We do not often think of the postrevolutionary American North in terms of slavery and emancipations. Such associations are typically reserved for the antebellum slaveholding American South. Indeed, the Northern emancipations—what are euphemistically called the gradual emancipations, 1777–1865—served to exonerate the American North from the general story of slavery. The institution of slavery that operated across the postrevolutionary United States depended on the participation of the Northern states, as much as on the expansion of the slaveholding plantation South. We are used to a triumphant abolitionist narrative that pictures slavery in scenes far away from the centers of industry and finance in the North; far from cosmopolitan cities such as Boston, Philadelphia, and New York. Yet, these cities, well into the nineteenth century, formed a circuit of power and wealth for the slavery economy.[1] Without these Northern centers, the plantation industries across the American South and the Caribbean could never have been as long-lived nor as lucrative. The international system of slavery depended on networks of commerce, finance, shipping, manufacturing, and consumption anchored in the North. Although the American North was not the epicenter of slavery, it was nevertheless deeply entwined, inextricably so, in the larger system of racial bondage and exploitation.

Slavery operated differently in distinct areas, but also in interlocking fashion across them. Plantation slavery looked very different from urban slavery, for example, even as these disparate arrangements of bondage fit together like the cogs in a great slave-driving machine. In 1619, slave-traders brought the first captive Africans to labor in the plantation colony of Virginia. Not long thereafter, slavery started to thrive in the Northern colonial urban centers, too. Slave-owners brought African captives to Boston in 1624, six years before the colonial town was officially incorporated. Dutch colonists brought enslaved people to New York City (then called New Amsterdam) in 1626. And 150 enslaved African people helped clear the land for the new colony of Pennsylvania in 1684, carved out of a Swedish settlement. In other words, enslavement was there from the very beginning across all of colonial Northern America, and not just in the South.[2]

A law legalizing slavery was passed in Massachusetts in 1641, and a number of subsequent laws regulated the activities of captive black people in the colony. In New York, the British implemented a severe slave code in 1702, the harshest one outside the South. This code stipulated that enslaved people could be punished "at the discretion" of slave-owners, and could not give evidence unless against someone else enslaved.[3] After a mass revolt by enslaved Africans in New York City in 1712, the slave code was tightened further. The Common Council of New York City published "An Act for Suppressing and Punishing the Conspiracy and Insurrection of Negroes and Other Slaves." After December 10, 1712, enslaved persons above the age of fourteen were forbidden from walking around the city after dark unless carrying a lighted lantern and from "assembling in groups of more than three, belonging to the militia, carrying a gun or other weapon of any kind, leaving their masters' houses on the Sabbath, or training a dog."[4]

By the 1700s, slave markets were in early operation in Boston, such as next to Faneuil Hall, and at the corner of Hanover and Union Streets. Similarly, around the same time in New York, slave-traders bought and sold African people at the official slave market on Wall Street. In Philadelphia, African people were traded in the London Coffee House at Front and Market Streets, and at other sundry locations. In this early period, more enslaved people were traded in these three big cities of the colonial North, together, than anywhere else in North America. The Northeast and New England were not distant from the history of slavery, but central to it.

Northern colonial towns and cities stimulated the expansion of the Atlantic slave trade in overt and covert ways. New England slaving vessels, owned by magnates in Boston and Providence, played a primary role in the trade. Boston sloops were the first to kidnap large numbers of people from Madagascar beginning in the 1670s, transporting them to plantations in the West Indies where African captives sold at high prices. Especially after the revocation of the British Royal African Company's trade monopoly in 1696, New England ships, and the sailors manning them, played a dominant role in purchasing captured Africans along the west coast of Africa and forcing them across the ocean to the plantation zones. New England capitalists were the most important section of North American shippers and conveyers of enslaved African people in the decades leading up to the American Revolution.[5]

Key industries and crafts of the colonial North depended on the industry and wealth produced by African bondage. By the 1700s, Boston, New York, and Philadelphia all fed on the profits from the industrial production of sugar in the Caribbean. Only thanks to the Caribbean plantations on what were known as the Sugar Islands, such as Barbados and Jamaica, could a group of British settlers in North America amass such tremendous wealth and assert their new genteel status. As a result of the sugar boom, many other enterprises took off, including shipbuilding, anchor making, and insurance. The Caribbean plantation economies also served as important markets for goods produced in the American North. In the 1760s and 1770s, New England exported the majority of its commodities—foodstuffs, tools, liquor—to the British Caribbean. In 1768, when 18 percent of New England's exports went to Great Britain and Ireland, a whopping 64 percent of its exports went to the Caribbean.[6]

Meanwhile, colonial proprietors of rum distilleries extracted the greatest derivative wealth from slave-harvested sugarcane. Rum was New England's largest manufacturing business before the American Revolution and was completely dependent on molasses from the West Indies. By 1700, more than sixty-three distilleries operated across the Massachusetts Bay Colony, producing 2.7 million gallons of rum per year. This rum was an important portion of the "pacotille," or the cache of petty goods, offered to slave-traders in Africa in exchange for human merchandise. In the early 1700s, New England slave-traders paid approximately £3 worth of rum for each African captive they imprisoned along the Guinea and Gold Coasts. They could then sell the captives who survived the transoceanic passage for £15 to £20 each at ports of call such as Kingston, Jamaica, or St. John's, Antigua. Slave-trading generated huge amounts of wealth precisely because slave-owners claimed the right to hold property in human beings. They sold this human "merchandise" for high marginal profits, and the wealth they captured went into building their estates, their civic institutions, and their reputations as "old and influential families." Almost all the colonial patricians—the Brahmins of Boston and the Honorables of New York and Philadelphia—had direct connections to slave-trade wealth. The Winthrops, the Belchers, the Faneuils, the Cabots, and the Pepperells, families after whom townships and official buildings across New England are named, all extracted ugly profits from human merchandising, then used that wealth to monumentalize themselves and their families across the colonial North. The wealth and estates of plantation magnates, such as Isaac Royall Jr., contributed to the endowments of the region's prestigious universities, including Harvard and Brown.[7]

NORTHERN SLAVERY AND RESISTANCE

In the North, enslaved and freed black people faced very different circumstances from those who lived on Southern or Caribbean plantation frontiers. African people living in urban environments worked primarily as laborers and domestic servants, but also as artisans and tradespeople. Cities created opportunities for black people, enslaved and free, to meet in common spaces, including taverns and market squares. Across Boston, New York, and Philadelphia, enslaved black people were farmhands, butlers, and maids, but also wharfmen, sailors, and building constructors. They were tobacconists, hatmakers, oystermen, and coopers. Enslaved African people comprised almost 20 percent of New York's population by the 1740s, making New York the nation's foremost slave city after Charleston, North Carolina. About four in every ten white households in the environs of New York City kept African people in bondage. In Brooklyn, African bondspeople were one-third of the population, and more than 60 percent of all white families held at least one person enslaved.[8]

The American Revolution created new opportunities to conjure and enact freedom among African communities. In 1775, American colonists across the thirteen colonies declared war on Britain, asserting their republican belief in self-determination and the universal "natural rights" to "life, liberty, and the pursuit of happiness."[9] Free and enslaved black people in the thirteen colonies fought on both sides of the war, although South Carolina and Georgia never permitted black enlistees. In fact, for a period in 1775, the Continental Congress banned black enlistment from all patriot militias, citing a fear of black insurgency. Certainly, the enslaved risked their lives on the battlefields, regardless of the side, with the primary purpose of achieving their liberty.[10]

In 1775, Lord Dunmore, the British governor of Virginia, actively appealed to enslaved people to flee their enslavers and join with British troops. Thousands of black people, as many as seventy thousand, made the flight to British lines in search of their freedom. Approximately five thousand black people, many of them enslaved, fought in the revolutionary army. They would have received manumission upon enlisting. After the British defeat in 1783, some three thousand black men, women, and children emancipated by the British troops boarded ships chartered for British Canadian Nova Scotia. Thousands more fled slavery and made it on their own to the Maritime coast. The countervailing story must also be told of the more than twenty thousand enslaved African people taken by British loyalists deeper into slavery, to Florida and onward to British slavery colonies, such as the Bahamas, in the aftermath of the Revolutionary War. The North American Revolutionary War, 1775–83, brought about limited emancipations. This kind of emancipation recurred during the War of 1812, and during the Spanish American revolutionary wars of 1814–21. In all these cases, the exceptional freeing of a small number of black enlistees served to strengthen the general rule of slavery.

During the revolutionary period, communities of black people petitioned Northern colonial governments to abolish slavery, but also to honor their rights to equity and to reparative justice. In petitions filed before the Massachusetts General Court between 1783 and 1796, groups of black people asked not only for the abolition of enslavement but also for land, education, and for social protection. In January 1773, a group of enslaved people wrote to the Massachusetts General Court, "We have no property. We have no wives. No children. We have no city. No country." In April 1773, a "committee of fellow slaves" asked for financial assistance, "until we leave the province, which we determine to do so as soon as we can from our joynt labours procure money to transport ourselves to some part of the coast of Africa, where we propose a settlement."[11] Large numbers of black people in New England in this period had been born in Africa and had been kidnapped away from family and native lands. They still spoke African languages as their mother tongues. It makes sense that they would dream of using their freedom to return home.

In January 1777, another petition by African people in Boston stated, "[We are] detained in a state of slavery in the bowels of a free and Christian country." After filing "petition after petition," they had received no redress and hoped they "may be restored to the enjoyment of that freedom which is the natural right of all Men."[12] In 1780, in Dartmouth, Massachusetts, a small group petitioned the revolutionary legislature "to relieve them of poll and estate taxes on the grounds that we are not allowed the [privilege] of free-men of the State having no vote or influence in the Election of those that Tax us."[13] They asked the governmental authorities to stop "[reducing] us to a state of Beggary." In 1787, another group of black people in Massachusetts asked for equal educational facilities, stating, "We therefore pray your Honors that in your wisdom some provision may be made for the education of our dear children."

None of these requests were granted. As we shall see, black voluntary organizations, black churches, and white-led abolitionist societies were left to redress the damage of slavery in the North. However, in this revolutionary period, even before the work of redress could properly start, the problem of slavery's abolition remained unresolved. There was certainly no widespread renunciation of the property rights in enslaved people across the new, independent United States of America. In fact, in 1787, a compromise at the Constitutional Convention in Philadelphia enshrined Southern slavery in Article I of the new national constitution. The stipulation provided slave-owners in the Union a slavery bonus. Major slaveholding states such as Georgia and the Carolinas, which could now count enslaved Africans as three-fifths of an inhabitant, were bolstered in their representation in the new Congress, as were their slaveholders.

Beginning in 1780, lawmakers in Pennsylvania initiated a new gradualist system of emancipation, which would soon serve as a model for antislavery endeavors across Britain and the Spanish Americas. Philadelphia served as a catalyst. Informed by the nonconformist and abolitionist doctrine of the Quakers, with international roots in Dutch Mennonitism, the state of Pennsylvania, and the Quaker stronghold of Philadelphia, emerged as a center for voluntary manumissions early in the 1700s. The rise of revolutionary republicanism and the natural-rights ideology of "life, liberty, and property" only served to further activate the commitment in Quaker theology to the "social gospel," and the recognition of enslaved Africans as persons and not as property.[14] Revolutionary war and social gospel combined in 1780 as the Pennsylvania General Assembly passed the first-ever act of gradual emancipation.

This act, however, for all intents and purposes, stipulated that emancipated people should pay compensation to slave-owners in the form of sentences of unpaid labor. In the very legal process to abolish slavery, the Philadelphia legislature confirmed the legitimacy of white property owners to enslave African people, while disregarding the right of enslaved Africans to obtain reparations for the damages they had suffered. Born of racist law codes, this "first emancipation" could only have racist outcomes. It contained fatal flaws that would replicate in subsequent emancipations across other Northern states, making the end of slavery into a process of continuation, not conclusion.

To understand this fatal legal regime, we need to pause here to explore the preexisting voluntary practice by which enslavers could release their captives from bondage. This practice was relatively widespread in Philadelphia in the decades before the Act for the Gradual Abolition of Slavery of 1780. Manumission—the word derived from the Latin *manumisso*—was a practice rooted in ancient Roman law and in European feudal legal arrangements. Beginning in the late 1700s, *emancipation* referred to government action to free enslaved people, while *manumission* signified the voluntary action on the part of individual slave-owners. Long before the 1770s when emancipations commenced, manumissions were taking place. Manumission stipulated the compensation of slave-owners for the "loss" of property rights in enslaved human beings. This legal instrument had been widely used across European slavery colonies since the 1600s, called *coartación* in the Spanish and Portuguese colonies. *Coartación*, or "gradual self-purchase," required black people to make long-term debt payments, in cash or labor, to their former enslavers. As a result of this arrangement, colonies such as Cuba and Brazil counted more free black people than enslaved by the nineteenth century. *Coartación*, as one kind of manumission, was designed to strengthen the overall institution of slavery, as slave-owners could offer individual freedom, according to their whim, without disrupting the general institution. The French plantation colonies had a similar arrangement, called *rachat*, and the Dutch had *vrijlating*. The actual scope and procedures for the voluntary freeing of enslaved people differed widely between colonial systems. The emancipations across the revolutionary US North, and then the revolutionary Spanish America, from the 1770s to the 1820s and beyond, scaled up the existing manumission system and made it a matter of government policy, even as slave-owner interests were protected.[15]

The British, French, and Dutch colonial states limited manumissions much more stringently than the Spanish. The British slave code was by far the most restrictive. Under the conditions of slavery, the greater the size of the manumitted black community, the greater the perceived risk to colonial slave-owners and propertied classes of disruptions to their social status. Manumission, in the British American colonies, signified a danger to the establishment.[16]

In New York City, for example, only thirty-one enslaved people were manumitted during the entire eighteenth century. This number is small compared to the more than eight thousand enslaved black people living in the city during this time. Government policy, based in British colonial law, actively dissuaded New York slave-owners from offering manumission to slaves.[17] Although the slave-owner could define the kind of payment he or she required of the enslaved person in exchange for the grant of freedom—such as additional unpaid labor for a set period of time, or a specific "redemption price"—slave-owners also had to agree to a £200 bond for each enslaved person they freed, which would have to be paid to the city government if the freed person ever became a burden on the public. In other words, freed black people were treated, from the start, as future assets for white property owners. They were "freed" into the condition of having to pay their oppressors.

Interestingly, a law from 1712 stipulated that slave-owners should pay £200 to the formerly enslaved person in increments of £20 per year, as "freedom pay" to the enslaved. However, this law was quickly struck down. The New York city council determined it to be "very inconvenient, prejudicial, in a manner a prohibition to Liberty, and will very much discourage and disheartened such Negroes, Indian, and Mulatto slaves from serving the Master or Mistress truely and faithfully as they ought to do."[18] Legislators, many of whom were themselves slave-owners, designed manumission to honor the property rights of the slave-owners and thereby also disregard the personal rights of freed African people.

The limited and voluntary manumission process in the American North provided the template for the general emancipations that began to unfold in the years after the Revolutionary War. Legislators also drew precedent from the early-modern "apprenticeship" laws governing how authorities handled destitute, or "pauper," children by assigning them terms of bonded labor.[19] As mentioned earlier, Quaker Philadelphia became a prerevolutionary epicenter for manumission, and it also legislated the first act of gradual emancipation in 1780. Two years earlier, a bill modeled on manumission stipulated that the children of enslaved people had to pay a debt to the slave-owner of up to eighteen years of bonded labor to "earn" their freedom. The *post nati*, or "freedom after birth," bill was finalized and approved as legislation in 1780, requiring all people currently enslaved to continue living under slavery for the rest of their lives. In addition, children born after March 1, 1780, would be required to live in bondage until their eighteenth birthday, after which they would be freed. This law was the first legislated "gradual emancipation" because it stipulated a deferred end to formal slavery. The law ensured that slave-owner property claims would change with as little disruption to their wealth as possible. Slave-owners maintained their ownership rights through the emancipation process because they exercised ownership over the process itself.

Emancipations in the North were deliberately slowed down and stretched out over decades. We can better think of these processes as deferrals, arrangements to ensure the slave-owners' right to power over African people for as long as was politically viable. For example, Vermont declared itself independent in 1777, officially joining the United States in 1791. Vermont's 1777 constitution banned slavery for men over twenty-one and women over nineteen. However, enslavement continued. Records show that some white Vermonters flouted the law, for which there was no oversight or enforcement, and continued buying and selling Africans for decades to come. Vermont slave-owners could redesignate their enslaved people as "servants," allowing them to continue benefiting from African people's bonded labor. Due to legal loopholes, black children in Vermont were kept in slavery until 1810, more than thirty-three years after the constitutional abolition. And because Vermont allowed enslavers to "transit" through the state with enslaved Africans, enslavement was condoned in the state as late as 1835, when planters from Alabama brought captives with them for seasonal stays. The story of the triumphant declaration to end slavery disintegrates under investigation.[20]

In Rhode Island, an Act to Abolish Slavery was passed in 1784, based on Pennsylvania's template. This act stipulated that only children born of enslaved women would be free, but, again, only after eighteen years—that is, not until 1802 at the earliest. Similarly, emancipation in Connecticut was also passed in 1784. Here, again, children born after March 1 of that year were termed "free," but were legally obligated to serve their slave-owners until the age of twenty-five. Paradoxically, gradual emancipation processes extended slavery in practice, even while abolishing the institution on paper.

In the case of Massachusetts, gradual emancipation happened quietly. Nothing was written down. The terms and protections of the enslaved were never recorded. Slavery was simply rumored to have ended during the time of the Revolutionary War, and eventually the rumor was presumed to be true. The constitutions of Massachusetts, as well as New Hampshire, did not ban slavery explicitly, and so the bondage of black people continued in informal and undocumented ways, such as in the widespread use of bonded, and thus unpaid, black domestic servants in the homes of patrician white Boston families. Possessing black servants became the euphemism for keeping people enslaved.[21]

So, in reality, across New England, those treated as slaves before the gradual emancipations continued to live as enslaved people for decades afterward. Northern emancipations, as with all those that would follow during the nineteenth century, passed on the property rights and the privileges of slave-owners to subsequent generations. Providing reparations for slavery would have required atonement for its harms at collective and societal levels. This never happened in the North, *not* because society did not know better, but because one caste of people held property rights to another, and this dominant caste was powerful enough to overcome the ethical pleas by the enslaved for justice and right relationship.[22]

The continuation of slavery in New England had huge consequences for black people as individuals and family groups. James Mars was born into slavery in Connecticut in 1790, after the passing of the emancipation act. He told his life story at age seventy-nine, recollecting the disfigurements of New England slavery as they persisted through emancipation. Mars, along with his father, mother, sister, and brother, had been owned by a man named Thompson, a minister who circulated between Connecticut and Virginia. After slavery was abolished in Connecticut, the law gave Thompson the right to keep the newborn child, James Mars, enslaved until he was twenty-five. And that's exactly what Thompson intended to do. Furthermore, he planned to take James and his older brother to the South, where his wife's family owned a plantation. There, Mars and his family could be brought back into the system of permanent slavery. This was all fully legal according to the Connecticut emancipation law.

James Mars's family spurned Thompson's plans. Most of all, they wished to stay together. Family separations—the removal of mothers and fathers from children, and of siblings from one another—were always the first and most egregious pains of enslavement. The Mars family escaped from Canaan, Connecticut, to the town of Norfolk. They hoped they would be safer there. James was eventually captured and taken from his family, just as his older brother succeeded in escaping to Massachusetts. When James Mars, still just a boy, was taken back to Thompson's house, his mother and father decided to relocate to a place nearby so they could still see him. James Mars, as a house servant for Thompson and eventually a field laborer, was allowed time with his parents only every two weeks. When Mars reached age fifteen, Thompson sold him to another Connecticut slave-owner named Mungers. Mungers used the lash with impunity and said he would keep James Mars in bondage for as long as the law permitted, until he reached age twenty-five, as approved by the Connecticut emancipation law.

As James Mars grew older, he argued, pleaded, and insisted on his freedom. Eventually, when Mars defied Mungers' rule, the slave-owner went to the town court and threatened to put Mars in jail for a year for refusing to submit to involuntary servitude. Only at this stage did the court decide in Mars's favor. All of this happened in the wake of so-called emancipation. Mars eventually became a well-known figure in the local church. He signed petitions to support the causes of fugitives who escaped from the South. Mars's life story provides a trace of the reality of gradual emancipation in New England, and the suffering required to endure it.[23]

MID-ATLANTIC AND SPANISH AMERICAN EMANCIPATIONS

In New York State, where emancipation laws were first passed in 1799, and where the letter of the law stipulated the final abolition of slavery in 1827, some black people continued to live in slavery well into the 1850s. Kept as "servants" and "indentures," or as "transfers" by enslavers claiming to take up temporary residence in the state, black people knew that emancipation did not represent the end. The long drone of unfinished emancipation was common across the Northeastern states, including in Connecticut and in Rhode Island. New Jersey's emancipation process began only in 1829 and ended in 1865. Pennsylvania's emancipation, which had begun much earlier, in 1780, ended only in 1850. Certainly, the focus on the long trajectory of slavery in the American South is a convenient narrative, allowing mainstream publics to disavow the active forms of enslavement, and the widespread social and political complicity, of Northern society. For contemporary Northerners, to forget about the North's involvement is also to shirk any need to take responsibility.[24]

New York State legislators innovated new legal measures that ensured New York's 1799 emancipation law was more proslavery than the earlier versions of Pennsylvania, Rhode Island, or Connecticut (the latter two were passed in 1784). New York *post nati* emancipation was for children born to enslaved mothers after July 4, 1799. Even then, these children would be forced to serve as "indentures" to their mother's slave-owners until age twenty-eight for men, and age twenty-five for women. Much as under slavery, property titles to indentured African people could be passed on as inheritance or sold. "Indenture" was just another word for slave-like human bondage. In practice, the experience of indentured people after 1799 was little different from that of the enslaved.

The capriciousness of emancipation in New York after 1799 is made clear by the records. Some black people received freedom "only after [the slave-owner's] death," or else only after the payment of a specific amount, such as "a consideration of $50." In some cases, slave-owners stipulated the future date of enslaved people's emancipation: "The children are to be free in twenty years from this day." The 1799 bill also included a cunning scheme for the monetary compensation of slave-owners—a policy that would become much more explicit in future emancipation processes across the Atlantic.[25]

Slave-owners had the option of "abandoning" enslaved children on their estates after they were one year old. New York State would then "bound out" these children as servants to other white families and pay these families $3.50 per month to compensate them for the wardship. The trick was that slave-owners could "abandon" the nominally freed black children, only to have the state return the children to them as wards with the monthly financial compensation paid at New York taxpayers' expense. New York slave-owners could count on almost thirty years of compensation from the state for the ploy of foster care for the same "freed" children the slave-owners had previously abandoned. Slave-owners benefited from the free labor of these children, too. White people who said they were being "robbed of their property" could receive both a state compensation and free labor of black people for decades.[26]

In 1817, the New York legislature passed a new emancipation act, pushing its own farce of freedom. This act promised to free all slaves born before 1799, but not until 1827. Again, another deferral; another legislated and legalized denial of justice. Again, the ghostlining of black people's demands for liberation. And as under the previous law, all enslaved children born after 1799 would have to serve as slaves for twenty-eight years so that the owners could benefit from their labor. Additionally, under the 1817 law, whites from the South who visited New York could keep their enslaved people with them for up to nine months. This created another loophole that some white New Yorkers quickly exploited. Some briefly took their enslaved people across state lines every nine months, thereby allowing them to claim the nine-month exemption, and to keep enslaved people in their households long after 1827.[27]

In New Jersey and Delaware, the gradual emancipation process promised even greater benefits for the slave-owners. New Jersey abolition was passed in 1804. The bill, like New York's, also contained a clause about "abandoned children" that allowed New Jersey slave-owners to collect state compensation while keeping "free" black children. By 1810, New Jersey was the only Northern state in which the number of enslaved people outnumbered the number of free black folk. Slave-owners in New Jersey, situated in close proximity to slave-holding Delaware and Maryland, facilitated the export of black people into Southern bondage for many decades of the nineteenth century. In 1812, the state legalized the "removal" of free black people into Southern slavery if conducted "with their consent." This opened the door to rampant fraud. Some of the powerful beneficiaries of ongoing slave tracking in New Jersey were its most prominent politicians and judges.[28]

By 1830, two-thirds of black people remaining in slavery in Northern states were held in New Jersey. Not until 1846 did New Jersey pass its "act to abolish slavery." Here again, however, enslaved people were not actually freed. The remaining enslaved people were made "apprentices for life." Not until 1865 did the institution of slavery in New Jersey come to an end, although what followed was a regime, like others across the Northern states, in which black people were still treated as legal aliens and as criminals.

In Delaware, the gradual emancipation bill, finally debated in 1847, was never passed. It was tabled indefinitely, and slavery remained in place until the end of the Civil War in 1865. "Gradual emancipations," the pride of the North, were marked not by freedom but by prolonged legislative debates and machinations aimed at conserving and transferring the property rights of the slavery era into the postslavery era, along the iron tracks of law.

In a time of worldwide revolutionary crisis beginning in the 1790s, the Spanish empire also quaked with the insurgency of revolutionary nationalists across South America. The Parliament of Cádiz, convened 1810–12, sought to establish a new understanding between the Spanish imperial government and the insurgent political leaders in its colonies. The agreement quickly broke down, leading to a decade of revolutionary struggle and the creation of independent South American nation-states by 1821, under the general leadership of Simón Bolívar. In this period of revolutionary warfare, as during the North American Revolutionary War, 1775–1783, enslaved people were enlisted on both sides of the battle and were offered freedom for putting their lives on the line. At the same time, the outline of general emancipation policies emerged. These explicitly drew on the precedent of the "gradual emancipations" of the American North, especially the 1780 Philadelphia scheme.[29] In 1813, the revolutionary legislature of Argentina passed a law granting freedom to all female children of enslaved people at age sixteen, and all male children at age twenty-one. This *post nati* (freedom after birth) emancipation in fact ensured that black children would continue to be born into captivity. This Spanish American "freedom" was little more than a promissory note.

The new South American nation-states—Gran Colombia and Peru in 1821, Uruguay in 1825, Bolivia in 1831, and Paraguay in 1842—widely adopted emancipation by the *libertad de vientre* (freedom of the womb) laws, with consequences for decades to come. During the Bolivarian revolutions across Latin America in the 1820s, local *juntas*, or commissions, administered small public funds to manumit small numbers of enslaved people.[30] Only in the 1850s did Colombia, Venezuela, and Ecuador (the successor states of Gran Colombia) and Peru make the first declarations of universal emancipation among Spanish American states.[31] And these emancipations also included cash payments to slave-owners. These early emancipations all made use of gradualism and long delays. *How* slavery ended, not just *that* it ended, should matter to us, as should whose interests governed the process.

BLACK LIBERATION ON THE STREETS

Black people responded to the changing legal injustices of the Northern deferred emancipations by seizing freedom for themselves and creating spaces for liberation from below. Many of the black men who sat atop the main voluntary organizations and black churches across the American Northeast in this early period of emancipation, in cities such as Boston, New York, and Philadelphia, had themselves been freed from bondage. In the 1790s, they began to break away from the white church institutions where they were treated as subordinates and established their own autonomous institutions. Achieving black liberation from within the institutional structures of white domination involved the underground construction of mutual aid organizations. This underground work also relied on alliances with white abolitionists who used their privileged positions in the American racial caste system to undermine that hierarchy.

Black people confronted the new legal opportunities of gradual emancipation, as well as the obvious, endemic injustice and lack of safeguards, by organizing themselves in communities of black care and grassroots redress. The New York African Society, a spiritual and benevolent organization of free and enslaved black men (one of the first African associations in the city), began meeting as early as 1780. In Boston, Prince Hall, the celebrated black preacher and advocate, originally from Barbados, established the African Lodge of Free Masons in 1784, as well as a Boston African Society for mutual aid and benevolence. In Philadelphia, Richard Allen and Absalom Jones organized the Free African Society in 1787. The Philadelphia African Society bought land at Fifth and Adelphi in 1792. The church they built in 1794 was the first black church in America.[32]

Black women played an increasingly active and visible role in underground black organizing precisely as the pretenses of patriarchal gentility and respectability politics disintegrated in the lead-up to the American Civil War. As black survival and freedom became a matter of emergency action in the context of the Fugitive Slave Act of 1850 and the Dred Scott decision of 1857, black women, such as Sojourner Truth, Harriet Tubman, Julia Foote—the first ordained woman preacher of the African Methodist Church—as well as many women in the black Baptist movement, stepped into the breach.[33]

Black voluntary organizations did not just care for their living members but also for their dead. This work of preserving relationships of reciprocity with the ancestors, and of observing rituals of reminiscence and reverence for the dead, was a profound aspect of the African cultural inheritance, preserved through families for generation upon generation after the forced removal from African homelands. As we recall, under the punitive slave laws of New York City, African burial sites were heavily regulated as authorities recognized these locations as important centers of African-centered cultural identity.[34]

In New York City, in the period of colonial slavery, enslaved African people were interred in one of four different kinds of burial sites. Many were buried in the common African burial grounds at Duane and Reade Streets. More than 250 burials took place here from 1680 until the grounds were closed in

1799. A much smaller number of black people were buried in the segregated section of white churches, such as the old Trinity Church at the intersection of Wall Street and Broadway. Alternatively, many enslaved people were simply buried on the colonial Dutch- and British-owned homesteads on which they labored, strewn across Brooklyn and the Hudson River valley. Finally, an unknown multitude were buried in the segregated areas of the city's pauper fields, such as at the common graves at Washington Square, Madison Square, and Bryant Square. All of these burial sites had something in common: none of them offered the living members of the African community protected places where the remains of ancestors could be visited and ritually revered. In this way, the insecurity that black people experienced during life also carried over into the structural vulnerability they faced in keeping hold of their material relationships with their dead.

The African voluntary associations arising in New York during the emancipation period focused on ensuring reverential burials, and on creating autonomous and protected burial grounds for the black community. In this climate of ongoing black social vulnerability after emancipation, the black church played an important role as an institution for collective security, not just for the living, but also for the relationships between the living and the ancestors.

The first black churches, dating to the 1780s and 1790s, were also burial associations, and in New York City the AME "Mother Zion" church built at the corner of Leonard Street and Church Street in 1801 became one of the most important of them all. With their own burial society and their own catacombs, emancipated and still-enslaved members of AME Zion were no longer thrown into unmemorialized common graves or sequestered in the untended segregated sections of white-owned churches. Their remains were not strewn and lost across the declining and disappearing homesteads of white yeoman farmers. Having their own vault to inter their dead represented a huge victory for freed people in the age of gradual emancipations. The prospect of burial with dignity, with a ceremony officiated by a black minister, in a black-owned church, was itself a form of redress "from below." The burial vault of the African Methodist Episcopalian Mother Zion Church also served as an important station on the Underground Railroad. The same catacombs that safeguarded the bones of deceased family members also served as a safe house through which fugitives from slavery found freedom. By land and waterways, they stole their freedom in clandestine journeys from the South on the Underground Railroad. Thousands of fugitives from slavery would have known the refuge of Mother Zion Church as a station of the freedom train.

Black communities practiced their liberation together. They created their own space for family, pleasure, and creative expression—all that was truly human that lay outside the inhuman regime of coerced labor and racial oppression. They made free space for themselves before the official end of slavery, and throughout its slow and deferred death in the North. In their new organizations, both the physical institutions and the newspapers and literary organs they established, freed black people wrote about their visions of freedom in the context of emancipation's unfreedom. They fought to keep hold of their own sense of reality and history. They critiqued the ongoing institutions of slavery in the South, *as well as* the injustices of the inequitable emancipations of the North. They highlighted slavery's ongoing life in the very places where white society was quick to announce its death.

On January 2, 1808, for example, Henry Sipkins, an emancipated black man and leader of the African Methodist community, delivered an oration on the date marking the abolition of the Atlantic slave trade by British and American states. He spoke of "the injustice and barbarity" of the slave trade. He identified the root cause of slavery in the greed of the early British settlers in the Americas, who, "surpassing the bounds of reasonable acquisition, violated the sacred injunctions of the gospel . . . and enslaving the harmless aborigines, compelled them to drudge in the mines." In his historical account, the settlers turned to the enslavement of Africans to meet their labor demand, striking a "mortal blow" to West African society. "O Africa, Africa! To what horrid inhumanities have thy shores been witness," he lamented.[35] Black interpreters used commemoration days to recall the trauma of slavery, and to grieve its continuities.

At the very same time, black people rejoiced in their new freedoms, however circumscribed and unjustly delivered. In New York, they celebrated in 1800, and in 1808, and in 1817, and in 1828, the coming of different incomplete emancipation laws. In July 1827, on the occasion of the end of the deferred emancipation and the arrival of universal legal personhood for black people, crowds gathered with pennants on New York City streets, played music, listened to speeches, and feted. They gathered on July 5 because the date of July 4 was guarded as a whites-only day for the public celebration of American Independence. A newspaper account of the 1827 celebrations reports:

> The blacks of the city and the vicinity had celebrations yesterday. . . . The procession passed through all the most public streets, and was followed by vast numbers of negro women and children. . . . There were four or five bands, comprising a great variety of instruments.[36]

On that same day, William Hamilton, a black carpenter and founding member of the New York African Society for Mutual Relief, exclaimed in a public address, "This day has the state of New York regenerated herself—this day has she been cleansed of a most foul, poisonous, and damnable stain."[37] For Hamilton, emancipation, even in its imperfection, was nevertheless part of an ongoing detoxification of the public soul. However, after the celebrations were over, black folk returned to the same homesteads they had left that morning. Many of them returned to the same condition of bondage and remained in such a state long after 1827.

Black people made their own meaning from emancipation and used the yearly observation of Emancipation Day to reflect on an unquenched promise of freedom. Peter Williams Jr., one of the most admired black pastors in the city, preached on Independence Day in 1830, "Alas! The freedom to which we have attained is defective."[38] Even as more time passed after the original legislation of slave-owner compensation, the problem of emancipation remained.

VIOLENCE AND HYPERVISIBILITY

Across the North, postslavery laws and policies excluded black communities from full participation in society. By the 1820s, black people were already overrepresented in Massachusetts prisons. A Massachusetts government report from 1821 warned that black migration to Massachusetts had to be banned to "protect the population of this Commonwealth from all dangers and injuries, whether affecting morals or health, whether introduced from foreign countries, or from the sister States of these United States." Black people were defined as a "species of population which threatens to be both injurious and bothersome" to society.[39] Massachusetts proscribed interracial marriage. Black workers across New England would often be "warned out," or denied settlement in towns and chased to the outskirts. They were forced to live on the margins of society, where they formed new families and communities, especially with indigenous peoples of the area.

During the 1830s, a full one-third of the fifteen thousand black people in New York City worked as live-in domestic servants in white homes.[40] The ongoing experience of many black women and men as domestic servants and indentured workers meant they were, in practice, unprotected by law. As a consequence, between 1827 and 1865, there are no recorded cases in New York City of black people seeking legal redress for abuse or infringements by white employers.

Adriance Van Brunt owned a homestead in Brooklyn near the Gowanus Canal. His diary from 1829 to 1832 sheds light on the continuities of slavery for a number of bonded black workers who lived in slave-like conditions on his property. He mentions Old Susan, a black woman who continued to serve as his *unpaid* domestic servant after 1827. He also makes reference to Nancy, a twelve-year-old black girl and an indentured house servant "bound" to his household. Van Brunt employed the labor of "bound boys" and "bonded" field laborers, Frank, Michel, and Harry. In his diary, Van Brunt refers to many black people as the possessions of neighboring white men: "Joseph Woodwards' woman," "Mr. Polhemus' boy." The domestic servants of Adriance Van Brunt, including the elderly woman named Susan, and the young girl named Nancy, were buried on his Brooklyn homestead, somewhere close to Third Avenue and Eighth Street.

Despite the deferred end of slaveholding in the North, the ties of Northern business and finance to the plantation economy grew closer and tighter over time, especially as the Southern cotton economy began its long-term boom in the 1820s. The textile factories of New England were dependent on Southern cotton, and wealth mushroomed as production exploded around this time. Between 1816 and 1840, the number of New England workers employed in large-scale cotton manufacture, in towns such as Lowell, Massachusetts, and Providence, Rhode Island, grew from five thousand to one hundred thousand, approximately one-seventh of New England's entire workforce. What the sugar and rum boom was to the 1700s, the cotton boom was to the following century. A group known as the Cotton Whigs, rich industrialists in the North, fought for the interests of their slave-owning business partners across the South, on whose slave-produced cotton their mills hungrily fed. The Cabots, the Browns, the Lowells, and other grandee merchant families made their wealth from Southern cotton, Northern spindles, and the 4 million African Americans living in slavery.[41]

Not only the New England industrial elite continued their investments in slavery. Small farmers did, too. In New England, long after emancipation, black people continued to be hired for "Negro jobs" and were also "bound out," or placed under indentureship, to do them. During the postslavery period, Northern merchants profiteered by selling free black people into slavery. Black people could be forced to migrate to the South and could then be enslaved in major slaving states such as North Carolina, South Carolina, Georgia, Virginia, or Maryland.

A captured black person in New York City could yield hundreds of dollars on the Charleston slave markets. A New York City kidnapping and reenslave-ment industry flourished, feeding the Southern demand.[42] Blacks working on the docks were especially vulnerable. Children on the city streets were also at significant risk. A November 29, 1835, article in the *New York American* warned, "There are at present in this city a gang of Kidnappers, busily engaged in their vocation of stealing colored children for southern markets!"[43] Black parents put out ads looking for missing children likely captured by enslav-ing kidnappers. Perhaps unsurprisingly, kidnapping rackets linked Southern businessmen, New York police, and New York judges in an unholy alliance to make money from the illicit slave trade.[44]

WHITE ABOLITIONISM

The 1820s and 1830s saw the rise of the white abolitionist press, anchored especially in Boston. Associated with the tireless work of William Lloyd Garrison and the famous *Liberator* newspaper (1831–65), the key planks of white abolitionism included the call for immediate abolition, the celebration of "amalgamation," or the intermarriage between blacks and whites, and the denunciation of schemes to deport freed people from the United States to colonies in West Africa. At the core of white abolitionism sat a yearning for reconciliation and union between the segments of American society torn apart by the legal codes and the customs of racial slavery. This wish for reconcilia-tion went along, however, with a strong tendency to displace the problem of slavery onto the slaveholding South, and to exonerate the "abolitionist North" as savior—liberator—in the painful American saga of the slave traffic.

This characterization is not wholly fair to Garrison, as especially in the early tracts of the *Liberator* he reserved space for the round critique of the hypocrisy of the North, and the injustice suffered by black people amid the so-called Northern emancipations. "If compensation is to be given at all," Garri-son said at the National Anti-Slavery Convention in Philadelphia in 1833, "it should be given to the outraged and guiltless slaves, and not to those who have plundered and abused them." An editorial from the very first year of publication reads, "New England is part of the great federal compact; the same laws govern, the same power protects. . . . In New England, then—proud, spirited, intelligent, patriot New-England—let the torch of emancipation be lighted, to avert the doom that otherwise sooner or later awaits this now prosperous and happy republic."[45] Garrison presents the cause of immediate emancipation in the South as a path for Northern moral redemption. Nevertheless, as the years went on, and perhaps as the problem of slavery in the South loomed larger and drew increasing support from Northern business leaders and political grandees, Garrison tended to externalize the problem, locating it down there, far away, in the Deep South. Identifying an external enemy often serves to distract from inner turmoil and, especially, inner complicity. Over time, the *Liberator* became simultaneously more radical and less self-critical. The goal was to mobilize "Northern sentiment" for immediate abolition down South. The problem of emancipation—indeed, the betrayal of abolition in the North—was far more insidious.

As the counterpoint to the abolitionist press, a virulent proslavery and antiblack press also burgeoned in Boston. Racist cartoons, called bobalition broadsides, mocked the liberatory aspirations and accomplishments of emancipation-era black people, and of revolutionary Haiti. Demeaning and derisive images of black people, especially in urban settings, represented a wish to void out the recent history of black social mobility and self-liberation, and to replace it with stock racist tropes.[46] The broadsides laughed off free black people as unwelcome intruders, evacuating them of their status as social counterparts. A key feature of the Boston press's "black jokes" was making fun of black civic life, especially celebrations, marriages, gatherings, and political meetings. Here, the cartooning of black people provided a trace for how intensely the anti-abolitionist white public wished to preserve and replicate the established order, squarely founded on slavery and colonialism.

At this same time, in New York City, white impersonations on the minstrel stages of black social life and music found audiences. In 1827, Thomas D. Rice, a white performer, developed a slapstick minstrel routine in blackface, in which he imitated African American speech and parodied black music for audiences of the white working class and the newly immigrated. Just as New York's twenty-eight-year-long emancipation process came to an end, white hardship and social resentment found some relief, or perhaps some distraction, in cheap entertainment based in depictions of black abjection.[47]

Rice made the Jim Crow character his signature by 1832, especially the song "Jump, Jim Crow," based on his rendition of a disabled black stable groom. Another of Rice's famous routines was the "shadow dance," in which he came onstage with a sack slung over his shoulder, then began to sing a version of "Me and My Shadow" while a child actor in blackface crawled out of the sack and danced behind him.

In response to the emergence of a free black population in the North, a virulent backlash of fists and bats spread across many cities during the 1820s and 1830s. Pennsylvania instituted a ban on black people entering the state. In 1837, the General Assembly voted to bar free black men from the franchise, restricting it to "white freemen only." White mob violence against black people and white abolitionists became a major feature of 1830s Northern urban experience. In Philadelphia, in 1834, antiblack riots burst onto the streets, targeting churches, meeting halls, as well as individual black community leaders. White mobs in Philadelphia committed five terror attacks against the black community between 1834 and 1849.

Widespread riots in 1835 led to the stoning of abolitionists in Concord, New Hampshire. In October 1835, in Boston, a mob captured William Lloyd Garrison and dragged him through the streets at the end of a rope. He was rescued by the mayor and kept in a jail for a night to keep him safe. In New York City, white anti-abolitionist publicist James Watson Webb warned that the "amalgamation of the races" would undermine the "genius" of his race. For people such as Webb, the loss of white supremacy was tantamount to "annihilation." According to him, racial hierarchy was a requirement for social order. On July 4, 1834, on the seven-year anniversary of the abolition of New York slavery, a black group gathered at Chatham Street Chapel to celebrate.

White vigilantes attacked those gathering at the church. Between July 9 and 12, 1834, white bands destroyed the homes of abolitionist Arthur Tappan and the minister Peter Williams Jr., as well as many homes and businesses of black people in the Five Points area. They burned the theater across the street from the AME Zion church on Leonard and Church Streets.[48]

NAMING THE MADNESS

Freed black thinkers dealt with this postslavery reality in fascinating and perceptive ways. They developed modes of interpretation and social analysis to name the madness of antiblackness that surrounded them. In 1829, David Walker, a black author raised in North Carolina but writing from Boston, wrote an "appeal to the coloured citizens of the world." His appeal included an inventory of racial injustices that persisted in New England society. He observed that black people were emancipated but left without land. "I ask those people who treat us so *well*, Oh! I ask them, where is the most barren spot of land which they have given unto us? . . . But I must really observe that in this very city, when a man of colour dies, if he owned any real estate it most generally falls into the hands of some white person."[49]

Walker indicted the postslavery regime of nonredress and inequity. "Now I appeal to heaven and to earth, and particularly to the American people themselves, who cease not to declare that our condition is not *hard*, and that we are comparatively satisfied to rest in wretchedness and misery, under them and their children,—not, indeed, to show me a colored President, a Governor, a Legislator, a Senator, a Mayor, or an Attorney at the Bar;—but to show me a man of color, who holds the law office of constable, or one who sits in a Juror Box, even on a case of one of his wretched brethren, throughout this great Republic!" David Walker died at his home in Boston under suspicious circumstances, aged thirty-three. Although the coroner attested that he died of "consumption," many in the black community believed he was murdered by agents of the proslavery cause. Legislators perpetuate an unjust social order not only by the inequitable laws they pass but also by the extralegal forces they tacitly mobilize—especially terror and murder—to keep critiques quiet, and to keep radical alternatives out of the public imagination.

Many black newspapers based in New York City were devoted to critique and the discussion of alternatives. Samuel Cornish and John Russwurm's *Freedom's Journal* (1827–29) provides perhaps the clearest example of how free black communities reasoned through the perplexity of "gradual emancipation" and the rising antiblack backlash of the times. Articles in *Freedom's Journal* compared different emancipation processes across the Americas, with particular attention given to *coartación* in Cuba, as well as the movement toward general emancipation in the British empire. The revolutionary liberation of the Haitian people received special attention in *Freedom's Journal*. Haiti represented the radical promise of full freedom—freedom on the terms of the formerly enslaved, not of the slave-owners.

The journal devoted significant attention to the development and activities of black voluntary organizations, black churches, and black benevolent societies involved in grassroots organization and mutual aid. And it also overtly advocated for compensation for freed people. "If compensation be demanded as an act of justice to the slave holder, in the event of the liberation of his slaves;—let justice take her free, impartial course;—let compensation be made in the first instance, where it is most due;—let compensation be first made to the slave, for his long years of uncompensated labor, degradation, and suffering." If white abolitionists focused on the incubus of the American South, black authors had a broader, comparative mindset, contemplating the diverse problems with and possibilities of emancipation in Cuba, Haiti, and Jamaica, as well as the limitations of emancipation in the American North.

Hosea Easton, a black and indigenous preacher from Massachusetts, published his own survey of legal inequities facing black people in 1837. Easton laid out an extensive political treatise showing that Bay State laws continued to advantage white communities, and to encourage the abuse and mistreatment of black peoples. In this remarkable future-oriented text, Easton surveyed the long track record of European colonial destruction, culminating in the "motely mix of barbarism and civilization, of fraud and philanthropy . . . or religion and bloodshed" across the Americas. He insisted that "merely to cease beating the colored people, is nonsense." He went on:

> Emancipation . . . must restore to them all that slavery has taken away from them. . . . Nothing short of an entire reversal of the slave system in theory and practice—in general and in specific—will ever accomplish the work of redeeming the colored people of this country from their present condition.
>
> Let the country, then, no longer act the part of the thief. Let the free state no longer act the part of them who passed by on the other side, and leaving the colored people half dead, especially when they were beaten by their own hands, and so call it emancipation—raising a wonderment why the half dead people do not heal themselves.[50]

Easton's voice echoed across the parched moral terrain of Puritan New England. The traces of unjust emancipation in New England grew stronger, not fainter, over time. In 1850, the Fugitive Slave Act was passed by the US House of Representatives and officially made all free black people in the United States vulnerable to enslavement. The law stipulated "that any person who shall knowingly and willingly obstruct, hinder, or prevent such claimant . . . from arresting such fugitives . . . or shall harbor or conceal such fugitives . . . shall for either of said offences be subject to imprisonment." The Fugitive Slave Act has been described as a yet another "compromise" to preserve the Union—a compromise made by the "abolitionist" North with the "slaveholding" South. However, as we have seen, slavery's circuits of wealth extraction crisscrossed the American North and South, binding them together. These two siblings, despite their feuds, were facets of the same national personality.

In 1851, Thomas Sims, a man who had escaped from slavery, took refuge in Boston. After his capture, he sued for his freedom. Edward Greely Loring, a probate judge in Massachusetts and a member of a Cotton Whig Boston family, ordered Thomas Sims sent back into slavery in the South. Three years later, in 1854, Loring similarly ordered Anthony Burns, a fugitive in Boston, to be returned to slavery in Virginia. When Anthony Burns was returned to Virginia, the slave-owner kept him tightly shackled in a slave pen for four months, permanently damaging his health. A group of black abolitionists in Boston purchased his freedom in 1855. Burns subsequently moved back North, eventually to St. Catharines, Canada, where he died at age twenty-eight.[51]

These kinds of eventualities made it clear to black people in New England that not only were they not safe from marauding "slave catchers" but the state and its judges would honor slavery's property relations and strip black people of protections against reenslavement. The message from the state was clear to black people: they had to watch their backs because white supremacy ruled the North, too. The business up North of catching black people, chaining them, and transferring them to the South was sanctioned under federal law between 1850 and 1864.

The *Dred Scott v. Sandford* Supreme Court case of 1857 exacerbated the situation. The majority of the Supreme Court justices decided that black people across all of the United States, from Maine to Louisiana, should not be considered citizens of the United States and should "therefore claim none of the rights and privileges which that instrument provides for and secures to the citizens of the United States." Wherever the abolition of slavery was left incomplete, the US Supreme Court had decisively and immediately allowed laws to dispossess the black population further.

During this period, New England's ties with slavery did not only range over land but also seas. The American North, in the cities of Boston, Providence, New York, and Baltimore, provided ports for slaving vessels all the way until the 1850s. The outlawing of the Atlantic slave trade by British, American, French, Dutch, and Portuguese empires in 1831 meant that the trade was categorized as "illegal," even as it exploded in scale over the subsequent decades. Slave ships, financed by New England investors and outfitted and manned from Boston's Long Wharf, played an important role in the forced migration of more than eight hundred thousand persons from West and Central Africa to Brazil between 1830 and 1856. An especially stealthy type of vessel, fashioned exclusively in Baltimore—the Baltimore clipper—became a favorite among slave-trafficking marauders in this period.

In 1855, just months before the slave ship *Mary E. Smith* was captured off the coast of Brazil, it had docked at Boston's port. Spending ten days at port, the crew of the *Mary E. Smith* procured wood planks, metal shackles, and a large number of water casks—equipment for slaving voyages and human captivity. The ship then sailed on a slave-trafficking mission to Angola. In Boston, the ship was identified by its scent: the smell of death and human cargo specific to slaving vessels. The smell of slave ships was so familiar and distinctive that people of that time had special ways of describing it: "the smell of the night"; the stench; the *catinga*. Despite the smell of slavery, no Boston harbor officials stopped the ship's onward journey.[52]

On January 20, 1856, the *Mary E. Smith* approached the shores of northern Brazil and was intercepted by an antislavery squadron. Escorted to the shore of Bahia, Brazil, the 387 African captives rescued from the *Mary E. Smith* were led to prison cells at the House of Correction in Salvador, where they were incarcerated again. Many of these African people subsequently died in detention because of diseases resulting from human caging. Only 146 of the "rescued" persons survived, and most of them were forced into hard labor or trafficked into the Brazilian plantation complex.

But the story doesn't end there. Captain Vincent D. Cranotick and his crew had tossed at least 133 Africans overboard, some already dead and others still living, during the ship's passage. Slave-traffickers commonly jettisoned African captives—the deceased, the ill, and the rebellious—into the sea.[53] Cranotick died in prison in Salvador, Brazil. The *Mary E. Smith*, the Boston schooner, continued to deliver cargoes for decades afterward between different ports along the Eastern Seaboard.

GHOSTLINING IN THE NORTH

Harriet Beecher Stowe's 1851 novel, *Uncle Tom's Cabin*, consolidated the Northern vision of slavery as something that happened at a distance. Stowe, a Boston abolitionist, begins her novel in Kentucky, with a slave-owner named Shelby selling a young black boy and a middle-aged black man to settle his debts. Stowe provides her audience a glimpse into Southern slavery, and she depicts the institution in gross detail. Shelby calls one of the enslaved children on the plantation his "little Jim Crow" and asks him to dance for a prospective buyer, Haley. Jim Crow, the generic name for the subservient slave, appears as a fantasy figure—the placeholder for a void—in the minds not just of the white slave-owners, but also the author and her intended readership. Beecher introduces this fantasy of subservient blackness in the novel's opening paragraph and suggests that it pervades the South—and not the North—like the scent of a poisonous night blossom.

New England historical narrations of this time commonly celebrated the abolition of slavery while also erasing black people from the depiction of New England society. A whole school of historians arose in the 1850s exonerating the North and praising New England's abolitionist "intelligence." William Sumner explained in his *History of East Boston* (1858) that "slavery was repugnant to the Puritans." Emory Washburn claimed (1857), "Slavery was sustained only by force of the policy and laws of the mother country [Britain], and was abolished by the people by the very first clause in the organic law of the state." These ways of writing history were not only about romanticizing the past but whitewashing the present. The New England mode of historical narration—which was also a way of perpetually deferring historical reality—was a practice of amnesia toward the past, and of political disavowal toward the present day.

At the same time, black people, in their art and advocacy, showed that slavery continued to live a long death in the North. In 1859, Harriet Wilson, one of the first African American novelists, gave witness to the continuities of slavery at the Boston fireside. Wilson, born in 1825 in New Hampshire, was a black child of the "gradual emancipations."

Although technically born free, Wilson was indentured until the age of eighteen and lived in slave-like bondage. She married twice, but both men died. She had to put her son in a poorhouse while she struggled to make ends meet as a maid in the homes of white Bostonians. Her son would die of fever just one year after she was forced to give him up.

In 1859, at age thirty-four, Harriet Wilson published *Our Nig.*[54] Wilson's autobiographical novel explores the Northern afterlife of slavery. In Wilson's depiction, emancipation did not mark a break in time, but a conveyance. In the very first words of the novel, a shadow falls across the page:

> Sketches from the Life of a Free Black, in a Two-Story White House, North.
> Showing that slavery's shadows fall even there.

Shadows tell us about the existence of things not directly seen, but that we know to exist. They provide evidence for the presence of entities that are otherwise out of view. Shadows can indicate a haunting presence. In *Our Nig,* Alfrado, or Frado, the main character, like so many of the approximately 1,250 black women living in Boston around that time, is a domestic servant. Frado, like Wilson herself, is an orphaned black girl. She grows up in the house of the Bellmonts, an upper-class white family. Members of the family nickname her Nig. The children in the family taunt her; the parents scold and punish her and lock her up in the house. The Bellmonts' children grow older and eventually marry. Frado, meanwhile, continues to wash and iron the clothes, bake and cook, and clean the house. As she grows up from a child to an adolescent, to an adult, however, the Bellmonts do not see her as a person, capable of growth and change, but as their unchanging property. She is part of the furniture of their lives.

The novel is not about deliverance from bondage in the North, but about its perpetuation. Frado is eventually transferred, effectively "loaned out," to another home. Long-term nagging illness continues to diminish and deplete her. Health is a social phenomenon, and Wilson shows how the long, unending death of slavery in New England causes Frado's slow physical deterioration. Infirm and unable to work, Frado receives the begrudging attention of the Bellmonts' doctor. As she regains her fragile health, she is again put in service. "Nothing new under the sun," writes the author in the last chapter. The plot of *Our Nig* is about recurring patterns: the addictions of white privilege and the continuities of racial property rights and the legal systems that underpin it.

Another very different analysis of the continuities of slavery in and through Northern emancipations unfolds in W. E. B. Du Bois's 1896 sociological study of the black community in Philadelphia. Du Bois, a leading black thinker and Pan-Africanist, was born in 1868 in Great Barrington, Massachusetts, to a mother who, like Harriet Wilson, worked as a domestic servant. Du Bois benefited from the support of his mother's white employers, who helped ensure the education of this "sentimental" youth. A graduate of Fisk and Harvard, Du Bois took up his first academic position teaching at a black college, Wilberforce University, in Ohio. Soon, he accepted a short-term research position in Philadelphia to study the "social problem" of the postslavery black community. The sponsors of the study, including Susan P. Wharton, of the influential Quaker family, and Charles C. Harrison, provost of the University of Pennsylvania, said they wanted "to know precisely how this class of [black] people live; what occupations they follow; from what occupations they are excluded; how many of their children go to school; and to ascertain every fact which will throw light on this social problem."[55]

Du Bois's research reinterpreted "the Negro problems of Philadelphia" so as to shed light on the social problem of white supremacy. Du Bois's resulting book, *The Philadelphia Negro* (1899), explores how the *conditions* of slavery remained in place long after the formal legal institution of slavery passed away.[56] Du Bois's work, in essence, investigated how the social affliction of systemic racism perpetuated itself—not primarily through individual acts of bias or prejudice, but through long-term, unremedied, impersonal legal structures of denial that impair reciprocity. Du Bois captured this problem of the ghost line, and its way of dismantling reciprocity, in the following excerpt of his concluding chapter:

> Other centuries looking back upon the culture of the nineteenth would have a right to suppose that if, in a land of freemen, eight millions of human beings were found to be dying of disease, the nation would cry

with one voice, "Heal them!" If they were staggering on in ignorance, it would cry, "Train them!" If they were harming themselves and others by crime, it would cry, "Guide them!" And such cries are heard and have been heard in the land; but it was not one voice and its volume has been ever broken by counter-cries and echoes, "Let them die!" "Train them like slaves!" "Let them stagger downward!"

Du Bois points to the "echoes" of the slave-owners' voices still heard long after individual slave-owners pass away. "This is the spirit that enters in and complicates all Negro social problems and this is a problem which only civilization and humanity can successfully solve." Du Bois leaves us to sit with the problem of deferred social afflictions and the ongoing denial of proper reparations for slavery. He observes, here, precisely through his study of *Northern*, not Southern, conditions, how the echoes of injustice reverberate from deep in the past and afflict the present.

CHAPTER 2

PUNISHING THE BLACK NATION IN HAITI

On New Year's Day, 1804, when the Haitian people smashed the chains of slavery, they walked into an international order seeking their return to bondage and oppression. The story of Haiti shows that imperial powers concertedly worked to disfigure black liberation, unleashing a destructive aftermath that lasted more than two centuries after the declaration of Haitian independence. A pact between France and other European and American states ensured that Haiti's postslavery future would be marked by debilitating punishments for daring to be free.

Twenty years after the people declared their freedom, in 1825, the French state enforced a retroactive emancipation process on Haiti before allowing it to gain access to the international community of nations. As part of this retroactive emancipation, Haiti had to pay reparations to the former slave-owners and accept a tremendous debt burden, making two things clear. First, emancipation, as a process to abolish slavery, is something different from and effectively antithetical to the black liberation struggle. And second, emancipations are processes owned and run by slave-owners and their states, often aimed at containing and constraining the future possibilities of black freedom. The nations of North America and Europe would not officially engage with Haiti as a sovereign nation until France had "emancipated" it; that is, until Haiti was reassigned a place in the international Euro-American regime of colonial rule and antiblackness.

* * *

Christopher Columbus, in 1492, reached the shores of the island that indigenous people called Ayiti. He returned a year later with *becerrillo* hounds and military weapons to wage war against the indigenous Taino people, and to conquer the island. He renamed it Hispaniola and claimed it as a Spanish possession.[1] In 1664, French emperor Louis XIV chartered a new enterprise, the Compagnie des Indes, to take sole authority over the French trade in enslaved African people to Ayiti and to develop sugar and tobacco plantations on the western portion of the island. This monopoly company allowed the French state to siphon wealth from the slave trade and the production of agricultural commodities. In late 1694, at a time of European competition for new colonial territories, France purchased ownership of the western portion of indigenous Ayiti, as if the land were Spain's to sell. France named their new colony Saint-Domingue and began transforming it in short order into one of the most intensive plantation economies on earth. During the coming century, an extensive web of investors and oppressors—planters, merchants, financiers, and political elites—stretching from the colony to the port cities of France, to the imperial center of Paris, fed from the bounty generated by the plantations.

French settlers in Saint-Domingue established and then expanded a system of slave production in which vast swathes of land stolen from indigenous peoples were enclosed and turned into mills for sugar, coffee, indigo, sisal, and tobacco cultivation. In the 1700s, as the European demand expanded for nutrients, intoxicants, and other chemical compounds from the distant tropics, the Domingois planters rapidly expanded production. One hundred sugar mills operated across the whole colony in 1717, increasing to more than 539 in 1754, and more than 800 at the peak of agricultural output in 1789. By the 1760s, production of coffee quadrupled in a decade, as plantation capitalists sold the fruit of 100 million coffee trees.[2]

Planters saw the land as a mine, and they sought to extract as much "rent" from it as possible in the form of sugarcane, coffee berries, indigo grass, and cacao beans. As the Brazilian historian Antonio Barros de Castro pointed out, plantation capitalists saw the enslaved African workers as extensions of land— as part of the exploitable environment. Along with the cane, berries, and nuts,

Saint-Domingue's planters extracted as much labor as possible from the enslaved.[3] Exhausted plantations were worked by exhausted enslaved African people, who had been captured and shipped in tremendous numbers to feed an insatiable European hunger for the products from the tropics.

Saint-Domingue's legal regime, the Code Noir, crystallized a colonial system that rewarded the squander of black people's lives. The code, established under Louis XIV in 1685, barred enslaved people from carrying money, selling goods, leaving the plantations, meeting in groups, reading books, carrying weapons, or practicing their religion. The edict made slavery hereditary under French colonial law, such that the "children born of the marriage between slaves will be slaves." Furthermore, planters could force Africans to toil without limit, except for "midnight to the other midnight" of Sundays and Catholic holidays. In Saint-Domingue, as in other El Dorado plantation colonies such as Jamaica and Brazil, the antiblack colonial legal system and the supercharged economic interests combined in the 1700s to produce extremely high death rates of the enslaved, requiring new captives to be continually imported from Africa. These colonies were places of death, out of whose decay the plantation capitalists filched the energy and creativity of African people along with agricultural commodities from the land to feed European demand.

Plantation production across the French West Indies surged from the 1730s to the 1780s, both stimulating and responding to the burgeoning industrial revolution in Europe and the American North. Big agriculture in the colonies and industrialization in Europe and settler America went hand in hand. Plantation sugarcane provided the cheap calories needed to feed Europe's proletarianizing laborers, while plantation cotton supplied the cheap fabric to clothe them. The rise of the European working classes depended on the extracted labor from enslaved Africans. And, conversely, the success of European capitalists in organizing and controlling laborers stimulated the demand for raw plantation goods, as factories arose in Europe to refine sugar, grind coffee, and prepare cocoa powder.

By the 1770s, Saint-Domingue had more than eight hundred sugar plantations, two thousand coffee plantations, and seven hundred cotton plantations. It produced approximately 40 percent of all the sugar and 60 percent of all the coffee circulating in the whole Atlantic economy, more sugar per year than all the sugar colonies of Britain combined. The island's sugar, cocoa, and coffee production generated more than one-quarter of the France's annual income.[4] The wealth of Paris, Bordeaux, Nantes, and Marseilles came from accumulated wealth of this slavery.

The eighteenth-century French mode of plantation production had no semblance of the "Protestant ethic" of Samuel Johnston's colonial North Carolina or Benjamin Franklin's colonial Pennsylvania. The eighteenth-century slavery economy of Saint-Domingue was devoted to orgies of human and ecological plunder. One Haitian historian, Pompée-Valentin Vastey, writing in 1814, recorded the "secret full of horror" of the old slavery regime. His text is a gruesome documentation of more than eighty-five specific incidents of brutality and torture in the years leading up to 1791, which he identified as symptomatic of the Domingois plantation system as a whole. The report is a catalog of mutilations, dismemberment, and sexual violation. The Code Noir prescribed public torture as an appropriate punishment for the enslaved people who resisted bondage, codifying cutting off ears, slicing hamstrings, burning with hot irons, and execution as "just" punishments. This definition of justice belonged to the slave-owners and amounted to a state-sanctioned terror regime.

"Yes, they all committed such horrors, participated in them and contributed to them," Vastey wrote about the planter class of Saint-Domingue.[5] The extreme tortures recorded in Vastey's account seem almost phantasmagoric. Similar practices were inventoried by the planter Pierre-Joseph Laborie.[6] Laborie recorded the forms of violence and violation he legally imposed on the African people on his enclosure. Mutilations, sexual violence, lynchings, sadistic humiliations, all formed part of the repertoire of rule cataloged by both Vastey, as observer, and Laborie, as participant. The plantation elite, known as the *grands* and *petits blancs*, big- and small-scale white planters, stole the labor of hundreds of thousands of African captives, resorting to spectacles of extreme violence as they tried to preserve a social system devoted to theft.

By the 1740s, slave-traders brought more than twenty thousand African captives to the colony every year. By the 1770s, more than 330,000 enslaved African people lived on the island, the vast majority directly kidnapped from their homes in the interiors and along the coasts of West Africa. West Africa is one of the most ethnically and linguistically diverse regions on earth. French slave-traders and plantation owners therefore inadvertently created a captive laboring population with a dense ethnic and linguistic diversity. War captives from more than twenty different African linguistic, ethnic, and cultural groups found themselves packed together on the Domingois plantations, where they began inventing new traditions and a new language together, metamorphosing through their dislocation.[7] The slave-owners did not perceive, let alone value, this tremendous African diversity. For them, there were only three types of black people: the *creoles*, born in the colony; the *bossales*, born in Africa; and the *anciens libres*, who were emancipated by their owners. These categories were centered in European ideas about race and slavery, not in African identities or cultures.

The plantation mode of production created the social contradictions that would cause the society to implode. Only forty thousand white and mixed-race property owners ruled over more than three hundred thousand African peoples torn from their families and lifeways, exiled to islands an ocean away, and dumped on the shores of a roaring, devouring plantation machine. The planters used their patrols and militias, and the armor of their laws, to rule by dread and by the discipline of universal fear. The enslaved were "constantly watched," wrote Elias Monnereau, a plantation owner of Saint-Domingue, in his manual from 1769. Laborie observed, "In order to make the best of the power of the negro, and to keep him in subjection, chastisement is often necessary." Monnereau and Laborie lived in a planter's fantasy world, though, because surveilled people do not submit, they resist. And chastised people do not cower, they revolt.

Captive Africans resisted primarily by running away from the plantations, in what was known since the origins of plantation slavery in the 1500s as *marronage*, from the Spanish word *cimarrón*, or "going into the wild." In the French colonies, *marronage* referred to flight into the mountains away from the plantations and patrols. Saint-Domingue, like Jamaica, was vast and craggy, its interior largely unsurveillable. Only a small percentage of the colony's land was taken for plantations. This left vast swathes of mountainous karst into which captive African people could flee.

The enslaved, banned from access to letters and arms, primarily resisted with their feet. The island of Hispaniola, as one of the first locations of African enslavement in the Americas, was ground zero for marronage. For hundreds of years, increasing exponentially with the growth of plantation production in the eighteenth century, black people liberated themselves by fleeing from the coastal towns and savannas into the mountainous interior. They formed Maroon village communities beyond the reach of the colonial state. Marronage was the root and first cause of the Haitian people's collective self-liberation.[8]

More than forty-eight thousand enslaved people escaped the plantations between 1764 and 1793.[9] In addition to the *grand marronage*, "permanent escape," many tens of thousands more Africans participated in the *petit marronage*, "small flight," by temporarily absconding from the plantations, whether for a night or for days at a time, for social gatherings, fetes, and respite. Small flights could also include everyday acts of disobedience—foot-dragging, sabotage, and secrecy, for example. The brutality of the punishment regime in Saint-Domingue, as recorded by Vastey and others, only reflected the growing loss of control by the white planters over the massive black undercaste.

PEOPLE'S REVOLUTION

By the mid-1700s, the plantation mode of production in Saint-Domingue gave birth to a society ready for mass rebellion. François Makandal, a Vodou bocor, or diviner and spiritual leader, led a revolutionary movement of Maroons and plantation captives in the 1750s. Makandal organized ceremonies, taught healing cures, and prepared toxins in a plot to orchestrate the mass poisoning of plantation owners and a large-scale revolt against the planters of the island. In 1758, the planter patrol captured him and publicly burned him at the stake in Port-au-Prince.

The Haitian people sparked off an insurgency some thirty years later, in what became the Haitian Revolution. On August 14, 1791, a *houngan*, or Vodou priest, Dutty Boukman, and Cécile Fatiman, a Vodou priestess, or *mambo*, held a large gathering to organize revolutionary action among the enslaved at a place called Bois Caïman in the northern interior of the island. The ceremony and the dancing lasted all night. Folk tradition recalls Boukman speaking these words:

> Our god, who is so good, so just, he orders us to revenge our wrongs. It's
> he who will direct our arms and bring us the victory. It's he who will assist
> us. We all should throw away the image of the white man's gods who are
> so pitiless. Listen to the voice for liberty that speaks in all our hearts.[10]

The unfolding drama set in motion a massive social movement, unique in world history, of abolition by revolution. The Haitian Africans rejected any kind of state-imposed freedom that compromised with the interests of slaveowners. Africans combined to capture the state apparatus and define political liberation on their own terms.[11]

For the crowd gathered around Boukman and Fatiman, the core contention was for immediate freedom—the total control over their own bodies, their own labor, and their family's lands. Freedom from slavery meant no longer being rentable by white planters. Le Cap became the hub for Boukman's revolutionary mobilization. The French colonial militia captured and beheaded him in November and displayed his severed head in an attempt to enthrall the enslaved in fear.

Freedom for Haitians had other meanings, too. About one year earlier, Vincent Ogé, a businessman of mixed race, known within the Domingois racial hierarchy as a "free man of color" (*gens de couleur libre*) because of his partial white parentage, attempted a rebellion against the planter class to demand civil rights, especially the right to vote, which under the Code Noir was reserved only for island whites. Ogé, once captured, was publicly broken on the wheel and executed in the northern town of Le Cap. However, the contention by Boukman and Fatiman for self-ownership and rights to land, on one hand, and by Ogé for civil rights and equitable participation in the state, on the other, outlived the physical lives of these revolutionaries. The interests of African and Creole groups combined into a broad definition of collective liberation. And from that new consciousness resulted unprecedented political developments.

The masses of enslaved black people took up an open revolutionary struggle beginning in August 1791. During thirteen years of revolution, the people continually reasserted their claim to the multiple facets of freedom, and their absolute unwillingness to compromise with the regime of white rule and plantation slavery. The Haitian Revolution was, at its core, a people's revolution, surpassing and surviving the limits of a succession of revolutionary generalissimos.

By 1792, a new leader emerged. Toussaint, a black person emancipated in 1776, was a military and political strategist par excellence. He renounced his slave-owner's surname, Bréda, and renamed himself Louverture, meaning "the breach" or "the opening." In 1793, large numbers of white slave-owners had already fled the island as Toussaint-Louverture's revolutionary army spread across the northern coast and hinterlands and swept southward toward Port-au-Prince. In August 1793, the French colonial governors in Saint-Domingue, overwhelmed by the uprising and fearful of invasions by British and Spanish forces, summarily declared the immediate abolition of slavery in the colony in hopes of quelling the African insurgency and staving off foreign conquest.[12]

This was not emancipation, or "letting free from the hand." This was liberation, or the claiming of freedom by the hands of the oppressed. A year later, on February 5, 1794, in the midst of the French Revolution, the National Assembly in Paris approved the abolition of slavery in the colony of Saint-Domingue. No emancipation process was implemented, since the black people of Haiti had already stolen freedom for themselves. But despite the unfolding Haitian liberation, the French state would continue to insist on an emancipation process—a slave-owner compensation scheme—for decades to come.

Toussaint-Louverture identified politically as a Jacobin, meaning he pursued a twin policy of revolution from slavery and reconciliation with the French imperial system. Louverture was both, and perhaps contradictorily, a revolutionary and a reformer. He wished to modify the French imperial order to make room for the Haitian nation of freed black people. For many years of the long revolution, he maintained allegiance and even admiration for imperial France, declaring the wish to be "black, free, and French."

Toussaint also took inspiration from the Maroon spirit of Haiti and Jamaica, and its insistence on black liberated space.[13] Toussaint was the leader of the people's political body, and the architect of a new Haitian government. In 1801, having successfully routed the French colonial forces, Louverture declared himself governor of Haiti. With words that would ricochet across the Americas and inspire enslaved folk and black and white abolitionists abroad, Toussaint-Louverture's constitution of 1801 declared, "There can be no slaves on the territory, servitude is therein forever abolished. All men are born, live, and die Free and French."

This first Haitian revolutionary constitution—six more would follow over the coming fifteen years—also defined the right of families to be "shareholders" in the cultivation of land. In addition to rights relating to land, labor, the "inviolability of the home," and to the protection of people's own bodies, the constitution outlined the rights of participation in the civil sphere. All Haitian citizens had the right to education, to the vote, and to fair trials. Resonating with the conception of freedom articulated by revolutionary movements in North America and in France, the constitution defined the protections and the privileges of a free people. However, the constitution went beyond these in its specificity: this was a constitution for free people collectively *liberated from slavery*. As such, it included unique and unprecedented articles in the comparative history of republicanism:

> Article 3—There can be no slaves on this territory; servitude has been forever abolished.
> Article 4—All men work at all forms of employment, whatever their color.

As of 1801, this new nation's constitution was anchored in antislavery, seen from the perspective of the black masses, and not the slave-owners. No indemnities for "property loss" in the form of enslaved persons, no phaseouts, no legal privileges. The constitution stipulated that forfeited plantations became the property of the state and would be used for common benefit. In the years after 1801, Louverture's deputies took things further by committing themselves to the total extirpation of slave-owners from Haitian society. This first constitution, still promulgated under the name of Saint-Domingue, and the subsequent ones after 1804 under the revolutionary and historical name of Haiti, defined slave-owners as perpetrators of crimes, and not as dispossessed owners of slave property. All other governments of Europe and North America, even as they eventually implemented abolition, adopted measures friendly to slave-owners and called these measures "emancipation acts." Only in revolutionary Haiti did abolition erupt without emancipation, through articles of liberation that held slave-owners accountable for crimes. In 1802, Louverture began articulating the ultimatum of total separation from France, in the face of France's insistence on reinstituting slavery.

In France, Napoléon Bonaparte rose to power in 1799, becoming first consul of the revolutionary republic. Soon after, he declared himself emperor. Napoléon directed his brother-in-law Charles Leclerc to travel to Haiti with forty thousand French troops to reenslave the Haitian people. Even after the French abolition of slavery in Saint-Domingue, Guadeloupe, and Guyana in 1794 in response to the Haitian revolutionaries, and after France's own revolution based on the ideals of "liberty, fraternity, and equality," and after the declaration of a new national constitution by Louverture in 1801, the French under Bonaparte spared no effort in the pursuit of reenslavement and recolonization. In 1802, Napoléon revoked the abolitions of 1794, rejecting the obvious fact of Haitian self-determination and black freedom.

In 1802, French forces invaded Haiti. After many of his closest generals surrendered, Toussaint also conceded defeat. In June, the French forced him and his whole family onto a ship called *Le Héros*, captives bound for France. French authorities then separated Toussaint from his family, taking him to the

Fort de Joux, a prison castle in easternmost France. Toussaint's wife, children, and ninety-two-year-old grandfather were sent to Bayonne, near the southwest border, some one thousand kilometers away. Louverture was stripped of his uniform and given convict's fatigues.

Toussaint, the black Jacobin, was accused of stealing from the French state, which provided the pretext for his interrogation and torture. The interrogations, continuing from September through January, 1802–3, had no other purpose than to derange a prisoner who dared claim he and his people could be black and free. The interrogator, Commander Baille, ensured that Toussaint's body was ruined, while also working to undo his mind. They put him in solitary. They prevented him from sleeping. They deprived him of blankets. After months of this treatment, Toussaint was "feverish and trembling from cold." They killed him slowly, and when he passed away on April 7, 1803, after nine months of horrendous treatment, they claimed he died a natural death.[14]

What happened next in Haiti can only be described as the second people's revolution. This time, the self-emancipated Haitian people rose up in a *levée en masse*, a spontaneous mass uprising, and rejected the reimposition of the slave regime. Over the next two years, from 1802 to 1804, Jean-Jacques Dessalines, one of Toussaint's generals, stepped in as generalissimo of the people's rebellion. He was known as "the African" because of his alignment with the undercaste of African-born people, and not primarily with the "free people of color" or the *anciens libres*. Dessalines became the new energy conduit for the mass mobilization, unleashing a pitiless counterattack against the remaining plantation elites and their auxiliaries. Unlike Toussaint, Dessalines professed no desire to be "black, free, and French"; instead, he wanted Haiti for the Africans, and Haitian Africans to obtain sovereign status in the world.

When Dessalines declared the final defeat of French forces and national independence on January 1, 1804, a thirteen-year-long struggle came to an end. The new constitution of 1804 again declared the liberty of the Haitian people, making no reference to emancipation. If emancipations serve to preserve the slave-owners' world of property and privilege, Haitian liberation exploded the contours and presumptions of that world. Black freedom pursued liberation *without* emancipation—a collective freedom of Haitian Africans stolen from out of the grasp of the French plantocracy. Dessalines called for a "Haitian empire." On May 20, 1805, he promulgated a new version of the constitution, declaring sovereignty from "any other power in the universe, under the name of the empire of Hayti."[15] Dessalines and the Haitians demanded international recognition as a sovereign people, even as European and American nations continued to honor France's ongoing pretensions to own Haiti.

SUCCOR FOR SLAVE-OWNERS

In France, the rush to provide succor to slave-owners began in the first years of the revolution and continued for a century. Starting in 1792, the year after the revolution began, French slave-owners began migrating as refugees to other parts of the Caribbean, to the United States, and to the Isle de France in the Indian Ocean. French planters fled to Martinique, Havana, Kingston, New Orleans, Charleston, Savannah, and Philadelphia as refugee slave-owners seeking asylum in other Atlantic plantation kingdoms. Many returned to France after the restoration of the Bourbon king in 1814. Through it all, they ceaselessly pined over their losses of property in land and in slaves because of the "perfidious Blacks and Mulattoes." Planter migrants from the former slave colony fled with their baggage of nostalgia for the olden days. French writers of the time commonly waxed poetic and melancholic about the "ruins of empires" and their lost grandeur. In the minds of the colonists, Haiti was a place of burned-down mansions, sacked churches, ruined cane fields, and their lost and stolen property.[16]

By this time, Le Cap, the main city of the white slave-owning elite, was burning. Scores of plantations had been sacked by the self-liberating Haitian people, with torched manor houses, cracked waterwheels, demolished sugar mills, broken coaches, and crushed aqueducts.

French slave-owners who were expelled from Haiti during the revolution (1791–1804) received compensation from the French government.[17] By

1792, the government was already providing assistance payments (the *secours*) to refugee planters. The French Assembly voted three times to expand the program, in 1794, 1796, and 1797. Planters had to file claims every six months to continue to receive the aid. Initially intended as a temporary scheme, the *secours* lasted for more than a century after Haitian independence. Not only slave-owners but also their descendants—many of whom had never stepped foot in Haiti—continued to receive *secours* from the French public purse until 1911. Some 25,838 French slave-owners or descendants of slave-owners received Haiti's ransom money during the nineteenth century, even as Haiti's national budget remained in chronic deficit.

In 1803, Napoléon forgave the debts of the refugee planters from Haiti.[18] These measures all established a long-term, intergenerational reparations program for the perpetrators of genocide. In their filings, erstwhile slave-owners presented themselves as deprived and abandoned. They blamed their moral and emotional position on black Haitians who stole their own freedom and converted themselves from legal property into sovereign persons through their own revolutionary actions. From 1804 well into the 1880s, the French planters and their children quixotically hoped that slavery would be reimposed. One official report from 1820 stated, "The old colonists remain interested, without doubt, in reclaiming their land and their slaves."[19] An 1831 collective letter from former slave-owners to the French secretary of state complained, "Despite the past half century, still victims, the colonists of St. Domingue have still not been asked to give their perspectives or to discuss their interests."[20] Referring to Haiti by its dead colonial name of Saint-Domingue, the "old colonists" of Haiti continued seeking reparations for the loss of "their" land and "their" slaves.[21]

The former slave-owners on the island of Haiti were not alone in this effort. An international alliance of states set out to force an ex post facto emancipation protocol onto Haiti—a set of arrangements that would force the young nation to pay in perpetuity to redeem the ruptured property claim of the slaveholders. A grand operation began to render Haiti's freedom defective, and to force it into the role of debtor and culprit, paying off the price of its freedom for generations.

BURDENING "FREEDOM"

Emancipations, regardless of whether we're talking about racial slavery or ancient Roman slavery, insisted on the indebtedness of the previously enslaved to slave-owning society. French diplomacy after 1804 normalized the perverse logic of slave-owners' grievances. France's antiblackness masqueraded as international justice, and it found significant support within the community of European and North American states.

Breaking with all precedents of international law, including those recently set by both the American and French Revolutions, France and its European and American counterparts refused to officially recognize Haiti's revolutionary independence for decades. Back in 1776, France was *the first* nation to recognize the United States' revolutionary independence. In 1783, two years after the last decisive victory of the American Revolution, the British empire acknowledged independence of its former colony at the Treaty of Paris. But these same countries denied this consideration to the first independent black nation.[22]

Haitian historian Jean Casimir captured it well, observing, "The state of Haiti was born into a world that considered its very existence inconceivable and undesirable."[23] Haiti was ostracized by an international community of French, British, American, and Spanish powers and treated as a political pariah of black "barbarism." At the same time, Haitian leaders provided inspiration and military support to the insurrectionary leaders of Spanish America, whether among the black crowds in Cuba, or the Creole elites, such as Simón Bolívar, in Venezuela.[24] In 1802, the French planter Baron de Malouet wrote, "The liberty of the blacks means their domination! It means the massacre or the enslavement of the whites, the burning of our fields and our cities."[25] French observers insisted that black people had "adopted liberty as an object of fanaticism," and that their liberation, worked out on their own terms, was a farce.

After the 1804 Haitian declaration of independence, the defeated French forces offered no acknowledgment of Haiti's independence. At the 1815 Congress of Vienna to reestablish the European international order after Napoléon's defeat, France negotiated with other European powers to use "whatever means possible, including that of arms to regain Saint-Domingue or to bring the population of that colony to order."[26] France's refusal to recognize Haitian freedom received support from all other European and North American states. Britain outlawed any official political or economic contact between Haiti and the British colony of Jamaica. American president Thomas Jefferson imposed a total blockade of political and economic engagement with Haiti during the first fragile years of its existence, from 1806 to 1810. Britain, Denmark, and the Netherlands recognized Haiti as an independent country only in 1826. Spain granted recognition in 1855. And the United States withheld diplomatic recognition until 1862.

Although Haiti was denied official entry into the "civilized community of nations," Britain, the United States, and other countries did permit trade with Haiti.[27] Even France allowed its seafaring merchants to participate in Haitian trade after 1809, stipulating, however, that French ships should lower their flags upon reaching the Haitian ports so exchange would remain unofficial. In other words, European and American powers fostered exchange and interdependence without recognition, and relationships without equity. This replicated a key dynamic of slavery—one in which it was legal to take from black communities without giving equitably in return—and projected it into international space, and into the postindependence and postslavery future.

In Britain and America, Haiti became a cipher for a variety of antiblack racist tropes. James Franklin, in *The Present State of Hayti* (1828), characterized each Haitian city he visited as "nearly demolished and tumbling into ruins."[28] After emancipation in the British empire in 1838, Britons took Haiti as a racial stereotype to signify the risk of "violent revenge." In 1849, the British popular writer Thomas Carlyle wrote, "Let the [black West Indian] look across to Haiti. . . . Let him, by his ugliness, idleness, rebellion, banish all white men from the West Indies and make it all one Haiti."[29] According to Spencer St. John, the British chargé d'affaires in Haiti in the 1860s, Haiti could only be redeemed by a return of white settlers.[30] James Anthony Froude, in his 1888 *The English in the West Indies*, recapitulated the common view that the black people of Jamaica have "revived their restless hope that the day was not far off when Jamaica would be as Haiti and they would have the island to themselves."[31] France, Britain, and the United States projected nightmarish visions onto Haiti. At the most essential level, the idea of black freedom prompted sweaty night tremors about the fall of other plantation societies.

At the same time, some white abolitionists came to Haiti's aid. Thomas Clarkson, the influential British abolitionist, corresponded directly with Henri Christophe, who rose to power after Dessalines's 1806 assassination, becoming leader of the northern Haitian imperial state from 1806 to 1818. In 1807, an opposing state, the Republic of Haiti, formed under another general, Alexandre Pétion, in the south. Clarkson even volunteered to serve as an unofficial diplomatic representative for Haiti in Europe. Clarkson advised King Henri Christophe to submit to France's untimely emancipation process as a route to acceptance within the Europe-centered community of nations. Christophe roundly rejected this advice. Other white abolitionists, such as William Wilberforce and James Stephen, campaigned against French plans to reinvade Haiti and published texts that celebrated the achievements of Haitian independence.[32] Importantly, white abolitionists tended to decry plans for Haiti's direct reenslavement, while failing to recognize and denounce the indirect ways in which antiblackness was being reconfigured through France's insistence on a slave-owner compensation scheme. By and large, white abolitionists tended to support emancipation processes, seeing them as necessary legal measures to achieve abolition. When confronted with Haiti's abolition *without* emancipation, figures such as Clarkson and Wilberforce cautioned about the supposed need to prepare black people for freedom so as to ensure their moral fitness. They took for granted ideas of European supremacy on the road to postslavery, instead of redressing the European cultural disrepair that underpinned *both* slavery and emancipation.[33]

EMANCIPATIONIST PUNISHMENT

As Haiti declared independence, it contended with an international regime insisting on its ongoing economic dependency—its enslavement by other means. By the 1820s, France, relying on the support of other Western countries, continued to insist on a retroactive emancipation process as the prerequisite for official access to the community of nation-states and the protections of international law. Per the terms of such an emancipation agreement, French banks would gain access to Haiti, extracting wealth directly from the Haitian people's treasury as compensation to slave-owners, and in interest payments and bank fees on the loans Haiti took out to handle the resulting debt.

Refusing to entertain Haiti's claim to independence, as though it were unthinkable, France insisted on engaging with postrevolution Haitians according to the archaic law of colonial slavery, the Code Noir.[34] In the 1820s, they succeeded. Haiti was thus subjected to an absurd emancipation professing to retroactively free a people who had freed themselves two decades earlier. With a massive indemnity serving as its invisible and powerful chain, France entrapped Haiti and dragged it back in time.

In 1825, French officials calculated that the reenslavement of the Haitian people was not militarily possible. So they conceived a new kind of colonization. France would seek to create a "commercial colony" out of Haiti.[35] French king Charles X, on April 17, 1825, "conceded" the independence of Haiti, but only if Haiti agreed to pay a redemption free to France, an *indemnité* of 150 million francs (approximately $37 billion dollars today), and to reduce customs duties on French goods by 50 percent, giving it most-favored-nation trading status. The French document made specific reference to a remedial "emancipation":

> The old French colony of St. Domingue was emancipated under the name of the Republic of Haiti. . . . The ordinance of the King recognizing its independence also establishes that it will pay an indemnity to the dispossessed colonists.[36]

As the French government conveyed the terms of the indemnity, fourteen French warships stalked the coastal waters of the Haitian capital, Port-au-

Prince. President Jean-Pierre Boyer of Haiti accepted the terms, eager to end the debilitating international diplomatic boycott and to protect against covert foreign military attacks on the Haitian state. In agreeing to the demands of emancipation, President Boyer symbolically and politically affirmed allegiance to the international order that slavery had built. And by agreeing to pay the indemnity, Boyer accepted a subordinated status for Haiti that was explicitly rooted in its past as a former French slave colony. Haiti would be treated not as a newly independent nation, but as a former French property and as such would pay France for its freedom. Instead of walking free, which it had done for over two decades, the Haitian state was made to kneel and crawl into the community of nations.

Haiti had to find a way to pay this ransom. French authorities instructed the Haitian government to take out a loan from the Ternaux, Gandolphe & Company bank in Paris to pay the first installment of 30 million francs. The terms for the loans were exorbitant, with an interest rate set at 6 percent and an additional 6 million francs in handling fees. This borrowed sum represented the beginning of the "double debt," as the Haitian state paid vast amounts of money to France as principal and to French banks as interest.[37]

Haiti defaulted on the loan after the first payment. A second attempt at paying the imposing *indemnité* came soon thereafter. The Haitian government now took out another loan from the banking syndicate of Laffitte, Rothschild and Lapanonze to repay 227 million francs, about half of which represented interest and bank fees, over thirty-five years, in yearly installments of 6.5 million francs. Once again, Haiti soon defaulted, leading the French to complain that the Haitian government was irresponsible and backward. After trapping Haiti in a vice of reenslavement through debt peonage, French officials used antiblack racial tropes to denigrate the Haitians for their entrapment. The *indemnité* and its financial legacy was not only Haiti's double debt at work but also France's double trap—a way of keeping Haiti chained to the past of white colonial domination and of promoting a future of white rule. The engineered financial failure of the Haitian state was used to assert the moral failure of the

Haitian people. Then as now, financial debt functioned to connect the realm of money to the realm of morals.

In 1838, a new arrangement for the *indemnité* was decided. The total amount for slave-owner reparations was reduced from 150 million francs to 90 million francs (approximately $22 billion in today's currency), with an additional 75 million francs in bank fees. Although the principal of the debt was finally repaid in 1893, the interest accrued on the debt rolled over onto Haitian national accounts long afterward.

Over the course of a century, the Haitian government took out a cascade of major loans, all with high interest rates, to finance the public debt. The ransom demanded by France on behalf of its slave-owners began a downward spiral for Haiti:

1875	Loan of 36,464,500 francs	5 percent interest
1880	Loan of 7,235,300 francs	5 percent interest
1896	Loan of 50,000,000 francs	6 percent interest
1910	Loan of $3 million	5 percent interest
1949	Loan of $10 million	5 percent interest

Haiti was the first nation-state laden with emancipation debt as the price for its self-liberation, in stark contrast to the claims of independence by white settler nations that were universally recognized under international law.[38] Beginning in 1825 and continuing for the subsequent 120 years, as much as 80 percent of Haiti's revenues went to paying off the slave-owner indemnity imposed by France. The invisible weapon of financial ruin, long after the overt use of gunboats, forced economic underdevelopment on Haiti. The burden of Haiti's payment to the French state was so extreme that, over its post-liberation history, there would be insufficient resources for its infrastructure: roads, ports, hospitals, schools. To pay the former French masters, Haiti would be forced to starve its children and deprive its communities for generations.

BLACK DEFIANCE

Despite the punishing loan payments, Haitian independence was a powerful symbol of defiance for black communities across the Caribbean and the Americas. Haiti's revolution, as both a concrete and abstract declaration of black liberation, sent shock waves across the Caribbean and the United States and quickened the spirit of revolt and rebellion in Guyana, Grenada, Jamaica, Cuba, Georgia, and Virginia.[39] In Cuba, enslaved people rebelled in 1795, openly testifying to Haiti's inspiration.[40] The story of Haiti ignited the Fédon rebellion in Grenada in 1795, and it was a talisman for future uprisings of enslaved people in Virginia in 1800, Louisiana in 1811, South Carolina in 1822, Virginia in 1831, Jamaica in 1831, and Brazil in 1833, among others.[41]

Black people from the Caribbean and the United States traveled to Haiti to take refuge from white supremacy in the world's only black republic. More than six thousand African Americans, mostly departing from Philadelphia, New York, and Boston, migrated to Haiti during the 1820s because they viewed it as liberated space.[42] In "Haitian leagues" formed in cities such as New York, black people could imagine together the full and spacious meanings of their freedom.[43] "Boyer Halls" of black Freemasons sprang up across the US North in honor of the long-serving Haitian president. The first African American newspaper, *Freedom's Journal*, published out of New York City, observed in the 1820s that Haiti "demonstrated that the descendants of Africa are capable of self-government" and thus refuted European supremacist claims to world ownership.[44]

But despite Haiti's reputation, the long death of slavery affected the Haitian people not only from outside but also from within. In Haiti, even though the "aristocracy of the skin" was destroyed, a caste society based on property ownership and the patronage of military patriarchs soon reconstituted itself. This created an oppositional division between the patrimonial leaders of the state and the large masses of the Haitian working people. The political leaders of revolutionary Haiti, military men intoxicated by their wish to impose their own order onto the revolutionary chaos of the new nation, sought to re-impose the plantation system. Toussaint's 1801 constitution, Dessalines's 1804 constitution, the Code Henry of 1812, and Boyer's Code Rural of 1826 all instructed the Haitian people to return to the plantation enclosures as bonded laborers cultivating sugar for the international market. Hundreds of years of colonialism had honed Haiti's economy for large-scale plantation production, and a long series of Haitian state leaders believed that the ongoing oppression of a nation of peasant farmers and small-scale producers was a necessary pathway to the liberation of the modern state.[45]

Again and again, however, working people reasserted what historian Jean Casimir called the "counter-plantation system" by creating fugitive small-farming peasant communities beyond the framework envisioned by state elites. Under the pressures of the oppressive postslavery state, the Haitian people again marooned themselves, fleeing the cities for the dense interiors of the island. The distinctive Haitian customary institution of the *lakou*, or the joint-family farming compound, expanded. And *lakous* served as shrines for the passing down of Haitian Vodou traditions and black healing arts. *Lakous* in different parts of Haiti came to be identified with the worship of different gods in the Haitian pantheon, as well as with music traditions associated with distinctive cultural groups from West Africa. This counterplantation system was mainly organized around the collective leadership of women. From Vodou *mambos*, or women priests, to women cultivators of farming plots, to the role of women in sustaining the extensive trading networks that crisscrossed the

Haitian interior, the freedom that Haitian people continued to work out for themselves from below was both collective and antipatriarchal. As historian Johnhenry Gonzalez shows, only a few years after the revolution ended, Haitian people began shipping new crops, including corn, beans, rice, millet, bananas, sweet potatoes, manioc, and yams, to neighboring islands as part of a trade in a free people's farming economy, instead of engaging in the sugar and tobacco trade of plantation capitalists.[46] The people's black liberation did not wait for the international order, or even for the state apparatus, to sketch out a path to social transformation. It grasped freedom for itself.

The Haitian revolution was not a single event, but an ongoing and open-ended process. Its roots went beyond republican ideals of reform and bourgeois property ownership and borrowed instead from black peasant and indigenous conceptions of freedom. At its core, the Haitian revolution was not based on the machinations or strategies of a few heroic patrimonial figures: not Toussaint, nor Dessalines, nor Christophe, nor Pétion, nor Boyer. The Haitian revolution was a revolt of the people, who did not intend to return to the conditions of their preliberation torment under any circumstances.

ANTIBLACK IMPERIALISM

In 1910, the Banque de l'Union Parisienne (BUP), a syndicate of French and German banking houses, took over the administration of Haiti's treasury and its national debt. The BUP formed the National Bank for the Republic of Haiti, which, though Haitian in name, was owned and directed by foreign interests. With the support of the US government under President Woodrow Wilson, the National City Bank of New York soon became a major stakeholder in this Haitian "national bank." In the high noon of America's Jim Crow era, the United States sought to take over the colonizer's mantle from France.

In late 1914, citing Haitian defaults on debt payments and concerns about the security of the wealth stored in the Haitian treasury, the United States stepped into the role of neocolonial "savior." At 1:00 p.m. on December 17,

1914, US marines invaded the shores of Port-au-Prince and went straight to the National Bank of the Republic of Haiti with rifles, armored cars, and a crane in tow. In coordination with the American director of Haiti's National Bank, eight marines commandeered $400,000 ($12 million today using historical inflation rates) in gold deposits from the bank's vault and transferred it to a waiting warship. Within two hours of the invasion, the captured lucre was on a ship sailing directly to New York City. Two days later, the marines delivered the gold to the vault of the Hallgarten & Co. bank in New York.[47]

The 1914 US invasion represented a breach of Haiti's sovereignty consistent with those of the preceding centuries. A few months later, in July 1915, Woodrow Wilson called on the US marines to occupy Haiti. Having disturbed the financial order of the country, the US president now proposed to interrupt the political order, too. During the bloody nineteen-year occupation that followed, US forces killed some fifteen thousand Haitian rebels and civilians.[48]

What can explain this recurring pattern of injustice; this inveterate resistance by the European and North American international community to leave Haiti alone to its freedom, and to recognize black sovereignty? Jamaican psychologist Fred Hickling pointed to the "psychosis" of the European preoccupation with "world ownership."[49] World ownership became a commitment of European states by the 1600s, dating back to the time of the international Peace of Westphalia in 1648. Around then, European state elites began believing that they had a political nation-state that was different from *and superior to* all other forms of government on earth. They began convincing themselves not just through their Christian theological writings but in their political philosophies that their form of governing was the future of the world, and that it was their right to take ownership of what was different and make it the same.

On a more intimate level, international white supremacy is about something much more quotidian: the interest of groups that are socially, economically, and internationally dominant to preserve that dominance, to stay at the center of it, and to make sure that others operate on the groups' terms. For Europeans and Euro-Americans, slavery provided the foundations for global wealth accumulation and world dominance. When the Haitian people disrupted slavery's international order—in a manner born out of their own insurgent need for liberation—such insurgent action was not just about the future of the Haitians, but about the architecture of a whole social and international system of white supremacy. In its most banal expression, white supremacy is merely the wish among groups who benefited from slavery to continue to enjoy its spoils and privileges long after its formal death. It is the wish by colonial elites to ensure that the social architecture of the future replicates that of the past. The United States and European nations, especially France and Britain, spent decades after Haiti's rebellion trying to bring it back into *their* idea of order, to ghostline Haitian sovereignty, and to reduce the scope of black freedom to the parameters of the plantation past.

CHAPTER 3

BRITISH ANTISLAVERY AND THE EMANCIPATION OF PROPERTY

Various emancipations across the hemispheric Americas—in the American North, Haiti, and South America—all broke with existing British, French, and Spanish imperial systems. Britain, in the period from 1770 to 1833, showed how antislavery and emancipation also developed in and through the sinews of empire and served its expansion. The final form of British emancipation, begun in 1833, set a model for other imperial powers to follow, including the French, Dutch, and Spanish. Britain's system of slavery, the most lucrative in the world in the 1770s, spanned the Americas, Africa, and Europe. The main economic center of the system was British Caribbean sugar production, especially in Barbados and Jamaica. Close to a million African people lived under British domination in the decade before the American Revolution.

The British abolition of the slave trade in 1807 paradoxically took place just as the British empire extended its hold over new slavery colonies, and new polities across Asia. Between 1785 and 1815, during a time of inter-European imperial warfare ignited by Napoléon Bonaparte's rule, Britain responded with its own ravenous appetite for colonial expansion. During this period, British militaries captured Guyana and the Cape of Good Hope from the Dutch, Mauritius from the French, and Trinidad from the Spanish. Britain also sent some eighty-nine thousand troops to Haiti and nearby French Caribbean colonies in attempts to put down the Haitian revolution and seize the plantation island as a British colony. British troops, routed in Haiti, were nonetheless successful in seizing the revolutionary Caribbean islands of St. Vincent, Grenada, and St. Lucia. In this way, Britain carried out contradictory policies of slave-trade abolition while expanding plantation slavery and colonial conquest, in order to promote the interests of its empire.[1]

This is not to say, however, that antislavery communities in Britain in the period from 1770 to 1830 were either monolithic or mere tools of the ruling classes. To the contrary, these communities were diverse and pursued varied objectives.[2] The radical antislavery of black and working-class advocates and of many women-led organizations in Britain contrasted with the elite abolitionism of well-known abolitionist parliamentarians, such as William Wilberforce. Wilberforce, not just heroized but beatified as the great emancipator in Britain's national canon, was the son of a wealthy Yorkshire business family, a graduate of Cambridge, and a member of parliament for forty-four years. He was one of the closest confidants to Prime Minister William Pitt the Younger. As the leader of the parliamentary abolitionists for almost a half century, Wilberforce pursued emancipation in ways that appeased slave-owner interests and prioritized the expansion of British imperial dominance worldwide.[3] As we will see, black abolitionists and their radical counterparts in Britain had a different vision of what abolition should achieve, and whom it should ultimately benefit.

The Caribbean economic historian Eric Williams argued, in 1944, that British antislavery was an inevitable cultural and political expression of a deeper structural decline in slavery's economic viability for Britain's imperial economy.[4] Later schools of historians countered Williams's claim, insisting instead that antislavery was a triumph of Britons' humanitarian willpower, and a testament to the potency of Enlightenment ideas.[5] Current research shows that the British plantation economy, and the profitability of slavery, was not so much in decline as in transformation from the 1770s to the 1830s. Antislavery in the British empire was symptomatic of a deep structural shift in empire from an old reliance on slavery to an emerging turn to new forms of racial servitude.[6] In this sense, Williams was close to the mark in recognizing the colonial compulsions that haunted British antislavery.

On the other hand, it is also true that millions of British people, of different classes, white and black, men and women, lobbied parliament from the 1770s to the 1820s to demand the end of slavery. Nonconformist religious groups, working-class vanguards, and women's advocacy associations traveled on separate courses but converged around antislavery during its peak decades. Radical British antislavery factions worked with and against the section of abolitionist political elites, such as Wilberforce, and his younger acolytes, such as Zachary Macaulay, Thomas Fowell Buxton, and Stephen Lushington. Britain's political elite could not, in the end, control the ultimate timing of abolition: protests at home and increasingly violent rebellion in the colonies pushed their hand in 1833. They did, however, control the fifty-year-long implementation of halfway abolition policies and a robust slave-owner reparations program. When it comes to giving people back the freedom that had generationally been stolen from them, and making restitution for the damage caused, the process of freedom and accountability matters most. Political elites of the British empire focused on attaining closure without accountability, and on safeguarding slave-owners' property rights. The British empire strategized to emancipate the *property held in* enslaved black people, instead of liberating black people themselves.

THE EXPLOITS OF PROPERTY RIGHTS

In the two centuries leading up to the British abolition of slavery in 1833, the British empire emerged as the largest and most powerful maritime empire on earth. Antislavery in the British empire overlapped with the consolidation of Britain's superpower status. Some three hundred years earlier, in 1656, political philosopher James Harrington envisioned what he called the rise of the "empire of Oceana." According to Harrington, this empire, with its body stretched across the world's seas, and its tentacles clutching lands and peoples across both hemispheres, would ensure the British people would "enjoy [their] own . . . property."[7] Less than a decade after the publication of Harrington's treatise, the

British government began its long-term, multigenerational endeavor to become the most powerful slave-trafficking empire on earth. In 1663, King Charles II chartered the Royal Adventurers of England Trading to Africa and placed it in charge of his younger brother, James, the Duke of York. The British Crown commemorated the occasion with the minting of a new domination of coinage, the guinea, named after Britain's term for the West African slave coast. In 1672, the Royal African Company took over the government's oceanic traffic in kidnapped African people, eventually delivering some forty-seven thousand captives per year to British plantation colonies, and to French, Spanish, and Dutch plantations in the Caribbean.[8] Another government-directed business, the South Sea Company, formed in 1711 at its impressive headquarters on London's Threadneedle Street, the City of London's financial heart. Some of the earliest directors and governors of the Bank of England directly invested in slave-trafficking, including Peter Delmé, Humphry Morice, Brook Watson, Beeston Long, and Charles Montagu.[9] The eighteenth-century economist Malachy Postlethwayt diagnosed "the Negroe-Trade and the natural Consequences resulting from it" as "an inexhaustible Fund of Wealth and Naval Power for this Nation."[10] Slavery was not merely an arm of Britain's emerging Oceana, it was its nervous system.

We can think of the "right to property" as the right to the exclusive use of valuable resources, or as what a state assigns to a subset of its population for their use.[11] Based on guarantees from the British government, people may hold rights in land, such as real estate, in movable assets, such as horses and cattle, or in intangibles, such as insurance and lotteries. Already in 1672, in the Barbados slave law, enslaved African people were categorized as a species of salable and heritable property, and not as human persons. In creating their ideal of Oceana, the British imperial elite, located between the British Isles and the Atlantic Americas, saw empire as the governmental structure legitimating the British right to claim property in the bodies of Africans.[12]

British merchants and militaries created property through marauding and predatory theft of land and people across Africa and the Americas. In the 1600s, the British established their first Caribbean plantation colonies in Barbados, Antigua, and Jamaica, along with plantations in Virginia and the

Carolina colony. These British plantation colonies had registries to delineate land ownership a century before such registries existed in England.[13] The market value of the sugar, coffee, cocoa, and tobacco harvested by laboring African people was captured by British plantation capitalists. The value of British plantation commodities jumped drastically from £7.9 million in 1660 to £89 million by 1760. By the mid-1700s, the British plantations in the West Indies and along the North American Chesapeake coast generated 80 percent of the total export value of the British Americas.[14] Because African people were trafficked as units of property, British bankers, merchants, and insurance agents also extracted huge profits from the slave trade itself. By 1800, Liverpool businessmen dominated European slave-trading, running 90 percent of European slave ships. Names of some of the biggest human traffickers of eighteenth-century Europe, including the Tarletons, the Gildarts, and the Cunliffes, adorn streets in Liverpool today.[15] An intricate web of investors and beneficiaries possessed derivative claims to property in enslaved people, especially as British planters often used enslaved Africans as collateral on their debt burdens. Brokers, insurers, bankers, and financiers, dressed in suits and quietly studying the latest shipping news and inventory lists, emerged as powerful hinges in the British imperial system of slavery.

These numbers and percentages index a history of hurt. In late-eighteenth-century Jamaica, black people's life expectancy was artificially reduced to an average thirty years, while white colonists, on average, lived to age fifty. The diary of British Jamaican plantation owner Thomas Thistlewood, from the 1750s to the 1780s, gives us a sense of the extremeness of everyday violence. Thistlewood, the son of an English petty farmer, was born in a small town in Lincolnshire in 1721. He boarded a ship to Jamaica at age twenty-nine to find work and climb the social ladder. In Jamaica, he began as a plantation field hand, then became a plantation overseer and finally a plantation owner on Jamaica's wilder western frontier. As of 1767, he joined the island's landowner class, albeit as a rough and rowdy newcomer. Plantation colonies were spaces for this kind of white upward mobility. An intricate caste-like hierarchy of privilege and license ranged from the old pseudo-aristocrats, to the parvenus, to the ranks of attorneys and overseers, and then on down to the mulatto castes of servants and artisans, and finally to the undercaste of the African masses toiling in the fields.

Although upstarts such as Thistlewood were seen as unrefined by the old white planter families, such as the Barretts and the Dawkinses, the plantation machine allowed white people to churn up new wealth and property rights, and to convert these rights into social status passed down for generations. In the plantation colonies, but not in Britain itself, poor white farmer boys could reinvent themselves through posterity as the moneyed cultural elite. For example, Hercie Barrett migrated from a small farm in England to Jamaica a century before Thistlewood, in 1655. After a century, one of his descendants, Edward Moulton Barrett, returned to Britain as a wealthy gentleman and built a country house called Hope End in the style of the landed aristocracy. The Barretts, over generations, converted plantation slave property into elite English cultural power. Elizabeth Barrett Browning, the daughter of Edward Moulton Barrett and Mary Graham-Clarke, daughter of a wealthy West Indian merchant, became one of the leading nineteenth-century poets of Britain. Her cousin Richard Barrett remained in Jamaica. He was the Speaker of the Jamaican Assembly, the owner of two thousand acres of plantation lands, and of five plantation estate homes. One of those estate homes, Greenwood Mansion, was run with a retinue of more than thirty enslaved African people. The mansion housed his library of three hundred books, containing tomes of British and European history, literature and travel writing, and many books written in Latin, French, Italian, and German. It also included the poetry volumes of his cousin Elizabeth Barrett Browning. Elite imperial families, dispersed over oceanic spaces, conserved their economic and cultural power over their Oceana—this is what the British imperial rule of property was all about.[16]

The power to secure and conserve property rights over generations relied on English domestic and colonial laws. And the spirit of that law was patriarchal. Thomas Thistlewood no doubt aspired to the social prestige of the

Barrett men. He set down his aspirations in his diary, a record of male license, using all other human beings on "his" plantation as "his" property. Thistlewood chronicled more than thirty-eight hundred times in which he had intercourse with 132 enslaved black women on his plantations. His diary is a record of sexual violation. We know that some of these women, such as Phibbah, were in coercive long-term relationships with Thistlewood, but that they also "worked the trap" to their own ends. Phibbah, for example, wielded a degree of power over Thistlewood, and she eventually attained some of her own goals through her intimate bonds to him. Phibbah "worked" Thistlewood to buy her manumission, and to build a house for her and her children. This was not an abstract and ideal kind of freedom by any means, but degrees of freedom exist within the practice of survival. Black women, such as Phibbah, sustained life for themselves and their children within these day-to-day, intimate cracks in the plantation regime of white-male property domination.[17]

To be clear, Thistlewood also recorded many, many tortures, whippings, mutilations, and serial murders of black women and men. As was common on all plantations, Thomas Thistlewood branded his initials on the enslaved people. In Thistlewood's case, no hint of bad conscience tints his diary; his plantation account reads like a comedy of consumption. Dispassionate descriptions of his violent acts are juxtaposed by notes on his meals. He records a meal of duck stewed in claret, roast turkey, ham and greens, cheese, bread, oranges, fine haddock, punch, Madeira wine, and claret.[18] This decadent lifestyle was furnished by the debt he owed to distant bankers in London and Liverpool.

ANTISLAVERY IN EMPIRE

Antislavery in Britain goes back to nonconformist religious associations of the late 1600s, such as the origins of Quakerism, and to the underground and underdeck resistance by black people trafficked through the ports of Bristol, London, and Liverpool beginning in this time.[19] The abolition and emancipation processes across the Americas, especially in the American North and in Haiti, played a significant role in galvanizing radical antislavery in British public discussion by the 1770s.[20]

The Haitian revolution, beginning in 1791, also had a tremendous effect on British antislavery. The supernova of black liberation in the French Caribbean incited fears among the British political elite—among abolitionists and anti-abolitionists alike. Beginning in earnest in the 1790s, through colonial "amelioration laws" and gradual-abolition acts passed by the British parliament, the British empire's established classes sought to avoid the fate of "St. Domingo" by reforming slavery and "regulating the punishments" imposed.[21] The idea, supported by well-known abolitionists in Britain including William Wilberforce, was that slavery could be mitigated by better administration, so that it would do less harm. In 1792, Wilberforce explained that the British slave-owners could even become good and benevolent educators to the enslaved. They first had to make the enslaved ready for freedom through a period of preparation and training. Thereafter, slavery should be abolished in order to obviate "insurrections."[22]

The true impulse for the extinguishing of slavery did not come down from on high—despite the romantic British national myth about the likes of William Wilberforce. Abolitionism bubbled up from below. The percolating legal origins of British abolition go back to the courageous acts of refusal and resistance by black people in Britain who sought to prove their legal freedom in British courts in the 1770s. They did so at the same time that black revolutionaries in the British plantation colonies were organizing rebellions. Jonathan Strong, Hylas, James Somerset, and others carried out courtroom rebellions in Britain, just years after Tacky organized the great 1760 rebellion in Jamaica. These courtroom rebels who came as enslaved people from the Caribbean to Britain were testing their chains.

More than fourteen thousand black people lived on the British Isles by the late 1700s. The majority worked as servants, pages, launderers, and housekeepers in a widespread system of undocumented enslavement in Britain.[23] Some were manumitted and thus nominally free, although they remained unpaid and subordinated in Britain's society. In April 1765, Jonathan Strong, an enslaved twenty-year-old man from Barbados, sought medical help for an attack he suffered from the British lawyer David Lisle, who claimed Strong as property. Lisle had bashed Strong in the head with his pistol and thrown him out on the street to die. Strong got medical attention from philanthropic doctor William Sharp at his Mincing Lane surgery in central London. William Sharp's younger brother, Granville Sharp, thirty years old at the time, met Jonathan Strong. Two years later, Granville Sharp, a trained linen draper and a complete outsider to the lawyers' guild, led Strong's legal defense against reenslavement when the slave-owner returned to try to sell Strong back into West Indian slavery.

Jonathan Strong's resilience in surviving and resisting his enslaver, and Granville Sharp's advocacy, led to a trial before the Lord Mayor of London in 1769. Sharp organized a public campaign in defense of Strong, even as Sharp, lacking barrister credentials, could not directly defend him in the courtroom. Sharp's 1769 treatise, *A Representation of the Injustice and Dangerous Tendency of Tolerating Slavery*, aimed to influence legal opinion in anticipation of a trial set for 1771.[24] Sharp, arguing from biblical authority, presented slavery as a perversion of "natural law," the inherent law governing God's creation. Sharp relied on historical arguments about the innate civilization of African societies as he insisted that the enslavement of other human beings contravened "natural equity." His text articulated the bad conscience that had always lurked silently within the British imperial mind. Sharp's writing articulated the collective unspoken.

Strong's appeal to an idea of natural rights was but one example of the stirrings of a new human rights discourse. Recall that this same decade of the 1770s saw a string of antislavery petitions by enslaved Africans in New England, as well as the manumission of black soldiers fighting on both sides during the American Revolutionary War. In other words, the origins of human rights law go back to the resistance and activism of black people seeking their freedom in courts of law and on battlefields in a time of revolutions. In the case of Jonathan Strong, no trial would ever take place. Strong, age twenty-seven, died in 1770 from the beatings he had received from Lisle, as well as, perhaps, from the ongoing trauma of his attacker's reenslavement campaign.

Jonathan Strong's death in 1770 is hardly ever mentioned in historical accounts. Historical records provide no adequate account of Jonathan Strong, no rounded exposition of his personality, his family ties, or his characteristic dealings and his gifts to the world. The records also provide no account of the many other African lives that were, like that of Jonathan Strong, stolen in situations of arbitrary capture and reenslavement in Britain. Amid the absence of documents there nonetheless lurks our collective awareness of incalculable human loss. Even in the case of Jonathan Strong, for which we have some account, the archival records sideline him as a footnote in the story of a white abolitionist's rise. Sharp's thesis of 1769—not Strong's life or death—has become iconically commemorated as a first ripple of legal abolitionism in Britain. Slavery, as a system, liquidated the being of black people into prices and texts, into numbers and letters, in ways that brought glory and repute to empire's men.

Jonathan Strong's resistance and the anticipation of his law proceedings ignited a set of other similar abolitionist cases in the early 1770s. A free black man in London named Hylas brought a case before the court of Common Pleas to secure the safety and release of his wife, Mary, from her former British enslaver. Under slavery, marriage and the legal protection of family unions were reserved for whites, forcing black families to invent creative ways to preserve their unions, such as buying enslaved spouses out of slavery. The slaveowner, according to Hylas, had forced Mary onto a ship and sent her back to Barbados, where she was to be sold back into slavery. British law, as a patriarchal code, did not seek Mary's testimony during the trial. A group of men held a legal process to determine the future of a black woman.

Chief Justice John Wilmot decided in favor of Hylas and ordered the slaveowner, John Newton, to pay damages to Hylas, and to return Mary to London within six months. We know that Mary was never returned to London, but remained on Newton's plantation in Barbados for the rest of her life. The historical records give us no insight into her volition. At the same time, the lasting injustice of the outcome is clear: even in one of the first British court cases that decided against slave-owners and ordered redress for enslaved Africans, both white supremacy and patriarchy won out. This case was a microcosm and premonition of what the British political and legal system would perpetuate at a macroscopic level a half century later: an unjust outcome resulting from an unjust process.

Since no legal systems existed to protect the freedom of black people living in Britain at this time, cases such as *Hylas v. Newton* began to set a new precedent. Granville Sharp attended the *Hylas v. Newton* case as an observer. In 1770, just months after Jonathan Strong's death, Sharp got directly involved in another case of a black courtroom freedom rebel in London, Thomas Lewis. Lewis had been kidnapped by a man claiming to own him and dragged onto a Jamaica-bound ship on the Thames. Lewis's cries for help alerted other servants of the house where he worked, who then roused the householders. They contacted Granville Sharp, and he swiftly secured a writ of habeas corpus—an order from a judge to return the prisoner so he could stand trial. The ship was intercepted downstream from London, and the case of Thomas Lewis eventually made its way to the highest British court, presented before Lord Chief Justice Mansfield in February 1771. Justice Mansfield explicitly avoided making any determination about the legality, in general, of holding people in slavery in Britain. "Perhaps it is much better it should never be finally discussed or settled," the judge commented.[25] Mansfield arranged for a jury to hear the case, and the jurors decided that no decision had to be made on the legality of slavery in Britain since no adequate evidence was provided to show that Lewis was indeed enslaved, except the verbal testimony of the enslaver himself. Lewis was set free; the regime of British slavery remained in place.

In 1772, the famous *Somerset v. Stewart* case followed with a similar outcome: an instance of emancipation within an otherwise untroubled sea of British bondage. James Somerset, a year previously, had fled his enslaver, Charles Stewart, the paymaster general of colonial Boston, while accompanying him on a trip to Britain. Reminiscent of the experiences of Jonathan Strong and Thomas Lewis, James Somerset was subsequently imprisoned on a ship chartered back to Boston. Advocates obtained a writ of habeas corpus, and yet again an emancipation trial reached the docket of Lord Chief Justice Mansfield. Again, Granville Sharp played an important role in articulating an abolitionist legal theory that guided the barristers' court arguments and helped to color public opinion. In June 1772, after four months of trial, Chief Justice Mansfield granted James Somerset's freedom, but also asserted that "the power claimed never was in use here or acknowledged by the law." The decision was ambiguous, since it was not clear what "the power claimed" referred to. Later on, in 1785, Mansfield suggested his phrase referred only to the power of *forcibly removing* enslaved people from Britain, and not the power *to hold* Africans as enslaved people in Britain. Indeed, Mansfield's 1772 decision had an enigmatic legacy. Just two years later, in 1774, the judge in *Knight v. Wedderburn* ordered the release from reenslavement of Joseph Knight, originally from Guyana, after he refused to continue serving slave-owner John Wedderburn. Knight was certainly inspired to demand his freedom by the actions of James Somerset, and by the outcome of the 1772 case.

However, in 1783, the limits of legal abolitionism in Britain became clear. Two years earlier, in December 1781, the captain of the *Zong* slave ship, Luke Collingwood, and his crew, deliberately murdered 142 African captives by throwing them overboard in order to later claim insurance on them as "cargo losses." The insurance company refused to cover the claim, leading eventually to a series of trials before Lord Mansfield. Lord Mansfield, who had issued the Thomas Somerset decision in 1772, saw the trial as a matter of merchant law: the status of contracts between insurers and slave ship owners. He did not adjudicate the case as a matter of criminal law: the mass murder of captive Africans and the forms of restitution required. He commented to the jury on May 22, 1783, that "the case of slaves was the same as if horses had been thrown overboard." Jurors returned with a decision in favor of the slave ship owners and ordered an insurance claim of £3,660 to be paid. Mansfield agreed to reconsider the case on appeal, but the trial was never held, nor did the insurers ever compensate the ship owners for the murders aboard the *Zong*.[26] In general, the legal guild of lawyers and judges refrained from decisions that could be seen to comment on the general legality of the slave trade. Most important, the decisions had no curtailing impact on the British international traffic in captive Africans. In fact, British slave-trading skyrocketed from 1770 to 1807, with more than 1 million more Africans captured and transported into slavery by British ships.[27] From 1770 to the British abolition of the slave trade in 1807, more British slave ships crossed the Atlantic than in the preceding century.[28]

Granville Sharp argued in his treatise of 1769 that the claim to property in African people "is the highest breach of social virtue" and a violation of "civil liberty."[29] In his subsequent writings, he turned to outlining a process for the abolition of slavery. In *Just Limitation of Slavery in the Laws of God* (1776), Sharp proposed that the enslaved should be required to serve their erstwhile owners during a six-year period of "apprenticeship." The enslaved should pay their oppressors for freedom, just as ancient Roman law prescribed slaves to pay a manumission debt. Sharp also drew on a well-established body of British law governing employment relations between persons of different statuses in the British social hierarchy, such as between "apprentices" and "masters" in artisan trades.[30] Granville Sharp's search for legal frameworks to govern the abolition of slavery pointed to the precedent of slave manumission and artisan apprenticeship. He failed to advance a strong legal argument that the African persons deserved restitution and reparations under the law as full-fledged legal persons.

Sharp suggested that emancipated black people, after a period of servitude, should be transformed into tenant farmers on the plantation estates of the former slave-owners. Planters, providing the freed people with plants, cattle, and stores, should then count on obtaining rent from their black tenants "on equitable terms." Under such a system, slave-owners' loss of property rights in African people would be compensated, and their right to enclose and entail plantation lands would be preserved. In other words, black freedom, for Granville Sharp and the majority of British white abolitionists of his time and subsequent generations, would be an unrestituted condition: a condition of ongoing social encumberment.[31] The point is not to reprimand an influential antislavery legal philosopher and activist of the late 1700s for the ways in which he was incapable of imagining African freedom. The point, rather, is to free our minds from the legacy of his mental trap, and then to look back on history to ask whose calls went unheard and unrealized, and what, then, is demanded of us today.

In the 1780s, Sharp's antislavery set a national tone. Thomas Clarkson, strongly influenced by Granville Sharp, became a new spokesman for a version of emancipation that would prolong African bondage. As a student at Cambridge in 1785, he won an essay competition with his contribution, *An Essay on Slavery*, which argued for abolition. In coming years, as he developed his views on how abolition should take place, Clarkson locked onto "gradualism." Africans should be "better fed," their daily labor would be "reduced," their persons should be "more secure," and they should have "a little time to themselves," he wrote. Enslaved Africans had to be made fit for freedom, the young man Clarkson proposed, which meant that time was required for planters and missionaries to civilize them.[32]

The 1780 Philadelphia model of slave-owner reparations and slow emancipation became a touchstone for British abolitionists by the 1790s. Clarkson, influenced by Granville Sharp, also found direct inspiration in the Pennsylvania abolitionists. Clarkson recounted that he studied "the Minutes of the yearly meeting for Pennsylvania and the Jerseys," for "the means not only of wiping away the stain of slavery from their religious community, but of promoting the happiness of those restored to freedom."[33]

In 1795, David and John Barclay, brothers from Essex, England, became long-distance owners of enslaved people in St. Ann, Jamaica. They freed all the enslaved Africans and selected twenty-eight emancipated people to send to Philadelphia. These freed people were then apprenticed to the Pennsylvania Society for the Improvement of the Condition of Free Blacks.[34] Around the same time, Joshua Steele, a plantation owner in Barbados, manumitted all the enslaved people on his plantations, only to then enlist them as "copyholders," or rent-paying tenants, on his lands. By the 1790s, an international nexus of white antislavery activists conferred on new ways to extend the subordination of black people.

HAUNTING THE EMPIRE

At the very same time, African intellectuals and political activists with direct experience of slavery in the Caribbean and of manumission in Britain developed African-centered theories of abolition and reparations in the 1770s and 1820s. These theories naturally insisted on immediate emancipation; validated resistance and rebellion; identified slave-owners as "robbers" and criminals and not as property owners; and demanded state-sanctioned reparations for the unjustly enslaved.

Ottobah Cugoano, born in Ghana (then called the Gold Coast colony), was kidnapped into slavery and sent to the plantations of Grenada. In 1772, a British merchant purchased the property right to Cugoano, brought him to Britain, and manumitted him. Cugoano, approximately fifteen years old at the time, worked as a house page to a white family and eventually became a well-known writer and outspoken abolitionist in the 1780s. In his autobiography, Cugoano's abolitionist arguments differed significantly from those of Grenville Sharp or Thomas Clarkson. Cugoano developed a theory of "reparation and restitution"—his words. He, unlike Sharp, dwelled on the requirements of reparative justice from the perspective of the victimized and assaulted. For Cugoano, reparations for the enslaved was not an afterthought, but a key feature of just emancipation.

> And so, likewise, when a man is carried captive and enslaved, and maimed and cruelly treated, that would make no adequate reparation and restitution for the injuries he had received, if he was even to get the person who had ensnared him to be taken captive and treated in the same manner. What he is to seek after is a deliverance and protection for himself, and not a revenge upon others.[35]

Cugoano envisioned the need for a "generous encouragement" to be given to freed people, in addition to their guaranteed protection.[36] Restitution, for Cugoano, was not a question of vengeance, but of "deliverance and protection."

He framed enslavement not as a property relation, but as a grave infringement of relations between beings—as an "abominable" form of robbery; of people "robbed of [themselves], and sold into captivity." Slave-owners and their society had to "repent" and "reform their lives." Cugoano also observed that it was a "duty of a man who is robbed in that manner [of being enslaved] to get out of the hand of this enslaver."[37] Rebellion and resistance, "revolutions and overthrows," were the natural right and the "general and grand duty" of human beings. Cugoano wrote before the outbreak of liberation struggle in Haiti, and he died in 1791, during the first year of the revolution. Nevertheless, he would certainly have perceived a "grand duty" in the burning of slave-owner plantation property, and the smashing of sugar works by the Haitians.

Cugoano conjured a different moral universe from the one formulated by white abolitionists. He grounded his arguments in his knowledge of the intolerable experience of slavery, in the righteousness of resistance, and in the meaning of reparations. Cugoano's moral universe arose from the mental orientation of the enslaved, of those "violently taken away to a perpetual and intolerable slavery," and not from that of the slave-owners.[38]

At the end of his text, Cugoano spells out a concrete plan for what redress might look like. To create a "general reformation" of slave-owning societies, after the declaration of immediate emancipation and the recognition of slavery as robbery, the next steps should include designating "days of mourning" to commemorate the harm committed and "the horrible injury of making merchandise of us"; free education for all those under slavery who had been deprived of the right to read and write; the elimination of Afrophobic representations in all corners of public life; and the guarantee of autonomous land.[39]

In 1791, the year of Cugoano's death, William Wilberforce put forth a parliamentary bill calling for the abolition of the slave trade. The issue of the abolition of plantation slavery would not be raised in the British parliament for another three decades. The British home secretary, Henry Dundas, citing the developments in Haiti, inserted the word *gradual* into Wilberforce's abolition bill.[40] Wilberforce agreed with the amendment, noting that a good British emancipation should be ruled by "law and order."[41] Meanwhile, starting in 1793 and extending until 1815, Henry Dundas, in the role as war secretary, along with his successors, embarked on a long-term campaign to expand the frontiers of slave owning in the British empire. In addition to the thousands of British troops sent to conquer revolutionary Haiti between 1793 and 1798, the British government fought to maintain control of other plantation colonies. In 1795, under Dundas's direction, the British attacked the free indigenous and black Maroon community at Trelawny Town in Jamaica. In 1795, they put down black revolutionaries in Grenada and executed freedom fighters. They attacked the Maroon community of Garifuna people, a mixed-descent indigenous and African community who lived beyond the plantations in the forested areas in St. Vincent. Some two decades earlier, in 1772, the Garifuna people had risen up in rebellion and forced the British to sign a treaty promising mutual respect. In 1795, the British, under General Ralph Abercromby, breached the treaty of 1772 and killed Joseph Chatoyer, the Garifuna chief. To this day, a calabash cup of Chatoyer, an artifact of the Garifuna people's political sovereignty, is held by the West India Committee in London.[42] What are believed to be the remains of imprisoned rebels from St. Vincent and Grenada, captured people whom General Abercromby sent back to Britain for trial, are held in a provincial museum on Britain's Devon Coast.[43] Material remnants from this 1790s period of British war and pillage in the West Indies turn up like shards of unclaimed responsibility in the holdings of Britain's institutions today.

After the British attack on the Garifuna, slave-owners on St. Vincent demanded compensation of £2.5 million from the British state. The government responded with £237,500 in "relief of persons connected with and trading to the Islands of Grenada and St. Vincent."[44] The British treasury stepped in further to sell enslaved people and lands in Grenada to compensate slave-owners who had lost property. The enslaved people were called the "Crown slaves."[45] A Commission for Forfeited Estates was established in January 1797 to accomplish this purpose. Britain carried out an inventory of what could be salvaged on the island of Grenada in slave value. The state provided assistance to slave-owners who wished to relocate to new slave-owning frontiers in Guyana and

Trinidad. Even as British abolitionists began embracing the official language of "gradual emancipation" in the 1790s, Britain was expanding its stake in African enslavement and slave-trading.

CROOKED AND TANGLED PATHS

British society from 1770 to 1830 was marked by extreme social contradictions, especially in conflicts between the mercantile and aristocratic elites, and the working classes.[46] By the early nineteenth century, imperial Britain, and its parliamentary leaders, were well versed in many abolition processes besides the abolition of slavery. *Abolition* was a key word of the 1790s in Britain, invoked for many different kinds of extinguishments, including of tithes, church rates, sinecures, and land rights seized by the government for the common good.

The British parliament abolished the property rights of many British subjects to own fenlands and pastures in order to build roads, canals, and, eventually, railroads.[47] The disparate abolition processes varied greatly in *how* they happened, in whose interest, and toward which ends. For example, the government paid landowners when it expropriated their lands for canal and road construction. Parliament abolished the tithe, or the feudal rent paid to church authorities and landowners, by compensating these tithe-holders with entitlements to government annuities lasting until 1976. On the other hand, the parliament's many Enclosure Acts of the eighteenth and nineteenth centuries closed off open fields from use by peasants and rural laborers, but paid no compensation to the common people who lost the collective right to pasturage. In other words, abolitions in Britain granted an "equitable" compensation to the elite classes, but none to the working and laboring classes for rights extinguished. The lines of class-based domination run through abolition processes, even before we come to the abolition of slavery.

The British parliament abolished the maritime Atlantic slave traffic in 1807. From 1807 until the abolition of plantation slavery in 1833, the British navy intercepted slave ships during the transatlantic journey, and the "captured

Africans" on board were inventoried and registered with the government as if they were salvaged cargo, not missing persons. The British state began generating reports on the names of "captured negroes," their nation, their age, their height, and distinguishing marks on their body. Because these black captives were still seen as property, or cargo, they were called "prize negroes."[48]

LIBERATIONISTS IN BRITAIN

From the 1790s, radical abolitionism was percolating in small and large cities of the United Kingdom. This abolitionism arose in mixed-race circles of workers' and women's rights advocacy groups. For example, the London Corresponding Society (LCS), established in 1792 under the inspiration of the French Revolution, coordinated thousands of artisans, tradesmen, and shopkeepers in a movement of anti-aristocratic radicalism. At a time when only 3 percent of the entire British population had the right to vote because of property requirements, the LCS's main objective was the expansion of the vote to the artisan classes, and the political education and mobilization of skilled workers. While abolition was not the central concern of the LCS, Olaudah Equiano, a famed black abolitionist, participated in the Corresponding Society and depended on its network to travel safely across the length and breadth of Britain to share his views on British antislavery.

Radical black abolitionists, such as William Davidson and Robert Wedderburn, played an important role in political organizations devoted especially to the working poor and the laboring classes. A group called the Spencean Philanthropists, founded in the 1790s by Newcastle firebrand Thomas Spence, demanded the expropriation of landowners, the public ownership of lands by local cooperatives, and universal suffrage for women and men. William Davidson, the child of an enslaved black woman and a highly placed colonial official in Jamaica, arrived in Glasgow in 1795 at age fourteen. His travel was purportedly sponsored by his slave-owning father. Davidson was meant to study law. He found it untenable to study and instead worked for some time as a wharfman alongside the many other black sailors plying the British coast. He tried his hand as a cabinetmaker in Birmingham, but was bullied out of that vocation because of his race. The vast majority of black people in Britain at this time worked as unpaid servants, whose condition was indistinguishable from that of the urban enslaved. By 1810, Davidson found himself working odd jobs in London when he joined the Spencean circle.

William Davidson, known as Black Davidson, rose as a Spencean activist. He participated in the Peterloo workers' protest in Manchester in 1819, when British troops injured more than four hundred demonstrators among the laboring classes, killing eighteen. Government spies eventually named William Davidson as a conspirator in a 1820 conspiracy to assassinate the prime minister and the cabinet. Davidson denied the accusations in his speech before his sentencing:

> I am a stranger to England by birth; but I was educated and brought up in England; my father was an Englishman and my grandfather a Scotchman . . . but I have not a friend in England, and it is hard that my life should be taken away; not knowing anything of the plot made out against His Majesty's ministers . . . for if I am to die, I can die with a clear conscience, that I know nothing of any assassination plot, nothing of any plunder or burning of the city, for those things I detest; I would get my living by honest industry, but I never was a man known to associate or keep any bad company.

Imagine Davidson standing in the dock before the King's Court, making a final plea of innocence as a black man, born under slavery. He wove the theme of racial injustice through his statement. He pointed to his slave-owner paternity, "my grandfather a Scotchman," only to soberly reflect on being black in Britain, "I have not a friend." Davidson was sentenced to death and executed the day after his testament.

Robert Wedderburn, also born of an enslaved mother and a white slave-owner, and William Davidson's contemporary, arrived in London from Jamaica in 1780. Wedderburn, like Davidson, took refuge for some time in the community of black sailors. He then took up tailoring. Wedderburn, always close to impoverishment, joined the Spenceans in 1813. He became a preacher and community organizer at the working-class Hopkins Street Chapel in London. There, he fanned the spirit of resistance among his mixed black and white audience from the underclasses.

Wedderburn did not shy away from using his autobiography as the basis for abolitionist reasoning. He took inspiration from the autobiographical genre of freedom writing popularized by London-based Cugoano, Equiano, and Phillis Wheatley.[49] Through the autobiographical mode, black writers dispelled the deceptions and denials about racial oppression endemic to the British white-supremacist worldview. Through autobiographical narratives, black people asserted the power of personhood *over* property. They drew back the veil that made their material life experiences ghostly and immaterial in British policy discussions.

In his sermons and his serialized writings, Wedderburn used his experience as the son of an enslaved woman and an outcast in London as grist for his radical vision of liberation. In 1817, in his newspaper, *The Axe Laid to Root*, he began his editorial with an indictment of his slave-owning father, tracing the imprint of ruptured and betrayed family ties:

> Be it known to the world, that, I, Robert Wedderburn, son of James Wedderburn, esq. of Iveresk, near Musselborough, by Rosannah his slave, whom he sold to James Charles Shalto Douglas, esq., in the parish of St. Mary, in the island of Jamaica, while pregnant with the said Wedderburn, who was not held as a slave (a provision made in the agreement, that the child when born should be free). This Wedderburn, doth charge all potentates, governors, and governments of every description with felony.

Wedderburn demanded truthful recognition from his slave-owning father's white family. His half brother, Andrew Colvile, the legitimate son of James Wedderburn, and an influential and powerful businessman in London, publicly denounced Robert Wedderburn for trafficking in libel. Andrew Colvile served as a member of the West India Committee and later became the London-based director of British Canada's Hudson's Bay Company.

Wedderburn connected the plight of the enslaved African people across the Caribbean with that of the "wage slaves" of British industrial factories, and the impoverished and oppressed Irish peasantry. He implored the enslaved in Jamaica to revolt through a general strike on the plantations. He instructed the enslaved to confiscate plantation lands of the felonious slave-owners and to redistribute them among themselves. "Above all," he directed, "mind and keep possession of the land you now possess as slaves; for without that, freedom is not worth possessing." According to Wedderburn, freedom without security and autonomy was not true freedom. In a time in which elite British abolitionists readily consented to the principle of reparations for slave-owners and the ongoing "apprenticeship" of the enslaved, black abolitionists in Britain insisted on the radical right of black people to immediate freedom and collective rights to land.

In 1819, government spies attended Wedderburn's lectures and transcribed his speeches, building up a case to eventually imprison him. In 1820, in the same year that British judges had Davidson executed, they put Wedderburn in prison for two years on charges of blasphemy. Justice Bailey said in his sentence that Wedderburn had a "perverted and depraved talent" for making speeches using "blasphemous and profane words." This necessitated the law to "remove [him] from society for some time." The blasphemy charges stemmed from sermons at Hopkins Street Chapel in which Wedderburn used scriptures from the Bible to attack the slave-owning British establishment. "Acknowledge no king. Acknowledge no priest. Acknowledge no father," Wedderburn proclaimed in one of the transcripts kept by London's secret police.[50]

A different kind of radical antislavery also arose to challenge the authority of Britain's fathers, priests, and king. British women's organizations were forceful proponents of radical abolitionism. Elizabeth Heyrick (1769–1831), an abolitionist in the city of Leicester, was a member of a "provincial network" of agitators against the London-centered, male-dominated, upper-class abolitionist hegemony. Leicester, like other British provincial capitals of the time, such as Birmingham and Newcastle, was an important site for resistance, especially for those in the abolitionist, workers', and women's struggles. Heyrick's husband, an army officer, died in 1797. As a widow without children, Heyrick lived the remaining thirty-four years of her life as a revered advocate of women's education, and of broadening women's social roles. She became a powerful and outspoken advocate of immediate emancipation. Heyrick converted to Quakerism soon after her husband's death. She practiced "rational dissent," which prioritized the freedom of conscience over custom or tradition. Heyrick emerged as a major antislavery writer of the 1820s, having participated in the cause since the 1790s.[51] She was known especially for her book, *Immediate, not Gradual Abolition: Or, an Inquiry into the Shortest, Safest, and Most Effectual Means of Getting Rid of West Indian Slavery* (1824). The end of the book contains a remarkable chapter, "Thoughts on Compensation," in which Heyrick argued for reparations for the enslaved. She wrote down what no one else, except black abolitionist writers, had been willing to articulate on paper since the 1790s. The widely circulated treatise, as well as the serialized excerpted chapter on compensation, made the forceful case for an abolition based on principles of "natural equity" and human rights, instead of patriarchal property claims of slave-owners. "Shall robbers, or withholders of their fellow-creatures' liberty be not only exempt from punishment, but entitled to compensation for the relinquishment of their human prey?" she probed.[52] After dismantling the argument for slave-owner reparations, Heyrick took the next logical step by insisting on "restitution" for the enslaved, echoing Ottobah Cugoano's call from the 1780s.

> But emancipation does not amount even to simple restitution—(alas, that would require a price which the riches of all the planters would be insufficient to repay: not the wealth of the Indies would suffice to make simple restitution for all the degradation, suffering and anguish involved in slavery)—but emancipation leaves the usurpers in undisturbed possession of the unrighteous gain he has hitherto acquired, and only interposes

in check to farther acquisitions. . . . Compensation, large compensation, larger far than the wealth of both Indies is sufficient to supply—is just due, but that it belongs not to *themselves*, but to their oppressed, their deeply, irreparably injured slaves.[53]

While it is true that abolitionist parliamentarians never raised the matter of restitution for the enslaved in the House of Commons, some radical advocates outside the charmed political circles were actively making the argument. Heyrick's arguments became the core of the Female Anti-Slavery Society movement, headquartered in Birmingham.[54] Even though women would not get suffrage in the United Kingdom until 1928, women's politics pressed far beyond the limits of the established organizations and parties led by men. British women played an especially important role in grassroots antislavery abolition, especially through sugar abstinence campaigns, petition writing, and organizing activities. From 1830 to 1833, hundreds of thousands of British women signed petitions demanding the abolition of slavery.[55]

The radical Agency Committee, led by Birmingham abolitionist Joseph Sturge, widely circulated Heyrick's texts in the 1830s. Slave-owner compensation "would reconcile us to the crime," wrote an Agency Committee contributor to the *Anti-Slavery Monthly Report* in 1829. Another contributor wrote in 1830 that compensation "would be a sap on public virtue." However, few white abolitionists were willing to state the case in writing as clearly and boldly as Elizabeth Heyrick's 1824 extended essay.

The radical and women-led fringe of British abolitionism, it must be said, reenacted the subordination and exclusion of black women in conversations about the breadth and scope of their liberation. The Female Anti-Slavery Society was almost exclusively a white community—the many black housekeepers and cleaning women were not invited to the meetings. Often, as members of nonconformist Christian denominations, such as the Quakers, Methodists, and Unitarians, white abolitionists, women and men alike, preferred to see black people as "powerless" and abject, as uncivilized and needing benevolent aid and Christian ministration. This was even the case as they, in many ways, imbibed and co-opted the original liberationist insight and spirit of black people fighting for their lives.

Consider the example of Mary Prince, an enslaved black woman from Bermuda who was brought to Britain in 1828. In London, Prince, despite suffering severe physical pain from the harsh conditions of Bermudan slavery, was subjected to intense daily physical labor as a charwoman. In her autobiographical account, taken down and heavily altered by a white editor named Susanna Strickland, Mary Prince recalled the heavy laundry loads and the continuous overwork. Prince finally fled her employers in London, but the slave-owning Wood household refused to manumit her. This meant that Prince could neither find a paying job in London nor return home to her family in Bermuda. She sought out the help of the Anti-Slavery Society, and with the support of its members, she became the first black woman, in 1829, to write a petition to parliament asking for immediate freedom. The petition received no response. Prince finally agreed to present her story to the public, and the heavily edited and altered account became a favorite of abolitionist campaigners across Britain. Scholars have shown that the editor, Strickland, eliminated portions from Prince's original testament that referenced her sexual agency and the politics of her multiple intimacies with men at different rungs of the patriarchal hierarchy of plantation society. Strickland's chaste account left out the ways in which Prince worked the trap of slavery to her own ends. The edited account portrayed Prince as respectable according to British middle-class concepts of gender and sexuality, and as powerless without the aid of white benevolence.

Yet, black women, such as Mary Prince, exercised the fortitude to flee oppressors, to try to make ends meet in a toxically antiblack British social climate, and to tell their own story. White abolitionists, through their exercise of aid, extracted the parts of those stories that they believed would best reach their reading audiences. The ghost line of antiblackness—the line separating those allowed to speak for themselves from those whose human experience is emptied and substituted with others' prices, values, and words—runs through British antislavery, even before we arrive at British emancipation.

CHAPTER 4

REWARDING PERPETRATORS AND ABANDONING VICTIMS ACROSS THE CARIBBEAN

Vibrating with the ambient energy of the Haitian revolution, major rebellions erupted in the British Caribbean colonies, in Barbados in 1816, and in Guyana in 1823. In Barbados, Nanny Grigg, an enslaved domestic worker and revolutionary leader, spread word that all enslaved people on the island were to be freed on New Year's Day of 1816. When the day came and went, she organized a group to plan a general strike and the destruction of plantation property. The rebellion, commencing on Easter Sunday, eventually engulfed a third of the island and flared for four days. Enslaved people gave shape to time not only by the celebration of calendar holidays but also by plotting insurgencies for freedom. In August 1823, along a twenty-five-mile coastal strip along the Demerara River of British Guyana, rebel leaders demanded "nothing more or less than their freedom."[1] In response, the British First West India Regiment and Rifle Corps fired on the crowd gathered at the standoff, killing more than 150 protesters. British authorities imposed marshal law for five subsequent months.

Instances multiplied of enslaved people flaunting white authority, and large internal economies of trade and local banking developed as people created grassroots structures within captivity that undermined control by the colonial state.[2] Black people did not wait for freedom; they fashioned it for themselves out of the wreckage they were given. The growing independence of enslaved communities fanned the spirit of rebellion.

A great insurgency broke out in Jamaica in 1831–32, bringing the island's sugar industry to a halt. Some sixty thousand enslaved people participated in the work stoppage and coordinated attacks on plantation sugar works. More than 226 plantations burned. The massive 1831 Jamaican labor strike, led by the black preacher Samuel Sharpe, began with maneuvers of small bands of rebels across the western parishes of Jamaica. Sharpe, born into slavery on a plantation in western Jamaica, benefited from missionary education. He learned to read and write. British planters banned enslaved people from accessing written words, and only by this period were some enslaved people allowed basic education. Sharpe eventually became a traveling Baptist deacon and educator. His ability to travel widely across Clarendon Parish, and to connect the concerns of people across different plantations, stirred up collective strength. In December 1831, hearing through Baptist channels of the mounting antislavery fervor in the United Kingdom, Sharpe and other leaders organized a general strike to demand a working wage and greater freedom. The protest began on Christmas Day. When planters resisted, the next step was outright rebellion. Tens of thousands of people took part in the effort to create liberated territory for family-based farming and collective protection and to destroy the plantations.[3]

In response, the British government in Jamaica unleashed a total war. The Jamaican militia imposed on-the-spot executions and courts-martial. Willoughby Cotton, the military chief, instructed the rebels to return to their plantations—to get back to their assigned place. "Negroes, you have taken up arms against your masters, and have burnt and plundered their houses. . . . I bring with me numerous Forces to punish the guilty, and all who are found with the Rebels will be put to death, without Mercy."[4] The British Jamaican militia killed more than 200 rebelling enslaved people on the fields and murdered another 344 by firing squads and the gallows. The revolutionary Samuel Sharpe, thirty-one years old on that day, was publicly hanged on May 23, 1832.

After the Jamaican militia suppressed the rebellion, the Speaker of the Jamaican Assembly, Richard Barrett, awarded Willoughby Cotton a special recognition, thanking him for "the humanity which has extinguished this rebellion with the smallest effusion of blood."[5] Despite Barrett's pretenses, all white Jamaicans knew that the colony depended on the constant exercise of violence. Jamaica, like all the British sugar islands, was a military state, sustained by punishment and predation. More than 70 percent of Jamaica's budget before 1834 went to cover military expenses, including prisons and paramilitary police forces. The Jamaican Assembly, comprised of white planters, merchants, and professionals, worried constantly about internal rebellion. The British Colonial Office's allocation of approximately £184,000 per year (£20 million in today's currency) for the West Indian military budget is an indication of the tremendous inhumanity of the system, as well as its inherent fragility.[6] Rampant state violence is a symptom of state weakness, and British plantation slavery relied on a constant and tremendously costly violence subsidy.

In the aftermath of the 1831–32 Jamaican uprising, the British parliament hastily set up two committees to make final recommendations for abolition and the emancipation process.[7] These parliamentary bodies, composed of individuals who stood to directly benefit from a hefty slave-owner compensation package, developed elaborate plans to end slavery in ways that emancipated the slave-owners' property rights in black people and ensured the continuity of the racist rule of property. Slave-owning members of parliament played an important role in the British abolition process. Because they—and not the enslaved—directed the process, the emancipation that resulted served the interests of perpetrators. A foundational principle of reparative justice is that "people cannot be judges in their own cases," *nemo judex in causa sua*. British emancipation is a study in the contravention of this principle.

The two parliamentary reports of 1832 drew the blueprints for the world's largest monetary reparations ever paid to slave-owners for lost property in African people. Britain's procedures set a gold standard for how to emancipate enslaved people in service of empire, one that influenced later emancipations by French, Dutch, and Spanish imperial powers. The plan was approved with the support of elite abolitionists in the British parliament, such as Wilberforce and Buxton, over the strong opposition of radicals such as Joseph Sturge and Thomas Cropper of the Agency Committee. In July 1833, one month before the bill became law, the amount of the reparations was inflated from £15 million to £20 million, £15 million of which was paid in cash and another £5 million meted out in government stocks. John Horsley Palmer, ex-governor of the Bank of England, said at the time that any hesitation to give the slave-owners what they wanted would tend "to shake the credit and confidence of the country."[8] For Palmer, deeply invested in the economics of colonial oppression, reparations for slave-owners were necessary to uphold the British guarantee of property rights for its elites. It would be better for business, he believed, for the state to enable slave-owners to liquidate their West Indian assets in enslaved people and convert the value into new investments in other parts of the empire.[9]

The decisions of the 1830s would saddle nine future generations of Britons, and nine generations of the descendants of the enslaved, with the financial burden of slave-owner reparations. To fund these reparations, the British government issued "gilts" or "consol bonds" in 1835, then reconsolidated the bonds with other government debt in 1888, repackaged them again in 1927, and only finally paid them off in 2015. This bond issue extended like a long wave across geographic space and historical time.[10]

The Abolition Act, published in August 1833, was clear in its intention. On August 1, 1834, all enslaved persons would be emancipated, and the slave-owners would receive reparations:

> Diverse persons are holden in slavery within diverse of his Majesty's colonies, and it is just and expedient that all such persons should be manumitted and set free, and that a reasonable Compensation should be made to the persons hitherto entitled to the services of such slaves for the loss which they incur by being deprived of their right to such services.

The act said that the commissioners administering the "manumission" would allot compensation to slave-owners "according to the rules of law and equity," invoking the principle of judicial fairness. The equity between property owners substituted for the imperative of equity and justice for the victims.

Thirty-seven of the sixty-six paragraphs of the Slavery Abolition Act, more than half, concerned the financial arrangements for compensating slave-owners. In other words, the document known as An Act for the Abolition of Slavery was fundamentally a document to define ways to liquidate and configure property value held in black people within the expanding framework of British world empire. The act also served as a great financial stimulus program for the British empire. The government poured financial liquidity into the open palms of tens of thousands of British slave-owners, allowing them to relocate their wealth and diversify their investment portfolios on new industrial frontiers. Former slave-owners used their reparations wealth to fund plantation enterprises across the Caribbean, South Africa, India, Ceylon, Malaya, and Mauritius. By 1860, British Guyana, Trinidad, and Mauritius were the largest sugar producers after Cuba's slave plantation complex. The British emancipation of property rights in enslaved people also allowed the former slave-owners to invest in new colonial ventures across Canada, Australia, New Zealand, South Africa, Mexico, and South America.

At the same time as slave-owners were being extravagantly rewarded, enslaved people had to contribute four years of unpaid work to their former enslavers. This was euphemistically known as apprenticeship, whereby white slave-owners and missionaries would supposedly train black people in moral fitness for freedom. In fact, the apprenticeship system provided slave-owners the reward of at least £27 million worth of forced labor (more than £200 billion in today's money) from black laborers between 1834 and 1838.[11] Apprentices were precluded from buying land, seeking other employment, or moving to other parts of the colony without permission. Conditions became even more brutal for the enslaved under apprenticeship, with more whippings, and the increased use of torture devices such as treadmills and iron masks in "sick house" prisons.[12]

On Emancipation Day, August 1, 1834, a proclamation by Howe Peter Browne, Marquess of Sligo, the governor of Jamaica, sounded similar in tone to the threats spread by the Jamaican military commander Willoughby Cotton at the start of the 1831 uprising:

> The People of England are your friends and fellow subjects—they have shewn themselves such by passing a Bill to make you all FREE. Your masters are also your friends, they have proved their kind feeling towards you all by passing in the House of assembly the same Bill. The way to prove that you are deserving of all this goodness, is by laboring diligently during your APPRENTICESHIP. . . . You will, on the first of August next, no longer be slaves, but from that day you will be APPRENTICED to your former owners for a few years, in order to fit you all for freedom. . . . Do not listen to the advice of bad people, for should any of you refuse to do what the law requires of you, you will bitterly repent it.[13]

After emancipation, black people were supposed to "prove they were deserving." Slave-owners wanted to feed on the physical and mental labor of Africans for as long as possible after abolition. In Browne's view, the freed were still indebted.[14] Emancipation Day, 1834, was marked not by celebrations but by widespread riots in Port of Spain, Trinidad; Guyana, St. Kitts, and Montserrat; and in Bridgetown, Barbados—and by the start of the brutal apprenticeship system.

Apprentices were officially subjected to an intricate schedule of punishments for disobedience to the former slave-owners. James Williams, eighteen years old, provided an account of the apprenticeship system in 1837. He recorded the repeated occasions on which he was punished for "insolence," "indolence," "vagrancy," working too slowly, not working long enough, "not taking orders," and "talking back." These were all punishments of black people for being out of their assigned place, outside the enclosed spaces and time schedules afforded by the British racial rule of property. A schedule of punishments, administered by the colonial state's magistrates, included fines, extra labor, incarceration in parish prisons, and floggings. Magistrates also imposed exile, forcibly sending prisoners off their native islands to other colonies. Many Jamaican prisoners, for example, were separated from their families and sent to the Bahamas, Grenada, and Cuba. "Apprentices get a great deal more punishment now than they did when they [were] slaves," observed Williams. "The master [takes] spite, and [does] all he can to hurt them before freedom [comes]."[15]

In an effort that would later inspire the creation of the Freedmen's Bureau after the American Civil War, the initial corps of special magistrates in charge of the emerging carceral system were sent directly from Britain: retired police officers, military men, and even schoolteachers.[16] The British Colonial Office recruited these personnel to oversee the doling out of punishments in the workhouses and prisons to keep black "apprentices" in order.[17] As the first one hundred magistrates initially recruited in Britain and sent to the West Indies proved insufficient, authorities drew additional magistrates from the ranks of plantation attorneys and owners. The perpetrators of slavery were thus not only the beneficiaries of the emancipation process, they were also in charge of it.[18]

As the stipendiary magistrates worked to keep "freed" black people unfree, another group of state officials, the commissioners, began calculating the monetary reparations due to the thousands of slave-owners living in the plantation colonies, in Britain, and in other parts of Europe. The process started with an inventory of "slave property" on the islands. In 1817, as part of the exercise to supposedly improve and regulate slavery, the British Colonial Office ordered a census of enslaved people by plantation. Beginning in 1834, administrators updated the census of enslaved people on each plantation across the seventeen British Caribbean colonies, Mauritius, and the Cape Colony to create a giant, detailed list of the property that slave-owners claimed to hold in individual Africans.[19]

Commissioners then determined the average prices for different "qualities" of enslaved people using the recorded average prices of human property on each colony's respective slave markets. The British government paid compensation to slave-owners proportionate to the number and the "quality" of the enslaved property they owned, and relative to the various slave markets in operation from 1822 to 1830.[20] Because of this, the property rights to enslaved people were converted into less per capita value for Jamaican slave-owners than for their counterparts in Trinidad, for example. In general, the younger the plantation colony, and hence the newer the population of enslaved people brought directly from Africa, the higher the price paid to the slave-owners. This intricate system of slave pricing was administered by the British state using public funds.

A Central Commission of Arbitration sitting in London oversaw the whole process and approved the respective amounts eventually paid to more than forty-four thousand British slave-owners. In a grand administrative exercise, the valuators in the colonies filled out "valuation returns," or ledgers that tallied the number and attributes of the enslaved people on each plantation, then submitted these documents to the colonial commissioners, who forwarded the reparations calculation to the Central Commission in London. This commission then physically disbursed the money from their bureau at the National Debt Office in the City of London.

In addition to the magistrates and commissioners, the "valuators" were charged with personally inspecting the enslaved people on each plantation across the colonies, and updating and confirming the value to be paid to each slave-owner. Planters, attorneys, and merchants were recruited by the Compensation Commission to carry out this work. The valuators calculated the price of freed people according to a calibration table in which gender, age, and disability were all priced out. For example, enslaved people working on the sugar fields were subdivided into five separate price categories: "head people, tradesmen, inferior tradesmen, field laborers, and inferior field laborers." The value for enslaved people in each of these categories was set on a descending scale. The "praedial attached" category included all slaves employed on the fields belonging to their owners. Meanwhile, the enslaved held on land owned by people other than their masters were categorized as "praedial unattached." Enslaved people who did not work in the fields were classified in the "non-praedial" group, which included domestic workers, dockworkers, and artisans. Valuators priced the enslaved who did field work higher than those who did domestic work. The Central Commission subdivided these grotesque categories further. At the bottom of the valuation scheme were the "aged, deceased, or otherwise non-effective." Persons in this category were typically valued at a third or a quarter the price of a "head person." According to the British government's protocol, slave-owners even made money from enslaved people who had run away, were absent from the fields, or had been killed. The valuation process was thus also a pursuit in grave digging and spirit possession, all to free the property rights that British society claimed to hold in black people's living, dead, and otherwise absent bodies.

GHOSTLY ACCOUNTS

Valuators used different designations to describe the property rights in black people whom slave-owners claimed were absent from their plantations, but still owned: "runaways," "maroons," "defectors," "deserters," the "absent," the "not present." Just as, under the regime of slavery, slave-owners received insurance policies for the "loss" of "slave property," so, too, here the British state transferred money to slave-owners for absent enslaved people. In Guyana, the valuators used a numbering system to monetize two kinds of absent slaves: number 1 was for absent slaves "with value," and number 2 for absent slaves "without value."[21]

A valuation return from Clarendon, Jamaica, includes the price for a fugitive who was last seen on the plantation in 1804—thirty years earlier—when he was five years old.[22] A slave-owner claimed him as property and received his price. In Kingston, a slave-owner received compensation for a child of eleven years who had been absent from the plantation since the age of three.[23] Many times, it was presumed that absentees were still alive and had fled to the Maroon communities. But other times the absented were either rumored or known to be dead. Reminiscent of the demands by the shipowners of the *Zong* in 1781, slave-owners claimed not only reparations for living enslaved people but also death insurance for those they themselves were responsible for killing. In either case, the reconfigured value of property in African people was credited to the accounts of the slave-owners. The British emancipation system replicated slavery's code using government funds and antislavery ideology. One return from Kingston, Jamaica, reads, "She would have been 17 in 1819. It is unknown if she is still alive."[24] In St. Andrew, Jamaica, a valuator inscribes, "8 year old boy, who would be 25 in 1834, doubtful he is alive."[25] The dead boy was priced as an adult male slave, his value entered into the valuation report and eventually paid to the slave-owner. Property prices reveal a society incapable of seeing the incalculable value of black life both during slavery and during the process that ostensibly sought to end it.

The return of James Roberts of Montego Bay, Jamaica, provides a vivid example of the British state's compensation to slave-owners for dead black persons. The property right to a dead enslaved man named Phillip was converted to a value of £15 through the inscriptions on Roberts's valuation form. Phillip's name was cruelly placed in quotes on Roberts's affidavit as if it were an identity tag stuck to a destroyed piece of chattel. Phillip reportedly died in 1837. One year later, his owner, James Roberts, signed the affidavit, "being duly sworn," that the dead Phillip belonged to him and was his possession on the date of emancipation on August 1, 1834.

Roberts's affidavit attached to his valuation reads thus:

Jamaica, St. James.

James Roberts of the parish and island. The aforesaid gentleman being duly sworn desposeth and saith [*sic*] that the apprentice named "Phillip" comprised in the annexed island registrar's certificate of the registration of two slaves by Deponent in the Year 1823 was a slave in the possession of Deponent to the first of August 1834 and from thenceforward an apprentice to him to the last Year 1837, when the said apprentice named "Phillip" died. That Deponent is included by and with the advice and consent of the recently appointed valuers Messrs George Gordon and Thomas Reaburn to testify an Oath to the truth of the contents of this affidavit.

James Roberts

Sworn to before me this seventh day of February 1838.

H. M. Plummer

The yellowing archival documents, with their smell of dust and mildew, do not describe what happened to Phillip and how he died. There is no information about his family and their experience of loss. These documents and administrative logs normalize the British state's cruel obliteration of black people's lives by numbers.

All told, property claims on more than eight hundred thousand black people were reconfigured into £20 million of financial value and distributed to more than 44,441 slave-owners located across the colonies and the United Kingdom.

FINANCING THE EMANCIPATION

The British government needed a generous line of credit to fulfill the terms of the Slavery Abolition Act and relied on banks to supply it. The Rothschilds, the famed banking family, stepped forward to finance the British government's plans to pay a huge compensation to slave-owners. In 1835, under the direction of family patriarch, Nathan Mayer Rothschild, who passed away soon afterward in 1836, the Rothschilds bank purchased £15 million in British government bonds on the condition of receiving various benefits. These bonds, called gilts or 3 percent consols, were perpetual. This meant that the bonds had no set redemption date and could conceivably earn interest for decades or even centuries. To finance the West India Loan, the Rothschilds also purchased additional short-term stocks worth £101,875. The government made the offer more favorable by giving the Rothschilds a 2 percent discount on the price of government bonds. This would have benefited the Rothschilds if or when they chose to sell the government debt on the bond market.[26]

The Slavery Abolition Act bonds, no trace of which seems to appear at the Rothschilds Archive in London, could have been resold, for a profit, by different members of Rothschild family or else kept in perpetuity. Records show that in 1835 more than fifteen members of the Rothschild extended family held consol bonds, and many children in the family had bonds purchased in their name.[27] The Rothschild bank has refused to comment on the West India Loan bonds, and the complete ownership legacy of the bonds is still unknown.[28] These bonds continued to earn interest for 180 years, financed by the British taxpayer. Abolition debt was repeatedly repackaged, creating a tidal wave of annuity interest and remittances. The government debt represented by the Slavery Abolition Act bonds came to be divided among 11,098 different accounts, and those accounts shared the total final redemption value of £218,388,715.22 in February 2015. Over almost two centuries, black people across the British Caribbean and UK taxpayers were forced to pay a host of undisclosed beneficiaries hundreds of millions of pounds in interest on the original 1835 principal.[29]

States sometimes choose to cancel their historical debts when they are considered immoral or illegitimate. Many countries since the late eighteenth century repudiated the "odious debts" of bygone regimes on the grounds that the payment of certain debts would be indefensible to their nation.[30] For example, the United States and France, after their respective revolutions, repudiated the debts of their old regimes; the Mexican republic in 1867 repudiated the debts associated with the period of French occupation (1861–67); and the Soviet Republic in 1918 repudiated the debts of the Russian empire. Governments repudiate old debts that their constitutions cannot morally justify. The British state never repudiated the slave-owner reparations, just as it has never apologized for the centuries of slavery that it sanctioned and promoted.

The British Treasury quietly announced the redemption of the Abolition of Slavery Act Loan in an online document in February 2015. A few months later, in July 2015, Prime Minister David Cameron, whose forefathers received slave-owner compensation for their plantation property in Jamaica, traveled to the island nation on a state visit. There, on behalf of the British nation, he stated that it was time to "move on from this painful legacy and continue to build for the future." A few years later, on February 9, 2018, the British Treasury resorted to social media, congratulating itself in a tweet:

> Did you know? In 1833, Britain used £20 million, 40 percent of its national budget, to buy freedom for all slaves in the Empire. The amount of

money borrowed for the Slavery Abolition Act was so large that it wasn't paid off until 2015. Which means that living British citizens helped pay to end the slave trade.

Indeed, generations of British citizens and Caribbean peoples have been co-opted into paying slave-owner reparations.[31] Meanwhile, the descendants of the enslaved have continually confronted the British ruling class's desire to "move on" from the crime scene, as if this history were past.

IMPERIAL FUTURES

Once slavery in the British empire was abolished, British slave-owners simply redirected their reparations windfall into new colonial pursuits, investing in the slave regimes in the American South, Brazil, and Cuba.[32] Slave-owners reinvested in railway stocks in Britain, South America, and the United States, shipping lines across the Atlantic and Indian Oceans, and in sugar production in Guyana, Trinidad, Dominica, and Honduras.[33] Other slave-owners diversified by investing in plantation frontiers across Africa and Asia, especially in new sugar and cotton plantation enterprises in South Africa, Sri Lanka, Malaysia, and Australia.

The majority of the compensation funds, 80 percent of the total, was paid to wealthy investors in slavery. Members of the British gentry, such as the Duke of Buckingham and Chandos, the Earl of Harewood, the Marquess of Sligo, and some thirty-four other English, Scottish, and Anglo-Irish peers received compensation.[34] Powerful businessmen, such as the Gladstones, invested their compensation funds in shipping networks to traffic indentured laborers from Africa, India, and China to British plantation colonies. Compensation money poured into tea plantations in Assam, railway construction in Bombay, and into setting up insurance companies in Calcutta.[35] At least twelve of the directors of the East India Company from 1800 to the 1840s received compensation for the loss of property in enslaved Caribbean people.

Wealthy Britons also used their compensation bounty to furnish their country houses, symbols of opulence and gentility. George Hay Dawkins-Pennant, a pro-slavery member of parliament, received reparations for the emancipation of 764 enslaved people on his four huge plantations in central Jamaica. The Dawkins-Pennant family had extracted wealth from captive African people since 1650. The family scion now used the funds to luxuriously appoint his family's Penrhyn Castle in Wales with Dutch, Italian, and Spanish landscape paintings and portraits. He also expanded his nearby slate quarry.[36] Meanwhile William Heaven, another wealthy London merchant and plantation owner, used his reparations money from Jamaica to buy Lundy Island in the Bristol Channel. He built a grand villa there overlooking the sea. Reparations recipient William Rutson purchased the Nunnington Hall country house in North Yorkshire with the funds he received.

The British plantation economy constructed a labyrinth of banking services across the Atlantic. By the 1820s, many of the holders of propriety rights to enslaved people in the British Caribbean were not individual proprietors, but banking firms. Of some sixty London banking firms operating around this time, at least thirty-five financed or ran plantations.[37] In the 1830s, when Britain started paying slave-owners with cash to liquidate their property rights in African people, banks received the dole, too. Lloyds Bank, Barclays Bank, the Royal Bank of Scotland (RBS), Baring Brothers, and the Rothschilds' bank, among others, are all implicated as historical recipients of slave-owner compensation.[38]

State-compensated slave-owners, padded with money, seized power and prestige across the British empire for generations to come. For example, in the 1852 parliament, some 40 of the total 654 members were of former slave-owning families, including the future prime minister, William Gladstone. Charles Trevelyan received slave-owner compensation and went on to become governor of Madras in 1859. Andrew Colvile, another compensated slave-owner, half brother of Robert Wedderburn, became the governor of Canada's Hudson's Bay Company in 1852, and his son, James, served as chief justice of Bengal in 1855. The two brothers George and Richard Booker, namesake of the Booker Prize, claimed compensation for enslaved people in Guyana and reinvested the money in more sugar plantations in the colony. By the late nineteenth century, the Bookers controlled three-quarters of Guyana's entire sugar industry.

MAKING NEW SPACE

The apprenticeship system ended on August 1, 1838, and black people across the plantation colonies celebrated this second coming of Emancipation Day with ebullient public processions. In the dawning postslavery period, the freed people, terrorized and abandoned by the emancipation process, found ways to keep hold of life and joy, and to define their freedom on their own terms. In the years after 1838, black people enacted collective redress for themselves by disobeying the planters, running away from plantations, and creating their own free villages. Some 40 percent of the black population was on the move in just the first two years after final emancipation. Others remained on the plantations but began occupying them in new ways and to their own ends, for example by claiming more land from the sugarcane fields for their own farming of marketable food crops, including roots and vegetables. In some cases, the formerly enslaved even took over the plantation estate homes and made elderly or isolated plantation attorneys and planters abide by their wills.[39]

In the years after 1838, thousands of acres of land across Jamaica changed hands, as twenty thousand new small farms arose within the first seven years after emancipation, many owned by emancipated people.[40] The vast majority of Jamaica's 2.5 million acres of land, however, belonged exclusively to the British Crown, forcing tens of thousands of free people to "steal" land on their own island by squatting. The Caribbean legislatures passed "vagrancy acts" in 1838, stipulating that free people who remained on their erstwhile plantations would be subject to arrest. Local magistrates, many times also local planters, had summary authority to implement these laws.[41]

Despite colonial designs, free people across the British plantation islands banded together to form new village communities. Some two hundred free villages emerged in Jamaica, many funded by local churches.[42] In some cases, as with Guyana's village movement, emancipated black people pooled money to purchase land tracts in common. As many as eighty people would come together to buy a land title. The villages lacked public works, such as roads and canals, and villagers struggled to pay the heavy taxes levied by the colonial state. Yet, the movement represented an important way in which the formerly enslaved fashioned their own space for freedom from within the cracks in the system. By 1840, according to one estimate, there were already eight thousand cottages and two hundred free villages across Jamaica.[43] From the 1850s onward, the colonial Guyanese government passed legislation to suppress the village movement. By 1861, however, some sixty-seven thousand people, about a third of the total population, lived in such villages.[44] Free villages also spread across St. Vincent, Dominica, Grenada, St. Kitts, Antigua, Bahamas, and other islands.

Freed people wanted space for their liberation, and they rebelliously sought out respite from the control of the colonial state and the matrix of planter ownership. They constructed villages in which the housing looked like the barracks on the plantations: simple wattle-and-daub constructions, fragile, precarious, makeshift. That's what postslavery survival looked like. It was often unassuming, small scale, vulnerable, and imperfect. The colonial planters called the freed people "squatters" and their villages "slums."[45] In these domains, trespassing on the matrix of planter property, black people nonetheless made their own lives and futures in everyday triumphs of resilience, kinship, and spirit.[46]

Emancipated workers also collaborated in "jobbing gangs": village-based labor unions. The freed people defined new ways to exercise their will over their bodies and time—over their work, their leisure, their sex, and their social engagements. At a certain level, postslavery freedom meant the ability to disregard the planters' orders, to squat on their lands, to leave the plantation enclosure at will, and to live in defiance. As the colonial state tried to restrict access to lands and to lock people in place, the forms of disobedient freedom multiplied. Intermittent strikes, independent farming, the expansion of inland marketing and local banking networks, efforts to educate children, fugitive seafaring between Caribbean islands, loud and disruptive festivals and amusements, the calculated irreverence to planter authority, and the growth of African-centered cultural practices marked different ways of creating imperfect, yet cherished, liberation.

The Jamaican colony displaced the cost of emancipation onto the previously enslaved in many ways. In Jamaica, the assembly raised taxes, placing new burdens on freed people to pay for the cost of government. In Barbados and Bahamas, planters introduced a "tenantry system" to exclude black people from small-hold farming, and to try to lock them in place as sharecroppers.[47] Under this system, the landowners could exercise the right of "ejection" at will to expel and banish tenants.[48] In the postslavery period, across all the plantation colonies, colonial officials greatly expanded the prison system as planter society tried to reassert control. The governor of Jamaica, James Bruce, the Earl of Elgin, demanded "degrading and humiliating punishments" for freed people who dared to act freely.[49] By the end of the 1840s, corporal punishment was reinstituted.

During postslavery, the influx of indentured African persons reinvigorated African Caribbean religious and cultural practices including Kumina, Obeah, and Myal, associated especially with the Congo region. These practices drew on African traditions for making antidotes, performing remedies, and calling on the protection of ancestors.[50] African-descended peoples drew on all their powers to create groundings together despite the ongoing exercise of violent colonial state oppression. The postslavery renewal of Afrocentric spiritual and cultural practices was also a way "to acknowledge the presence of and to thank ancestors for past kindness . . . see[ing] and respect[ing] the alternative world that our grandparents knew to exist," as Jamaican philosopher Erna Brodber says.[51] The compensated enslavers were spirit thieves. Postslavery black society was committed to getting back what had been stolen.

African traditions lived alongside, and also inside, the Christian faith, widely adopted by the majority of free black people thanks to the extensive British missionary campaigns across the plantation islands. Black people visited Obeah women for cures on "balm-yards" and practiced funeral rituals based on indigenous African traditions. Women played leadership roles in the traditions of Obeah, Myal, and Kumina, including in public healing and divination practices.[52]

Black people in the postslavery British Caribbean lived amid unresolved histories of trauma—histories still embedded in racist property ownership. This gave rise to an ancestral anger that descendants of enslaved Africans still feel today.[53] This ancestral anger comes from the inherited memory of enslavement, but also from British society's commitment to deny the theft and destruction, and to compensate perpetrators for posterity.

Michel Maxwell Philip's novel of 1854, *Emmanuel Appadocca*, captures the postslavery moment of black transgenerational anger and black liberation. Maxwell Philip, who was Trinidadian, born to a white slave-owning father and a once-enslaved black mother, came of age in the emancipation period. Twenty years after the abolition of slavery in the British empire, Maxwell Philip meditated on the meaning of historical trauma and redress. The action of the novel takes place along the coastlines of the Caribbean. The main character, Emmanuel Appadocca, sails his pirate ship around the islands of Trinidad and Tobago, St. Thomas, and Haiti, and onward to the Venezuelan coast. The plot inverts the procedures of slave emancipation and imagines what it would be like to impose them on slave-owners. Like the novel's author, Appadocca is the child of a slave-owner and an enslaved mother. He sets up a "pirates' courtroom" on his ship, the *Black Schooner*. When he locates and captures his white father, Appadocca imprisons him on the ship, mirroring the prison regime of the apprenticeship period. Appadocca's men "divide" and "distribute the shares" of the rum and sugar of his slave-owning father's cargo, again reflecting, but inverting, the slave-owner compensation process.

Appadocca holds a trial of his father on the deck of the *Black Schooner*. James Willmington is tried not according to the laws of England, but the laws of "great Nature." After judging his father guilty of wrongs by a "higher law," Appadocca affixes him to a wooden "machine" resembling a wooden horse, alluding to the torturing treadmill wheels introduced to West Indian prisons during the apprenticeship period. Appadocca propels his father, affixed to the machine, overboard into the sea. Willmington survives, however, and the rest of the novel is structured as the quest of the black Ahab to poach the elusive white father-creature.[54]

As a counterpoint to Appadocca's crusade of revenge, the novel also suggests a different path for healing a hurtful history. Appadocca veers off the course of his struggle to embark on "black contemplation." Feliciana, a Venezuelan woman, instructs Appadocca in a different approach to redressing historical trauma. Feliciana's actions are grounded in ritual acts of commemoration and communing with ancestors. By the end of the novel, Feliciana travels to Trinidad in search of Appadocca and is told by a black Myal priestess, named Mother Celeste, to wait "amidst the tombstones" for his arrival. Feliciana eventually implores Appadocca to give up his compulsive search to punish his father, and to "fly with me to some wilderness" to embrace a fugitive life.[55] By the end of the novel, Feliciana is called the "Mother of Succour," and the distributor of healing.

At the end of the nineteenth century, a real-life historical figure emerged who combined qualities of Appadocca and Feliciana. Marcus Mosiah Garvey was born in St. Ann's Bay, Jamaica, in 1887. Like Appadocca, he was a sea journeyer and a seeker of historical justice. Like Feliciana, he believed that remedy lay in transforming collective consciousness and adopting an ancestral orientation toward the future of black social life. Garvey, still a teenager, traveled to Costa Rica as a timekeeper on fruit plantations. From there, he journeyed across Guatemala, Panama, Nicaragua, Bocas del Toro, then farther into South America—to Ecuador, Chile, and Peru. In all these places, Garvey tried to organize West Indian migrants and inspire diasporic solidarity. In 1913, he took a steamship to Britain, where he worked as a sailor on the London docks.

Black people had spent decades making cities such as London their own. By the late nineteenth century, London was a center of Pan-African solidarity and organizing. Garvey found his way into the circle of Dusé Mohamed Ali, an African Egyptian political organizer and journalist. One of Marcus Garvey's first published essays appeared in Ali's *African Times and Orient Review* in October 1913. Garvey remembered the slave-owner compensation, and contemplated its significance for his present day:

> Twenty millions sterling was paid to the planters by the Imperial Government for the emancipation of the people whom they had taken from their sunny homes in Africa. The slaves got nothing; they were liberated without money, proper clothing, food or shelter. . . . I may not apologize for prophesying that there will soon be a turning point in the history of the West Indies; and that the people who inhabit that portion of the Western Hemisphere will be the instruments of uniting a scattered race who, before the close of many centuries, will found an Empire on which the sun shall shine as ceaselessly as it shines on the Empire of the North today.[56]

Garvey's Pan-Africanist vision of a world of sovereignty and freedom for black people across the whole African diaspora became the inspiration for the formation of the Universal Negro Improvement Association (UNIA) in Jamaica in 1914, as well as a steamship line, the Black Star Line, in 1919. The Black Star Line aimed to facilitate the circulation and reconnection of kindred African people across the Americas, Africa, and Europe—communities of people long fragmented and torn apart by the international property matrix of white supremacy. Garvey's organization sought to "unite the Negro people of the world into one great body to establish a country and a government of its own: an incipient shipping line; factories to feed, clothe, and employ black people; a newspaper; anthems; style of dress; a flag." As if combining the characteristics of Appadocca and Feliciana from Maxwell Philip's 1854 novel, the UNIA insisted on the need to link "up the sentiment and wealth of the four hundred million Negroes of the world," and to uplift both the "spirit" and the "material production" of black people. Garvey envisioned collective recovery from the centuries-long experience of spiritual and material robbery and division.

Marcus Garvey's UNIA opened chapters across the Caribbean, the United States, West Africa, and the United Kingdom, seeking to put broken pieces back together. "I am called an alien," Garvey said. "We are no aliens. We were taken away from Africa in chains against our will, and scattered around the world in slavery. We are now searching for one another."[57]

In another speech, Garvey reasserted the principle of ensuring equity between human communities, as opposed to the equity of racial property. "I feel that we are nearing the point where all the races will get together and compromise [sic] the issue of life. . . . Not until the Negro is given the privileges and opportunities of other races; not until then will we sit around the table of peace—the table at which humanity will end its troubles." Coming out of the experience of postslavery, Garvey saw liberation as still unfinished and imperfect and located in the bodies, beliefs, struggles, and memories of diverse black peoples. Marcus Garvey's action and thought represents a practice-based theory of reparations and redress. No matter how persistently the British empire disavowed the claims of equity and justice, black people continued to envision a world of abundance and of truth.

1

Left: Portrait of Ottobah Cugoano, or possibly of Olaudah Equiano, both of whom led black liberation workers in London, c. 1780s.

2

Right: Portrait of Granville Sharp, famed abolitionist and legal theorist in London, c. 1780s.

3

Coronacion de Juan Santiago Desalines primer Emperador de Hayti

Left: Coronation of Dessalines, the first emperor of Hayti. Engraved by Dubroca, c.1806.

Below: Iconic image from 1820s Britain of the brave white abolitionist and the supplicating enslaved person.

4

THE PETITION FOR ABOLISHING THE SLAVE-TRADE.

IMMEDIATE,

NOT GRADUAL

ABOLITION;

OR,

AN INQUIRY

INTO THE SHORTEST, SAFEST, AND MOST EFFECTUAL
MEANS OF GETTING RID OF

WEST INDIAN SLAVERY.

LONDON:

SOLD BY
HATCHARD AND SON, PICCADILLY; SEELEY AND SON, FLEET STREET; SIMPKIN AND
MARSHALL, STATIONERS' COURT; HAMILTON, ADAMS, AND CO. PATERNOSTER ROW;
J. AND J. ARCH, CORNHILL; W. DARTON, HOLBORN HILL; W. PHILLIPS, GEORGE
YARD, LOMBARD STREET; HARVEY AND DARTON, GRACECHURCH STREET.

MDCCCXXIV.

David WALKER'S

APPEAL,

IN FOUR ARTICLES;

TOGETHER WITH

A PREAMBLE,

TO THE

COLOURED CITIZENS OF THE WORLD,

BUT IN PARTICULAR, AND VERY EXPRESSLY, TO THOSE OF

THE UNITED STATES OF AMERICA,

WRITTEN IN BOSTON, STATE OF MASSACHUSETTS,
SEPTEMBER 28, 1829.

THIRD AND LAST EDITION,
WITH ADDITIONAL NOTES, CORRECTIONS, &c.

Boston:
REVISED AND PUBLISHED BY DAVID WALKER.

1830.

Above: Front page of Elizabeth's Heyrick's influential *Immediate, Not Gradual Abolition*, 1824.

Below: Front page of David Walker's *Appeal, in Four Articles*, 1830. Walker, a leading black abolitionist and a conductor of the Underground Railroad, was born to an enslaved father and free mother in North Carolina. He migrated north and wrote his *Appeal* from Boston.

7

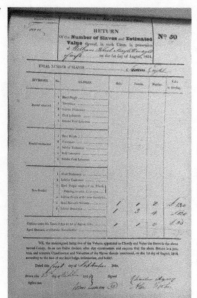

Left: An 1834 valuation form of enslaved people on a planation in Saint Catherine Parish, Jamaica. Based on this form, slave-owner William Robert Haylette received £147 9S 5.5D in compensation for eight enslaved people.

Below: An emancipated person performing in an 1836 Jamaican festival as "John Canoe," an irreverent antislavery persona wearing a white mask, military outfit, and a miniature plantation as his headdress.

8

JAW-BONE, or HOUSE JOHN-CANOE.

9

AN INTERIOR VIEW OF A JAMAICA HOUSE OF CORRECTION

Right: After abolition in the British Empire in 1833, black people in the British Caribbean suffered from punishments on new kinds of torture instruments, such as the recently introduced "treadmill."

10

Left: Portrait of seafaring self-emancipation. In 1833, at a time of heightened revolts on slave ships, including the revolt on the *Amistad* on the coast of Spanish Cuba, Edouard Antoine Renard completed this abolitionist image. Over the next decades, it circulated across the Atlantic as a symbol of the black struggle for freedom.

Right: A form from the Washington, DC, emancipation of April 16, 1862, in which two slave-owners Ellen and John Ashby attest that Alice Harris, an enslaved woman, received freedom "under [their] hand." With this document, the Ashbys obtained $525.60 in compensation from the US Government for their loss of "property."

Above: Emancipation by Thomas Nast (1863), celebrating Abraham Lincoln's Emancipation Proclamation of January 1, 1863.

Below: A view of labor on the cotton plantations in 1881, almost two decades after emancipation.

Eine Baumwollpflanzung: Das Pflücken.

yours Affectionately
David Livingstone

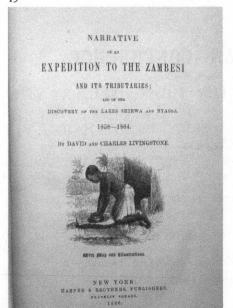

Above: Portrait of David Livingstone appearing in his popular 1866 travelogue, *Narrative of an Expedition to the Zambesi*. Livingstone, as a proponent of British colonization in Africa, styled himself as Christian missionary, abolitionist, and promoter of European commerce overseas.

Below: Frontispiece from Livingstone's 1866 travelogue drawing on the trope of the kneeling African.

Top Left: Portrait of Nora Antonia Gordon, Christian missionary and Pan-Africanist from Spelman College who worked in East Africa in the 1890s.

Top Right: Portrait of Emma Beard Delaney, Christian missionary and Pan-Africanist from Spelman College who worked in East and West Africa in the early 1900s.

Below: Announcement of the international 1900 Pan-African Conference in London, organized by the Pan-African Association led by Alice Victoria Kinloch, a South African activist living in London.

18

PAN-AFRICAN CONFERENCE.

WESTMINSTER TOWN HALL,

ON THE

23rd, 24th and 25th JULY, 1900.

This Conference is organised by a Committee of the African Association for the Discussion of the "Native Races" Question, and will be attended and addressed by those of African descent from all parts of the British Empire, the United States of America, Abyssinia, Liberia, Hayti, etc.

YOU ARE CORDIALLY AND EARNESTLY INVITED TO ATTEND.

CONFERENCES—Morning, 10.30 and Evening, 8.

H. S. WILLIAMS, *Hon. Sec.*,

139, PALACE CHAMBERS, S.W.

CHAPTER 5

FROM CIVIL WAR TO DIRTY WAR
AGAINST BLACK LIVES

Emancipations were never administered in peace. Sometimes they even arose as the aftershock of apocalypse. So it was in the United States by the 1860s, three decades after British emancipation. The American Civil War saw more than seven hundred thousand soldiers die in the sweat, blood, and dust of ten thousand battles. The four-year-long slaughter between the people of the Union and the people of the Confederacy sucked more than 3 million soldiers into its vortex, 10 percent of the entire US population at the time. Soldiers in the war spoke English with many accents. Some had been born in nations outside the United States, including in the sovereign homelands of the Cherokee and Creek peoples, in Germany, Sweden, and Britain, and, due to slavery, in many nations of Africa. The Civil War arose from and dissolved back into a complex North American social system of reciprocity and bondage, of attachments and losses, binding together strangers in the intimacies of battlefields and hospital camps, humanitarian campaigns and treatise rooms. If the war began in 1861 with the breach of a civil relationship between two large solidarities—the Union and the Confederacy—it ended with the symbolic repairing of a civil relationship, with Lee's signing of surrender documents at Appomattox in April 1865. The rending and mending of American civic attachments during the Civil War is a story of army maneuvers and battlefields. It is also an epic story of the breaking and forging of relations, and the racial ghostlining of black people amid the tumult.

Ideas about civic relationships and bondage, and how slavery plays into them, go back to the constitution of revolutionary America. In 1787, in the aftermath of the American Revolutionary War, participants in the American Constitutional Convention drafted a document to federate the thirteen existing US states. Heated debates ensued about the nature of civic relationships between American citizens, and between the independent state governments and the newly established federal government. The celebrated authors of the influential *Federalist Papers*, published in 1787 and 1788, Alexander Hamilton, James Madison, and John Jay, sought to define American civic relationships for the future. They argued that good relationships liberate participants from "accident and force"—from the arbitrariness of fortune and the despotism of tyrants.[1] Good relationships give people something to trust in and to depend on in their social lives together. Civil society should be marked by "balanced interests," wrote James Madison. Societies are composed of divergently motivated social groups, rooted in different religions, different opinions, and "the various and unequal distribution of property." So good civic relationships depend on a fair system of give-and-take, and mutual respect among interested parties.[2] Federalists, such as Madison, naturally argued that the role of the federal government was designed not to domineer, but to support and enhance respectful relationships between the thirteen states. And Alexander Hamilton, in *Federalist Papers* no. 17, argued that good governance fundamentally allows very different kinds of people to nevertheless form "attachment." Through the mutual protections of their persons and property by the state, Hamilton argued, citizens contribute "affection, esteem, and reverence" toward their government. And this mutual affection toward the thing they share in common—their federal state—thereby allows strangers and opponents in the realm of personal interests to nevertheless coexist in the peace of civic "friendship."[3]

Slavery provided a limit on the revolutionary-era American ideals of civic friendship. At the same Constitutional Convention at which the "founding fathers" established the primordial civic and emotional attachments for the newborn nation, they also agreed to the three-fifths compromise. Article 1, Section 2, Clause 3 of the Constitution (1787) read:

> Representatives and direct taxes shall be apportioned among the several states which may be included within this Union, according to their respective Numbers, which shall be determined by adding to the whole number of free persons . . . *three-fifths of all other persons* [my italics].

The compromise gave white US citizens of major slaveholding states, including Virginia, Maryland, Delaware, the Carolinas, and Georgia, the power to use the hundreds of thousands of enslaved black people under their control as political surrogates. Under slavery's property regime, black people's labor power, intelligence, and reproduction was already forcibly commandeered, never without resistance, by the slave-owners. With the three-fifths compromise, black people's political personhood was now also co-opted by the white planter class. Relationships of "balanced interests" among American free citizens rested upon an agreement to destroy the political interests of almost seven hundred thousand enslaved black people. American civic reciprocity was conditioned by American bondage.

The bondage on which slavery depended relies on the threat of violence to ensure that the "master" can take but not give, touch but not be touched, speak but not listen, and use but not be used by the "slave." Social bondage is the opposite of social reciprocity. Through force, 700,000 black people were held as captives, eviscerated of their political representation, and transformed into 420,000 population units to bolster enslavers' voting power. Here was a civic order based on imbalance; a system of attachments made possible by the ghostlining of the true interdependence between all persons in society. In this system, the bonding among American citizens depended upon the bondage of African Americans.

The dilemma of a civic peace reliant on ongoing warfare is not unique to the United States of America. All European empires, and by now all the postcolonial nation-states that emerged from them, are caught in this double bind. The American case simply adds vividness to the study, since many of America's founding political leaders hailed conquest and colonial domination as central, and not incidental, to the ascent of the young nation. Ever since the first British settlers arrived on the North American coast in the 1600s, they saw themselves as living on frontiers where the realm of civic relationships butted up against the extended "wastelands" of native peoples. From the time of their earliest arrival, whether at Jamestown in 1607 or Boston in the 1630s, settlers waged war to find their peace.

Fast-forward to the postrevolutionary period in the United States, in the 1780s, and American political thinkers already envisioned the western "frontier" as the growing edge of the nation, and as an advancing horizon of warfare. In 1781, even before the Revolutionary War ended, Thomas Jefferson, a wealthy slave-owner from Virginia and future president of the United States, wrote a whole treatise on the frontiers of American civil society in his *Notes on Virginia*. At a time when the United States comprised a string of coastal states hugging the Eastern Seaboard, Jefferson identified the Mississippi River as the prime geographical, political, and spiritual frontier of the new nation. The Mississippi "will be one of the principal channels of future commerce for the country westward of the Alleghany," wrote Jefferson.[4] He dreamed of making the Mississippi and the Tennessee Rivers "opened for constant navigation." Frontier fantasies of "opening," "owning," "mining," and of exercising "boisterous passions" flash through Jefferson's meditations.

Between 1807 and 1812, the US government sold more than half a million acres of enclosed "public lands" to its settler colonists—lands forcibly confiscated from indigenous peoples. American frontiersmen drew property boundaries around land and around enslaved human beings as the nation expanded. If American settlers sought a "balance of interests" and civil rule among themselves, they based this pact on fully uncivil relationships with their designated racial Others.

The origins of the Civil War can be located in the emergence of the New South, the expanding frontier across the Mississippi River, which inspired planter visions of a new empire beyond the control of the Northern union of states.[5] Between the 1790s and the 1830s, almost a million enslaved African people were transported from the Upper South into the newly conquered frontier zones of the greater Mississippi Valley region. Plantation capitalists of the New South, who counted more millionaires among themselves per capita than the commercial elites of New England and the mid-Atlantic states by the 1850s, transformed the Mississippi River arteries and alluvial lobes into the greatest cotton-producing region on earth. Human densification reached unprecedented proportions by 1830. For example, the total population of Mississippi increased by 75 percent during the 1820s alone. During that decade, of the seven thousand who settled in Mississippi, 53 percent were brought there against their will as plantation captives. By 1860, Alabama, Mississippi, and Louisiana produced 5 million bales of cotton annually, up from only six hundred thousand in 1820. The Mississippi frontier was not just in theory, but also in practice, a hub of American imperial expansion.[6]

The American New South emerged in the 1820s as a center of the world economy. The export of raw cotton from the Southern states became the single most important source of export wealth for the entire United States from 1820 to 1860. By the 1850s, the US South produced two-thirds of the world's cotton. Similar intensifications of plantation production feature in the two other slavery-based mega-economies: Cuba produced 60 percent of the world's sugar, and Brazil most of the world's coffee.[7] The planters and potentates of the US South's Cotton Kingdom, organized around the main artery of the Mississippi Valley, wished to command their own expansionary future, west to the Pacific and south to the Caribbean, without Northern interference.[8]

Distinct African ethnicities came together at an unprecedented scale within the New South's plantation machine. As we have seen in earlier chapters, enslaved people in the Caribbean were brought from West and Central Africa, two of the most genetically, ethnically, and linguistically diverse regions of the globe. More inter-African ethnic mixing took place in the lower Mississippi Valley than anywhere else in the Americas, besides Cuba and northern Brazil.

In 1822, Denmark Vesey, who had once been enslaved on the Caribbean islands of St. Thomas and Bermuda, orchestrated one of the largest black rebellions of the time in Charleston, South Carolina, by organizing guerrilla battalions according to their "country marks," or their distinct African ethnic heritages.[9] Slave-owners saw only an undifferentiated category of captives when they looked upon the enslaved. Thomas Jefferson, for example, himself a slave-owner, commented on what he saw as the "eternal monotony" of black skin.[10] His judgment tells us how the practice of social bondage impoverished the mental world of enslavers. Mande, Bambara, Gullah, Malinke, Wolof, Igbo, Fulah, Sereer, Fulbe, Berber, Ewe, Fon, Yaruba, Hausa, Ahsante, Akan, Mende, and other kidnapped African peoples and their descendants found themselves imprisoned on Southern plantations where they made new families together and developed new identities.

ON SOCIAL BONDAGE

Frederick Douglass, one of the most illustrious sons of the nineteenth-century black abolitionist cause, gives us a close-up understanding of the forms of relationship characterizing American slavery in the decades leading to the Civil War. Born into slavery in 1817, Douglass published his autobiography in 1845, in which he took the measure of various destructive relationships and severed attachments experienced during his childhood. Douglass keenly observed the ways slavery depended on thick and intimate interpersonal bonds among different strata of the racial caste hierarchy. Yet, despite this intense interdependence, there was no possible "balance of interests." Instead, he experienced the continuous tearing apart of human bonds through regular and everyday acts of violence, and the deprivations and uncertainty that resulted. Soon after his birth, the slave-owners separated him from his mother—a common practice designed to weaken family groups—thereby plunging him from infancy into the experience of vulnerability, separation, and anxiety. He recalled, as a boy, witnessing the "exhibition" of the brutal lashing of his aunt Hestor by the plantation overseer, and the way this scene haunted him for the rest of his life.[11] As a teenager, Frederick Douglass was sent to the household of another slave-owning family in Baltimore. He remembered how the householder was initially "tender-hearted," but the longer he remained, the more she "hardened." He witnessed her change before his eyes, and he noted, "Slavery proved as injurious to her as it did to me."[12] Douglass's autobiography is filled with many such subtle observations of the inner change, the hardening, inside various slave-owners. He escaped from slavery through the Underground Railroad to New York City in 1838.

Douglass, in his inventory of hard-heartedness, described the experience of slavery at an interpersonal level. This was the experience of force and abuse, not reciprocity. Reciprocity, at the level of publics and politics, was the subject matter of Hamilton and Madison in their 1788 meditations on civil liberties, protections, and the balance of interests through governance.[13] At the interpersonal level, this reciprocity is made up of tenderer stuff. At higher magnification, reciprocity creates mutual recognition, mutual trust, mutual gratification, and mutual protection. Social philosopher Michael Blakey maintains that reciprocity is the kernel of all justice.[14] To touch and to be touched; to call and respond. The basic law of societal serenity is precisely what slavery destroyed on the imaginary frontier between whiteness and its Others. This is also why slavery injured the humanity of the slave-owners, too. Social bondage warps the inner world of the master caste, not just of the enslaved.

From the 1820s onward, new states entering the American union encoded the language of franchise for "free white men only" in their constitutions. States such as Arkansas, Iowa, Wisconsin, California, and Oregon all did so. As W. E. B. Du Bois pointed out, the promulgation of explicitly exclusionary state constitutions coincided with rising mass immigration from Europe. Whiteness, as a political category, guaranteed racial caste privileges for European migrants, many of whom were otherwise poor and vulnerable.[15] The category of whiteness also appeased the struggling working classes and migrants, attracting westward migration toward the Mississippi frontier and beyond. The rise of this new, more explicit, political commitment to whiteness during westward expansion, 1820s to 1860s, also shows how dominant communities often project visions of their future, using other human groups as their projection screens. Oregon's 1859 constitution articulated white futurism clearest of all: "No free Negro, or Mulatto, not residing in this state at the time of the adoption of this constitution, shall come, reside, or be within this state." If reciprocity brings social peace, the destruction of reciprocity portends social strife. Attacks on black people on the plantations of the South, on the frontiers of the American West, and in the cities and towns of the American North generated within white society the forces for its own internecine war.

BLACK RESPONSES

The slave-owners' practices of bondage called forth counter-responses. In the decades before the Civil War, enslaved people in regions of the South organized their own internal economies of subsistence crops, which they grew on their plots and sold in their Sunday markets. A service economy also emerged, whereby black people sold services as herbalists, healers, musicians, folk artists, and artisans and banked their money in informal financial associations, such as the *sou-sou* system transferred from West Africa, in which a group of acquaintances would contribute money to a common fund, then rotate the payout among members of the group.

In many other ways, too, black people created insurgent networks of reciprocity within the plantation machine. This could be heard in the work-gang songs on the plantations that drew on the sonic-scape of West and Central African musical traditions, the rhythms of the plantation, and on biblical jeremiads. In their worship, sometimes carried out in the Sunday light, other times practiced in the dead of night, participants moved and danced in ring formations of "shout circles" as a way of making space for the ancestors to join.[16]

Black people also practiced arts of strategic deception and duplicity vis-à-vis the slave-owners and their enforcers—social code-switching that allowed the enslaved to keep their true thoughts and intentions, and their worldviews and culture, unto themselves.[17] As the plantation machine continually forged and sundered new human intimacies, the enslaved developed their own ways to derive pleasure, humor, succor, and enjoyment from within the trap. When they could, the enslaved withheld their labor and dragged their feet while working in the backbreaking fields of thorny, two-foot-high cotton bushes. Or, they ran away through the Underground Railroad leading north to New York and Canada, or south to the Caribbean isles, or west into Indian country. When you withhold reciprocity from people, they do not acquiesce, they fight for what was stolen, and for the reclamation of severed attachments.

LONG DEATHS

America's emancipation, more explicitly than perhaps any other emancipation process we have thus far seen, marked not a jubilee date to end slavery, but an ongoing and expanding dirty war against black communities. Born in the chaos of war, American emancipation took place in scattered fashion through warfare, policy changes, legal innovations, and terrorization, from 1861 into the long decades that followed. If we consider America's wartime emancipation as an epic canvas of momentous episodes, we see Abraham Lincoln delivering the Emancipation Proclamation on January 1, 1863; the Union troops belatedly announcing the news to the enslaved people in Galveston in June 1865; and the ratification of the Thirteenth Amendment outlawing most forms of slavery in December 1865. We see a close-up of the 1867 Reconstruction Act, which forced rebel states to rewrite their constitutions, ushering in an unprecedented wave of black participation at all levels of state government. We note the ratification of the Fourteenth Amendment in 1868 that granted citizenship to all persons born or naturalized in the United States, including the formerly enslaved. We gaze on the scene showing the Fifteenth Amendment's ratification in 1870, guaranteeing universal male suffrage without regard to race.[18]

On this epic canvas, we notice the warring spirits at work: the 1865 establishment of the Freedmen's Bureau, which helped lock black people back into coercive labor contracts under their erstwhile slave-owners; the Black Codes of 1865 and 1866, which reconfigured the bondage of black communities across the Southern states through unjust labor and vagrancy laws, and the restriction of civil liberties; the 1865 reparations of property to slave-owners by President Andrew Johnson; the many interventions of the Supreme Court to promote the interests of the Southern planter class; the long-term rise of Southern lynching campaigns; and the sharecropping, convict-leasing, and segregation laws of the Jim Crow era.

Yet, the way we have come to view the emancipation process in the Civil War era is wrong. In so many ways, it served to codify and extend the brutal racial caste system that existed before the war. The chaos of the war generated conditions for emancipation to begin, but the civil rights breakthroughs in the war's aftermath were quickly undermined by dirty wars waged by judges, politicians, and the planter class against the fledgling achievements of black civic freedom in the United States.

In comparative terms, the American war emancipation, beginning in the 1860s, differed starkly from emancipation processes coming before, during, and after. The US North's gradual emancipation, beginning in the 1780s, introduced the practice of paying universal reparations to slave-owners—a new practice that would become second nature as the nineteenth century went on. The North's gradual emancipation, unlike the explosive insurgency in Haiti, was long-term, slow-moving, and designed by slave-owners for slave-owners. Gradualism meant that the extinction of slavery could be deferred for generations, without end.

The British empire's compensated emancipation of the 1830s took universal reparations for slave-owners to its highest form. In 1848, the French empire abolished slavery and paid 126 million French francs (approximately $27 billion today) to slave-owners. In 1862, during the American Civil War, the Dutch empire abolished slavery and paid slave-owners in Surinam 5 million Dutch guilders (approximately $6.8 billion today) and guaranteed ten years of additional forced labor from the freed people. On the other side of the Civil War, in 1871, Brazil began a gradual emancipation process with a public manumission fund and stipulated that children born into slavery had to remain enslaved until age thirty-one. In 1873, the Spanish government paid slave-owners in Puerto Rico 25 million pesetas (approximately $170 million today), and prescribed three additional years of forced labor. A few years later, the Spanish Crown emancipated the enslaved in Cuba, but first granted slave-owners seven additional years of forced labor from the *patrocinados,* the "apprenticed" ex-slaves, in addition to anticipated monetary compensation of 120,000,000 pesos (approximately $2.4 billion today). In all of these cases, emancipations were designed with slave-owner continuity in mind, and not the imperatives of black freedom.[19]

Emancipation during the American Civil War differed from all these earlier and later processes because it emerged through the wartime suspension of civil law, as opposed to its peaceful adjudication. It arose amid the breakdown of reciprocity among the nation's free white citizens. The violence of the plantation frontier inscribed itself at the center of the domestic nation. Fundamentally, this meant that a much different relationship played out between the government and its slave-owners in the American case than in the comparative cases surveyed above. African Americans, once drawn into this vortex, forged new kinds of relationships with military and government entities. However, through a long, tortuous, and splintered process, American state and society avoided any meaningful readjustment of relationships across the color line. The fog of war and the haze of its aftermath helped cover up all the ways that the war led not to long-term reconstruction, but to slavery's repetition in new forms.[20]

A WARRING KIND OF FREEDOM

As W. E. B Du Bois once said, the "North was not Abolitionist."[21] The Civil War did not begin as a war over the abolition of slavery. The North was "overwhelmingly in favor of Negro slavery, as long as it did not interfere with Northern moneymaking." The causes of the Civil War are to be found in two competing visions of the American frontier: one intent on acquiring the "free soil" of the West and integrating the continent into a Free Trade empire, and the other intent on the expansion of the neo-mercantilist Cotton Kingdom across the Caribbean and into South America. This futuristic kingdom could thrive through state protection of slavery on land and at sea, and the expansion of the Atlantic traffic in captive African peoples. These two visions of the frontier and of the future, one Liberal and the other Mercantilist, one anchored by Northern banks and factories, and the other by the Southern plantation machine, stoked a war that resulted in hundreds of thousands of deaths. The Civil War, at its origin, had nothing to do with slavery and abolition. It was a struggle over the future of the American frontier.

After it broke out, and as it continued, the war increasingly transformed into a struggle over emancipation. The actions of masses of black fugitives, soldiers, and advocates played a major part in making the Civil War about slavery. As Frederick Douglass resonantly put it in 1865, "The Negroes of the South . . . comprehended the genius of the war even before you did."[22] They worked in and through the chaos of war emancipation to assert their core demands for voting rights, education, civil protections, and reparations. In sum, all of these demands stemmed from the demand for social reciprocity—the demand to be able to touch the social order and its representative bodies of statecraft, and to be touched by them.

A close look at the chaos of the war emancipation leads us to Abraham Lincoln, the Civil War president. Although the Civil War did not begin as a battle over slavery, Lincoln's actions, starting in the first months of the war, already began contributing to the patterns of starts and stops, of half freedoms and recurring compromises, on the crooked path to the Emancipation Proclamation. Lincoln, fifty-two years old when he took office one month before the raid on Fort Sumter, had spent many years studying the gradual and compensated emancipation processes of the US North and Britain. He, like other young politicians from Illinois, believed that a peaceful transition from slavery to postslavery could be engineered through slave-owner reparations, the "apprenticeship" of freed black people, as well as the deportation of black people to colonies overseas. The expulsion of black people become a mainstay of the "conservative emancipation" movement. Key representatives included Kentucky senator Henry Clay, one of the founders of the American Colonization Society, and one of Lincoln's mentors. Henry Clay's cousin Cassius Clay also believed the deportation of African American people to Africa and to Latin America would help preserve the civic peace. In 1861, Lincoln named Cassius Clay his ambassador to Russia, and later a Union army general. Lincoln, like Clay, insisted in 1862 that freedom for enslaved people would remain "far removed from being placed on an equality with the white race."[23]

As a member of Congress from Illinois in 1849, Abraham Lincoln had already begun preparing a resolution to abolish slavery in the District of Columbia. Lincoln's proposed emancipation bill (which never made it to a vote) was hardly a study in moral courage. He envisioned a conservative emancipation: black children born after 1850 would become "apprentices" and serve in bondage until adulthood; all living enslaved people would live out their lives in slavery unless manumitted; and all fugitive enslaved people found in DC would be imprisoned and returned to their owners. Lincoln believed slavery should die a long death, "a natural death," as he put it.[24] Principles of conservative emancipation would recur in Lincoln's opinions throughout the war, even as the chaos of the war pushed him, often against his grain, toward final decisions beyond his individual choosing.

By November 1861, Lincoln proposed a gradual emancipation plan for slave-owner reparations in the border state of Delaware. The plan would have delayed final emancipation to 1867 and paid $400 per enslaved person in reparations to slave-owners. The bill failed in the Delaware legislature in February 1862. In December 1861, Lincoln announced the compensated emancipation of enslaved people in the District of Columbia. This arrangement freed some thirty-two hundred people from official slavery. Slave-owners claimed $300 per emancipated black person. A group of three commissioners disbursed a total of $900,000 (approximately $28 million today, using historical inflation rates) to DC slave-owners over two years, after the British model.

Masses of black people were pushing Lincoln's hand on government action to end the institution of slavery. As curtains of war fell across the North and South, draping the Appalachians and the Mississippi watershed, tens of thousands of black women, men, and children began fleeing the plantations to the picket guards of Union camps asking for refuge from their slave-owners. Some Union generals, such as Henry Wager Halleck of New York, insisted on returning enslaved people to their owners, thereby upholding the Fugitive Slave Act of 1850. Other Union generals, initially Benjamin Butler, a Massachusetts lawyer, and later Oliver Howard, William Sherman, and John Frémont, among others, put fugitives to work in Union camps. Often enough, however, they also turned fugitives away when space was lacking, surrendering them to their fate in the rebel Confederacy.

In May 1861, General Butler made an on-the-spot decision to absorb black fugitives from the plantations in his camp at Fort Monroe, Virginia. Butler, in his memoir, recorded the experience of directly encountering black people's political demands during war. He wrote about three black men, Frank Baker, James Townsend, and Sheppard Mallory, who sought help from the camp's picket guards. They pleaded for refuge. Butler "immediately gave personal attention" to the matter and decided to harbor the fugitives. Instead of interacting with them as legal persons, however, he decided to treat them as a form of confiscated property, as what he called "contraband." In his memoir, Butler explored his dilemma. As a representative of the American federal state, he was constrained by the Fugitive Slave Act to return black fugitives to their slave-owners. He decided that his only option under the "exigencies of war" was to exploit a loophole in the Slave Act by accepting black men, women, and children as a "special instance of property." Butler's decision to categorize fugitives not as persons but as "contraband" prompted the Congress to pass the Confiscation Acts of 1861 and 1862, clarifying that black fugitives were not to be returned to rebelling slave-owners.

Another general, Oliver Otis Howard, in his autobiography, recalled a personal encounter with a fugitive woman in Virginia. "A tall, straight, healthful" woman came to him at the picket guard of his camp.

"What do you wish?" he asked.

"Sir, I'm a slave woman and this [here] is my child. Let me and my child go free!"

Howard recorded his perplexity when the slave-owner, "a white woman of middle age," intervened to demand the return of her "property." Howard noticed how "the [fleeing] woman kept pressing her child to her breast." Unlike Butler, Howard opted to honor the stipulations of the Fugitive Slave Act. He returned the woman and child to the slave-owner. In retrospect, he congratulated himself for at least not providing a military escort for the slave-owner back to her plantation. "I will never use bayonets to drive a poor girl and child into bondage." Howard said he felt "heart ache . . . but I became comparatively helpless." We have no record of how the black woman felt, and what she or her child experienced due to Howard's decision.[25]

The US government, with its military officers as the first line of contact, had to respond to the on-the-ground realities of the war theater. The government had to adjust its policies to reports that black people, through the rebellion of their feet, were proving central to Union strategy. African Americans in the South were shutting down the Confederate economy through their massive work stoppages. During the war, the eight hundred thousand formerly enslaved people who fled behind Union lines labored to build ditches, lay rail lines, nurse soldiers, spy on enemies, and eventually fight with Springfields and sabers on the battlefields. In the chaos of war, a transitory and bloody public intimacy and responsiveness emerged, born of urgency and need.

As it became clear by mid-1862 that the black population of the South was fighting its way to freedom, Lincoln again explored opportunities for black emigration to Central America, to Panama, and to Colombia. In August 1862 at a meeting called by Lincoln with black representatives, including Frederick Douglass, Lincoln said, "You and we are different races. . . . It affords a reason why we should be separated." Pointing to the devastating war, he shook his head and repeated, "It is better for us both, therefore, to be separated." A month later, in September, Lincoln seemed to change course. He issued the preliminary Emancipation Proclamation, effectively declaring all enslaved people held by rebels to be free, while also protecting slave-ownership in the border states and among planters who pledged loyalty to the Union. The proclamation permitted the continuation of slavery in Delaware, Kentucky,

Maryland, and Missouri, as in any sections of the Confederacy that accepted the North's authority.

Lincoln signed the final version of the Emancipation Proclamation on January 1, 1863. The proclamation fully legalized the protection offered to tens of thousands of black fugitives dwelling in Union army camps—recognizing them as persons instead of as contraband human property. By July 1863, Lincoln again began developing plans for a gradual emancipation of all enslaved people across the South with reparations for slave-owners, and with a probationary period of continued compulsory labor for freed people. He continued to promote the idea of a gradual emancipation into late 1864. By this time, the Congress already was working on the Thirteenth Amendment to the Constitution, abolishing slavery "except as a punishment for crime." The amendment left a crucial criminalization loophole that Southern states soon used to reenslave large numbers of black people in prison complexes and the convict-leasing system.

The actions of Union generals, Congress, and the president were chaotic, conducted in response to the torrential foot traffic of black people fleeing the plantations in an unpremeditated and unstoppable extended general strike. Vulnerable and in disarray, the US state flailed its various arms and joltingly made gestures of assistance, if not embrace, to black war fugitives.

As government and military officials took halting steps toward emancipation during the war, black liberation from below also arose. In the war camps, black communities constructed temporary neighborhoods and practiced mutual aid. At the camp at Corinth, in northern Mississippi, for example, refugees ran their own housing barracks, gardens, school, hospital, and community safety operations. Corinth's superintendent, John Eaton, a pastor from New Hampshire, enjoyed his reputation as the enlightened administrator of a model camp. Eaton was the first organizer of the Freedmen's Department, which would become the Freedmen's Bureau in 1865. Even as people took refuge in the camp, however, Eaton was busy labeling the fugitives as "bewildered and stupid." He maintained that black people needed to be trained up from their "veritable moral chaos."[26] Eaton's approach and language informed the orientation of the Freedmen's Bureau. He treated black people seeking liberation as indebted and debased subjects who needed to be made fit for freedom. This fitness training, unsurprisingly, involved leasing fugitives out to plantation owners to cultivate the "disciplines" of dependable field labor. Eaton carried out the work of care and "succor" in the mode of a paternalistic Christian savior. Saviorhood destroys reciprocity, too.

In 1864, Eaton received orders to move his military camp up toward Memphis. The army burned down the houses, gardens, and school buildings constructed by the black people to prevent the Confederates from making use of them.[27] Camp members watched as the life they had constructed together over two years went up in flames.

Congress began deliberating the creation of a new federal office to provide temporary care to the millions of black people coming out of slavery. It would take two years to finally establish the Freedmen's Bureau, and then the struggle to fund it continued until its demise in 1872. Personnel of the Freedmen's Bureau codified the pedagogy they wished to impart to black people. Isaac Brinckerhoff, who taught in one of the state-run Freedmen's schools, published his *Advice to Freedmen* in 1864. Jared Bell Waterbury's *Friendly Counsels for Freedmen* (1864), and Clinton Bowen Fisk's *Plain Counsels for Freedmen* (1866) also contributed to this "Self-improvement, or else!" genre. These manuals read just like the "amelioration laws" in Britain of the 1790s, or the 1820s.[28] Black people had to guard against "idleness" and had to "pay their debt" to society for their freedom through dependable labor and the dutiful performance of obligations. Emancipation literatures everywhere carried out the same ghostlining trick: they projected the disrepair of the racist social order onto the very people targeted by the order. The Freedmen's Bureau would eventually run schools, form a bank (which went bankrupt in 1874, losing the savings of sixty thousand black account holders), and surveil the work of black people after the end of the war.

RELATION AND LIBERATION

During the Civil War and in its aftermath, African Americans defined liberation in terms of what it meant for social relations, and they asked for the state and its representatives to transform themselves—to cease saviorhood, and to start sharing civic power. Black communities demanded new terms of engagement with the US state based on civil guarantees and protections. Unsurprisingly, Frederick Douglass, the attentive student of social and political relationships, emerged as the de facto national black spokesperson for Civil Rights in the 1860s. As an itinerant speaker, he stated repeatedly the demand to be "admitted fully and completely into the body politic of America"; to receive "elective franchise in all the states"; and to obtain "immediate, unconditional, and universal enfranchisement." He found a hundred ways to demand, essentially, one singular prized social good: the guarantee of reciprocity: "We claim that we are, by right, entitled to respect; that due attention be given to our needs." Amid the expulsion fantasies of conservative emancipationists, including Abraham Lincoln, the 1864 National Equal Rights Convention, organized by black political representatives including Douglass, declared, "We claim the right to remain upon [the land]: and that any attempt to deport, remove, expatriate, or colonize us to any other land, or to mass us here against our will, is unjust."[29] Black people insisted on their right to use their own wills, and their own freedom, on their own terms. Fundamentally, they wished for their interests to touch the state and to change its balance.

The demand for reciprocity is evident in the demand for reparations by a group of black leaders in Georgia as the war was barreling to an end in favor of the Union Army. On January 12, 1865, on a cool evening in Savannah, twenty black church leaders met with Secretary of War Edwin Stanton and Union general William T. Sherman. The chief representative of this contingent of black leaders, Garrison Frazier, a Baptist minister, defined the condition of freedom in terms of safety and autonomy. Freedom was a place "where we could reap the fruit of our own labor and take care of ourselves." In opposition to the US government's emerging policy of returning black people in the South to the plantations, Frazier asked for the state to fundamentally change its relationship to black communities, to treat them not as wards or inmates, but as a harmed citizenry with a case for reparations. The request for material recompense was part and parcel of a more encompassing request for a readjustment of the relationship between the US state and black communities.

For a short time, General Sherman and War Secretary Stanton opened new space for this readjusted relationship. Sherman issued Field Order No. 15 on January 16, 1865, setting aside a large portion of land along the South Carolina, Georgia, and Florida coasts for the settlement of black families and independent farmers. In 1865, black families on the Sea Islands in Georgia, and Edisto Island in South Carolina, received forty-acre plots in compensation. Other instances of land redistribution to the enslaved include the dividing up of plantations at Davis Bend, Mississippi, among freed people for independent farming.

This reorientation of the US state toward freed black people was fleeting, however. The Bureau of Refugees, Freedmen, and Abandoned Lands, officially established by Congress within the War Department on March 3, 1865, took charge of the matter. In March, the bureau became the holder of lands abandoned and confiscated from Confederate planters. In total, the bureau controlled some 768,590 acres of abandoned lands. On July 28, Oliver Otis Howard, the bureau's director, declared that "all confiscated and abandoned land, and other confiscated and abandoned property," was to be distributed to "loyal refugees and freedmen."[30] However, the Freedmen Bureau's agents often prioritized "organizing the freedmen" as lessees, and selling the confiscated lands on the open market, instead of the large-scale redistribution of lands to black communities. By the time the land redistribution program was officially shut down by President Andrew Johnson in September 1865, some forty thousand black people had claimed possession of redistributed plots in South Carolina, Georgia, and Florida. Howard traveled down the coast to personally deliver the news to the landholders at Edisto Island that their acreage would be reclaimed by the government and turned back over to the erstwhile white planters. The Freedmen's Bureau, Howard promised, would help get fair terms for the tenants—another unkept promise. Despite its early flare as a reparative body, the Freedmen's Bureau quickly settled into its dependable role as an office of black labor control.

From 1865, "forty acres and a mule" circulated as a byword among African Americans for the government's broken promises, and for what was owed to the enslaved more generally. Oliver Otis Howard, the founder of Howard University, titled a section of his autobiography "Abandoned Lands." The debacle clearly weighed on his mind. Howard observed that the "positive adverse action of President Johnson and the non-action of Congress caused a complete reversal of the Government's generous provision" for the free black people.[31] The Bureau was expected to "make bricks without straw," he chastised. Indeed, Congress supported the Freedmen's Bureau when it acted paternalistically to "organize" and "control" black people as laborers. Congress starved the Bureau when it was charged with land redistribution to the freed people as persons, equal before the law.

AFTER THE WAR

After the assassination of Abraham Lincoln in April 1865, Andrew Johnson, his vice president, assumed presidential office. By May, President Johnson began a massive reparations program for the expropriated rebel slave-owners of the former Confederacy. He exonerated all Confederate officers and ordered the return of all confiscated lands to the Southern planters with their pledge of loyalty. Although slave-owners did not receive a monetary compensation, they did reclaim land and town buildings. By 1890, the majority of these returned lands still belonged to a small set of wealthy planters—the Southern plantocracy. Their immense wealth and social privilege would continue to pass down through generations, Johnson having ensured no break in the chain.[32]

Johnson himself came from a small-holding white farming family in the South. Johnson's suppression of reparations to the formerly enslaved was perfectly in line with the basic tenets of emancipation as they had been worked out internationally over the previous century. Johnson did not redirect American wartime emancipation, but advanced its already crooked course—reasserting the government's goals of deliberate black dispossession and slave-owner compensation.

On February 7, 1866, Johnson met with black representatives, including Frederick Douglass, to discuss his policies. Eerily, the transcript of the encounter is reminiscent of Douglass's experience with slave-owners as narrated in his autobiography from twenty years earlier. New opportunities for black men to engage directly with federal representatives played to the tune of old tracks. Black male delegates from twelve states came to Johnson to demand the vote, "equality before the law," and the full protections and privileges of civil rights. President Johnson's response, even in transcript format, exposes the social void that had opened up in that room.

He began with a note of absolutism: "I feel and think—not to be egoistic—what should be the true direction of this question [i.e., equality before the law for African Americans], and what course of policy would result in the melioration and ultimate elevation, not only of the colored, but of the great masses of the people of the United States."[33] He explained how much he had already done for black people, and how much this current meeting was testing his patience. After preparing the stage, he got into the heart of the matter. Adopting the stance of the conservative emancipationists, he said that his interest was to prevent "a contest between the races," and that the continued subordination of black people was the only guarantor of a peaceful civic community among the white mainstream. Johnson expressed white settler frontierism in this view, with roots going back to Jefferson. He also spoke like the western expansionists of the 1830s (when he would have been in his twenties), entranced by the promise of a white patriarchal westward future.

Douglass tried to interject a question: "Mr. President, do you wish—"

Johnson cut him off, "I am not quite through yet." Johnson said that the real "enmity" was between black people of the plantation South and impoverished white communities—he wished to leave the question of plantation capitalists out of the discussion. Unlike any other group, white men were "part and parcel of the political machinery," Johnson observed. Johnson's greater duty was thus to cater to the needs of the white masses, apparently by serving the interests of the Southern planter elites. Next, he adopted another favored justification for ongoing black oppression: states' rights. "Each community is better prepared to determine the depositary of its political power than anybody else, and it is for the legislature . . . and not for the Congress of the United States," he barreled on. Johnson finally stopped his monologue to catch his breath and to ask, "Is there anything wrong or unfair in that?"

Douglass wryly and minimally responded, "A great deal that is wrong, Mr. President, with all respect."

The meeting was a study in nonreciprocity and the reverberations on social bondage. President Johnson wished to speak to the black people gathered in his office without listening; to decide without heeding their consultation. Johnson meant to tell Douglass and the other representatives that *Johnson's* future—the future of white men like him—existed in an impervious relationship to the deprived and terrorized black people coming out of slavery. He proposed to Frederick Douglass that the millions of black people in the South should find some way to leave. The balance of his emancipation and deportation views echoed those of Abraham Lincoln from as late as 1864.

BLACK RECONSTRUCTION

Reconstruction after the American Civil War was about new laws and institutions, but it was also about sorting through material ruin. The battlegrounds of the war, especially in the Southern frontiers such as Georgia, Kentucky, Tennessee, Mississippi, and Louisiana, were mounds of churned earth and rubble by 1865. The war left a landscape of suffering for all involved. More than a third of Mississippi's seventy-eight thousand soldiers were killed in battle or died from disease. "Of the railroad bridges . . . only the high stone piers remained," remarked John Trowbridge, a Northern traveler surveying the "bruised and battered" South at war's end. While in the town of Corinth,

Mississippi, where a Union camp had once been, he observed, "The [white] citizens were bitterly hostile to the Negro garrison which occupied Corinth."[34] Carl Schurz, a Union war general, recorded the "singularly bitter and vindictive feeling" among white Southerners toward the free black people during his tour of the Southern states in December 1865.[35] The war transformed and inverted relationships, and now combinations of Southern whites began clawing the relationship back to resemble what it had been before.

A series of acts by the federal government sought to change the relationship between black people and the state, and to bring black people into the system of civic representation. In 1867, Congress passed legislation requiring all rebel states to pass new state constitutions before regaining admission to the Union. In response, black communities across the South established Union Leagues to talk about their political business together and to organize their voter bases and platforms. Union Leagues spread throughout the South after 1867, as black people planned marches, held conventions, ran cooperative stores, and provided advice to free people about labor matters and contracts. Black churches expanded and extended across the South and were joined by other black civic organizations, including literary clubs, mutual aid societies, and fraternal and sororal orders.

Black people in the South did things they could not ever before have done, including gathering in large groups without white surveillance. They changed their names in rejection of the slave-owners' patronymics. They formed their own enclaves and business districts in cities and even established black free towns. Family reunions took place as loved ones separated on distant plantations found one another again.[36] The decade of congressional Reconstruction, 1867 to 1877, was a taste of participatory democracy for black people after more than 230 years of American oppression and exclusion.

In 1867, 70 percent of the black people registered in Georgia voted, as did 90 percent of those registered in Virginia. African Americans rose to become lieutenant governors, secretaries of state, and treasurers in Southern states. State governments were remarkably biracial by the early 1870s. For example, Pinckney Benton Stewart Pinchback, a black man, became the acting governor of the state of Louisiana for six weeks, from December 9, 1872 to January 13, 1873. He would be the last black governor of any state in the United States of America until 1990. In total, during Reconstruction, sixteen black representatives joined Congress and two black members joined the Senate. Among the highest-ranking representatives were the black lieutenant governors: Alonzo Ransier of South Carolina; and Oscar Dunn, P. B. S. Pinchback, and Caesar Antoine of Louisiana. Ransier went on to become a congressman (1873–75). Meanwhile Hiram Rhodes Revels served as a senator from Mississippi (1870–71), and Blanche Bruce also served as Mississippi senator (1875–81). After this brief decade, there would not be another black representative in the US Senate until Edward Brooke's election from Massachusetts in 1967.

DIRTY WAR

Congressional Reconstruction unfolded over a decade, ending with the Compromise of 1877, when Union armies, sent in to occupy and administer the defeated states, withdrew completely from the South. Already by the early 1870s, Mississippi officials sent black prison inmates to the Mississippi Delta to be leased for coerced labor on "plantation farms." Mississippi set up several carceral plantation farms in the delta in this time. Parchman Farm, the Mississippi state penitentiary, emerged on one such cotton-farming incarceration site. Laborers worked under the supervision of prison "drivers," and whippings were a sanctioned form of discipline.[37]

Sharecropping was a way of generating new debts to encumber black people's freedom. Black tenants, emerging from slavery, were tied by the rope of obligation and unpaid dues to white landholders. This tenancy system, heavily promoted by the Freedmen's Bureau, organized and monitored black workers as they tilled rented lands and split the harvest with the owners. Sharecroppers received their paltry portion, or share, minus the cost for their food and rations. Landowners charged sharecropping families exorbitant interest on tools and other goods and systemically underpaid them for their labor, deepening their dependency on the white proprietors. Sharecropping families depended on the landowner's store for victuals and daily necessities and paid on credit. White landowners thus trapped landless black people, just as they were coming out of slavery, into the weir of perpetual debt. Debt rolled over and grew more burdensome, year after year. Across the South, approximately thirty thousand black people owned land, while almost 4 million did not. More than 95 percent of black Southerners contended with this debilitating debt regime.

The police and the courts forced sharecroppers to work on the plantation to which they were assigned. Those who refused could be arrested as "vagrants." Laborers leaving their jobs before the contract expired would forfeit all wages up to that time. Recalling the slave codes, the law empowered every white person to arrest any black person who deserted the service of his or her employer.[38] Some states introduced apprenticeship laws allowing them to take children from parents whom the state declared incapable of offering proper support. The children would then be sent to white employers, who forced them into uncompensated work.[39]

White employers and plantation owners had a practice called "bulldozing," whereby they forced black people out of urban trades to the benefit of the white working class. The planter class of the South pushed black workers out of the urban centers and into the countryside as landless laborers. After the urban white people bulldozed them, black people might then be "white-capped" by the country-dwelling whites. Terror mobs expelled black families again to the margins of country townships. As before the Civil War, the social order conspired to deprive black people of land, capital, money, and civil rights. These developments marked not an interruption of emancipation, *but its promulgation*. Emancipation represented an effort in continuity, a process that perpetuated the war on black people, rather than ending it.

Beginning in 1865, lynching became a political tool of war emancipation that would remain in use for a century. Terror groups emphasized their role in upholding what they called "righteous society." The lynching era in the United States marked an extended period of state-sanctioned terrorism; historians estimate that at least four hundred African Americans were lynched between 1868 and 1871 alone. The 1870s were especially deadly for African Americans. During the twelve years of Reconstruction, "at least 2,000 black women, men, and children were victims of racial terror lynching," and their deaths were never redressed by any law court.[40]

The Jim Crow laws, designed to constrain black people's civil liberties and to hold black communities in "legal" forms of bondage, militated American war emancipation for decades, well until the 1960s Civil Rights movements. Southern state legislatures after the end of congressional Reconstruction drew a line of racial segregation across all aspects of life: education, marriage and intimacy, housing, food systems, public transportation, and the use of public space. Black people could be imprisoned for riding the train in the "whites only" compartment, or using the wrong water fountain, or entering the wrong theater, or sitting at the front of the bus. Black people were barred from schools, deprived of the vote, and excluded from public facilities and institutions. These included the department stores, symbols of a modern era, popping up all across the United States. Jim Crow laws said that black people were to be looked through, looked past, and eviscerated as civic beings. If emancipations are long historical processes meant to normalize ongoing state-sanctioned antiblackness and ghostline the experience of people subjected to it, Jim Crow laws represented a perfect tool for denying black people their humanity in the wake of America's wartime emancipation.

The federal courts already started to abandon Reconstruction by the early 1870s, adopting a "states' rights" stance on the protection of black people. The Supreme Court invited the Southern states to overrule the constitutional amendments without recourse. The *Slaughter-House Cases* (1873) provided an important step in this process. The Supreme Court decision limited the role of the federal government in regulating business, wages, and work conditions, and from intervening in the semislavery imposed on black people in Louisiana. A succession of cases followed, from *US v. Cruikshank* (1876) to *Pace v. Alabama* (1883) to *Plessy v. Ferguson* (1896) to *Hodges v. US* (1906)—more than fifteen cases—that vindicated racial rule, segregation, and Jim Crow white supremacy. These cases established that federal courts would not intervene in cases involving the actions of Southern white lynching mobs; that "anti-miscegenation statutes" were legal; and that states had the right to disenfranchise black voters. War emancipation did not succeed by a single, violent blow. It was slow, crooked, and dirty.

REPARATIONS AND RECIPROCITY

In response, black communities developed social movements to create civic reciprocity and mutual protection from below, in ways parallel to the exclusionary institutions of the state. Black social movements also served a memory function: they provided space for black people to remember the meanings of their liberation together, and to work out how they would attain the liberation yet to come. Callie House, born under slavery in Nashville, Tennessee, in 1861, organized one of the most impactful social movements of the late nineteenth century. It was so powerful that the federal government surveilled her for decades and eventually imprisoned her. House organized the National Ex-Slave Mutual Relief Association, which demanded reparations for slavery from the federal government. At its peak in the early 1900s, the organization counted some three hundred thousand subscribers, and the monthly dues they paid supported the political activities of the association, as well as the collective burial fund for the benefit of all members. Drawing on the reparations formula from a white Southerner and ex-mayor from Council Bluffs, Iowa, named Walter Vaughan, Callie House connected the monetary demand to the taproot of a deep African American tradition of liberation struggle.[41]

House's organization, active from 1896 until 1918, proposed that free people who had been born into slavery and were over seventy years of age should receive a $500 bounty and $15/month for life. People over sixty should receive $12/month. People under sixty, $10 per month. She argued that the broken promise of "forty acres" from 1865 had to be fulfilled. In addition, the unpaid labor by black people under slavery had to be acknowledged and redressed. She did not ask for a one-off payment, but for a pension, that is, an asset that generated income into the future. Slavery, and the war emancipation that followed it, had imposed debt-bearing liabilities on black communities. Incarceration, sharecropping, vigilante terrorism, and segregation laws all forcibly encumbered black people with social liabilities that gave rise to future debt. House asked the federal government to repair this debt avalanche by providing a lifelong income stream for those born under slavery. In this request, she also demanded a new long-term program to remedy social abandonment through guarantees of reparations, reciprocity, safety, and sustained attachment.

By 1912, her organization had filed a federal suit for $68 million to be paid in pensions. The US government harassed Callie House by opening a long-term investigation of her organization for mail fraud. House was eventually labeled a felon by the government for the "offense" of insisting that reparations for slavery was a legitimate case to present before Congress and the courts. In 1916, House was convicted by an all-white male jury for mail fraud. She spent eighteen months incarcerated at the Missouri State Penitentiary in Jefferson City. When released, she returned home to Nashville, Tennessee, and spent the last ten years of her life in private.

Anna Julia Cooper, a black feminist philosopher born in North Carolina, was born just three years before Callie House. Around the same time House was laying the groundwork for her reparations movement, Cooper published her book *A Voice from the South*. Cooper had studied at Oberlin College in the 1880s and would complete a dissertation at the Sorbonne in 1925, at the age of sixty-seven. In *A Voice from the South*, Cooper broke new ground alongside other black women authors of her time, including Ida B. Wells and Charlotte Grimké, by insisting in print that the struggles facing black communities during America's long emancipation specifically required black women's leadership. Cooper wrote that women's leadership provided a "vitalizing, regenerating, and progressive influence . . . on the civilization of today."[42]

In the last section of the book, she addressed the question: "Has America a Race Problem; If so, how can it be solved?" Her observations shared theoretical grounding and liberationist insight with her contemporary, Callie House.

At the basis of the race problem, both women recognized, was fundamentally a problem of ethical relationships.

Through their very different kinds of work, both sought to shed light on the severed attachments left by slavery and emancipation. In Cooper's magisterial treatment of the issue, she observed that solving the race problem in the United States could never result from attempts to "fix" or "improve" black people. The illness pertained not to their minds or bodies, but to the larger, racist civic body that engulfed them. Only a commitment to "a general amnesty and universal reciprocity" could remedy the social ill, she wrote. She pointed attention back to white society and asked for it to solve its reciprocity problem. Cooper proposed that America's long, indeed endemic, experience with frontier wars might actually prepare it for a change of heart, and for the turn toward the reciprocity needed to end the agony. "Universal reciprocity [is] born of universal conflict with forces that cannot be exterminated," she wrote. She continued, "The principles of true democracy are founded in universal reciprocity."

Reciprocity, not as an abstract concept, but a physical, emotional, and political quantity feels like a balance of interests, access to the vote and to education, and social reparations for social harm. It feels like the recognition of the social attachments that exist between us, and the recognition of the differential privileges that structure how those attachments affect each of us differently. Reciprocity is something other than hard-hearted projections of one's own vision of the future onto other people's visions of *their* futures. Put simply, reciprocity is another word for justice. And when black people, in their effort to survive America's long dirty war of emancipation, repeatedly demand reparations, they are using concrete language to restate and reiterate an essential demand to find again what has been denied and decimated.

CHAPTER 6

GLOBAL JIM CROW AND EMANCIPATION IN AFRICA

History is the study of social currents that flow across time, and the search for signals that tell us about the interdependence between these currents. This study of emancipation processes, and of the voids they created, has moved from the Caribbean to the mainland Americas, to Europe, and back. All these processes—whether gradual, retroactive, compensated, or wartime—comprised developments that also circulated across coastal and mainland Africa. Emancipations belonged to a hemispheric transoceanic system. And the seaboard and hinterlands of Africa played a pivotal role in this system, both in the history of how emancipation processes unfolded, and how black people responded to the emerging postslavery regimes.

Oceanic interdependence provides an ideal metaphor for the flow of ideas and people around the African Atlantic, between the African continent, the Americas, and Europe. Look inside the blue holes pockmarking the limestone island crust of the Bahamas and you find they contain a record of continuous connections with the African desert. Blue holes swallow sediment carried by Atlantic Ocean currents. Sedimentary layers build up over geological time—thousands of years. These red sedimentary layers are the sign of a distant connection: the winds from the African Sahara driving North Atlantic Ocean currents westward, delivering the Sahara's ultrafine red sand from more than ten thousand kilometers away into the voids in the Bahamian karst. This movement is only one part of what oceanographers call a "great ocean gyre." The gyre, or circulation, continues as ocean currents flow clockwise up the North American coast and are amplified by the eastward-flowing wave energy of the Gulf Stream. On the other hand, the coasts of West Africa exhibit extremely rich oceanic ecosystems only because of their interconnection with the North Atlantic gyre. While ultramarine currents from Africa bring fine red desert sand to the Bahamas, the currents from the Caribbean, North America, and Atlantic Europe enable a flourishing of sea life along the West African coast.[1]

Oceanic systems are characterized by circulating interconnectedness. We can apply this insight from environmental history to the realm of human history. If governments and slave-owning interest groups engineered the long death of slavery across the Americas and Europe, we must also explore the ways that the diverse people of Africa were caught up in the currents of slavery's long death, and the new kinds of circulations that black people across many continents created in the midst.

To look at the impact of emancipation on Africa, the lens must open wider, to include a discussion of how African coasts and heartlands were affected by successive "gyres" of transoceanic emancipation from 1775 to 1915. All the previously described emancipations involved interconnections with peoples and places on the African continent. Considered together, they reveal a singular observation: across Africa, all colonial emancipations, in all their forms, were linked through the colonial imposition of new forms of bondage and colonial servitude to a global war on black lives and sovereignties.

In Africa, even more overtly than in the Caribbean, the continental Americas, or Europe, the processes designed to abolish slavery inherently entailed measures to destroy—not to redress or repair—the historical coherence of black people's personal, social, and political lives. Conquest, or the will and actions to rule and sequester another people, to exploit their life forces and to steal the bounty of their homelands, informed successive emancipation processes across Africa, although with various modulations and intensities. Emancipations, despite their humanitarian pretensions, were fundamental acts of conquest. Black people across Africa and the African diaspora withstood and navigated these colonial vortices in search of a future made to new dimensions.

AFRICAN SLAVERY

The Guyanese historian Walter Rodney, in 1966, advanced a set of influential and enduring arguments that continue to inform how we understand institutions of slavery in Africa. First, Rodney recognized that slavery had a long African history predating the onset of European transoceanic slave-trafficking in the 1400s. As with almost all societies on earth, including Mediterranean and Northern European polities, slavery was a feature of ancient and medieval African history, in line with premodern societal norms from around the world. Second, Rodney noted that overseas slave-trafficking transformed the nature and scale of slavery in Africa. The expansion of African slavery and slave-trafficking over five hundred years was intimately connected with the forces and relations of the European slave trade. As just one example, beginning in the 1600s, African states started to import firearms from Europe, often exchanged for enslaved people. Guns in Africa transformed and destabilized political alliances between West African states, prioritized commerce to benefit Europeans, and further expanded markets for enslaved people.[2] Finally, Rodney observed that the African "ruling classes joined hands with the Europeans in exploiting the African masses—a not unfamiliar situation on the African continent today."[3] There can be no reckoning with the devastating consequences of slavery in Africa, Rodney noted, without recognizing the particular role of African elites in selling women, children, men, war prisoners, ethnic minorities, disabled people, and other vulnerable persons down the rivers and across the oceans in class-based gambits to accumulate power and status. This wager built up the short-term wealth of African kings and patriarchs, while corroding social and political fibers of trust and stability in the long term.[4]

Slavery, wherever it exists, is essentially defined as a social institution that threatens designated groups of people with the catastrophic violence of sale and relocation as mere commodities on markets. If human beings find meaning through reciprocity with others, and through participation in durable communities of collective memory, then the slave market attacks the essence of being human by obliterating reciprocity and alienating people from their people's memory traditions.[5]

Especially in the 1700s and 1800s, the number of African people subjected to slavery's catastrophic violence expanded, as networked trans-Saharan, sub-Saharan, and transoceanic trafficking markets drastically increased. The expansion of slavery in Africa was not an isolated artifact of African societies, but a response to the explosion of European and American industrial demand for human merchandise. The western coast of Africa, the epicenter for the removal of enslaved people across the ocean, commanded about 80 percent of the total volume of Africa's slave exports. West coast African societies suffered a severe long-term population decline from 1750 to 1850, as nearly one hundred thousand persons disappeared each year from their coasts for a century. By 1850, the number of people held in different kinds of slavery in Africa itself roughly outnumbered the enslaved African population in the Americas, located primarily in the American South, Cuba, and Brazil.[6] About a quarter of the population of West Africa was enslaved by the late nineteenth century.[7] Meanwhile, in East Africa, Arab slave-trafficking across the Sahara and Central Africa funneled captives toward the island of Zanzibar and then over the Indian Ocean. Deportations of kidnapped and merchandized human beings through Zanzibar date mostly to the 1800s. From 1850 to 1870, demand soared for enslaved people on Omani-owned date, clove, and spice plantations along the Red Sea.[8] Merchants delivered large portions of these crops to Europe. Meanwhile, during the 1800s, European sugar and palm plantations swiftly expanded across islands of the Indian Ocean, such as Réunion and Mauritius, and eventually across India, Southeast Asia, Australia, and the archipelagoes of the Pacific.

European plantation capitalists, many enriched by the slave-owner compensation from the 1830s West Indian emancipations, initially fulfilled their labor demand by buying indentured African people and holding them in renewable five-year servitude contracts on plantations.[9] The arrangement had a similar effect on the family bonds and life experiences of indentured African people as transatlantic slavery. By the late nineteenth century, through the smoke and mirrors and daggers of emancipation policies and expanding hemispheric industrial-agriculture regimes, more than two hundred thousand African, Asian, and Pacific Islander people per year entered the "second slavery"—the legalized servitude known as indentureship.[10] European traffickers, in partnership with merchant elites across Africa, Asia, and the Pacific, "blackbirded" people onto ships chartered for distant plantations and mines.[11]

CREATING EMANCIPATION COLONIES

Each of the four major sequences of emancipation in Africa had a contemporary corollary in the Americas. In 1786, at the end of the American Revolutionary War, a small group of antislavery entrepreneurs in Britain established an emancipation colony on the west coast of Africa. By 1807, the west coast became a global center for adjudicating the abolition of the maritime slave trade. By the 1840s, in the aftermath of the recent British abolition of slavery across the Caribbean, European colonizers unveiled a whole new approach to abolition in Africa and Asia. This approach relied on a consortium of merchants and missionaries. Finally, by the 1880s, the era of Global Jim Crow dawned, as European and American states unleashed all-out terrorization and destruction campaigns against a kaleidoscopic range of black and indigenous people across Africa, the Americas, and the Pacific. The global war on black people intensified not just in the aftermath of emancipations, but in the name of emancipations.

Ideas connecting emancipation with efforts to conquer African states and peoples developed at the beginning of British and North American emancipations in the 1770s. These ideas transformed over time, like the rills and eddies of waves across an expansive sea. Ideas about emancipation and conquest did not move perfectly in parallel, nor were they motivated by shared intent. But projects for emancipation by colonial conquest did amplify over time, growing from small improvisations in the late eighteenth century to massive state-funded military projects by the late nineteenth century. Despite their manifold, errant, and anarchical directions, colonial ideas about emancipation in Africa all moved with overwhelming momentum. That momentum was toward the exploitative rule by Europeans and Americans over African homelands.

British abolitionists created the first emancipation colony in the world on the banks of the Sierra Leone River in West Africa in 1786. The end of the American Revolutionary War in 1783 provided one key condition, as British generals penned "freedom certificates" for more than eight thousand black men who had served the loyalist military cause. The vanquished British navy and other refugee vessels retreated from the North American seaboard, taking along thousands of white and black loyalist veterans to Nova Scotia and Britain. Some were even relocated to New South Wales, today's Australia.[12] As the number of black people in London spiked in the years after the war, and as they funneled onto the streets and the tenements of the East End, a group of wealthy British merchants set up a philanthropic society, the Committee for the Relief of the Black Poor. Alongside a proliferation of other such endeavors in "poor relief," this committee offered daily soup and clothing to black castaways in London.[13] A new spirit of philanthropy, increasingly organized by the wealthy of industrializing British society, responded in ad hoc ways to the problem of the impoverished masses threatening the ruling order. Finally, a series of antislavery court cases championed by Granville Sharp over the prior fifteen years brought the plight of black Londoners to the attention of the city's genteel classes.[14] Postwar veterans' relief, upper-class philanthropists' concern for maintaining order, and the rising tide of antislavery sentiment made possible an unprecedented, and improvised, attempt to create a settler colony of emancipated black Londoners in Sierra Leone. Amid all these conditions, the Committee for the Relief confessed its main motivation: "It was necessary [impoverished black people] should be sent somewhere," one member told a parliamentary inquiry, "and be no longer suffered to infest the streets of London."[15] The committee envisioned a project of both relief and deportation.

Henry Smeathman (1742–86), an amateur, mercurial plant and animal collector, had lived for four years on the Sierra Leone peninsula beginning in 1771, followed by four years in the West Indies. Smeathman had long proposed the creation of a plantation colony in West Africa that would grow cash crops, especially rice, cotton, and tobacco, to compete with the West Indies. In 1776, he suggested a new colony of plantations and small farms, in which "many black persons . . . disbanded from his Majesty's Service by sea and land" could freely choose "quiet cultivation of the earth," or else work for daily wages on the commercial plantations.[16]

Smeathman's sketchy vision of a peaceful colony of emancipated black war veterans and their families, carved out of the peninsula of Sierra Leone, was utopian. As plans developed, no one thought to consult the black war veterans in London about their interest in emigrating four thousand miles to an ill-resourced settlement on a slave-trafficking coast. The Sierra Leone coast was one of the most active centers for British slave-trafficking. European slave-traffickers transported away more than 389,000 African people from the Sierra Leone coast between 1581 and 1867. All the Committee for the Relief wanted was a plan to swiftly remove large numbers of black people from the city.[17]

In the spring of 1786, Granville Sharp, the most prominent British antislavery advocate, learned of the plans and published a document with a proposed constitution for the new colony. Sharp had consulted with black representatives in London, and his long and detailed *Short Sketch of Temporary Regulations* emphasized the need for black emigrants to be granted land titles, and for a form of community self-determination, in which each group of ten families would name its own representative (the tithingman), and then groups of these representatives would name their own spokespeople (the hundreders), who would sit on the colony's senate. The British Treasury, which initially sponsored this experiment in Sierra Leone, rejected the proposal of self-government. Instead, plans to settle black people from London in Sierra Leone were marked, from inception, by extreme administrative neglect and underfunding. Olaudah Equiano, who worked for a year as the commissary for the resettlement project, complained that the Committee for the Relief and the British Treasury had underprovisioned and underfunded the black emigrants.[18]

Arriving on two ships during the rainy season, the emigrants—a group of black women, black men, and a number of white women married to black men—met no arrangements for shelter, nor for their collective safety. Of the 376 original emancipated veterans and family members who disembarked at the experimental township named after Granville Sharp, only 130 persons remained part of it by the following year, with some having escaped to neighboring African villages, and many having died of disease and neglect. However, those who remained and survived formed their senate and organized themselves against the dangerous surrounding European and African slave-trafficking agents along the peninsula. Within three years, in 1790, the settlement of Granville Town was totally burned down by the local Temne king.

Colonies, unlike self-determining nations, are sites of rule, not of representation. By design, colonies are administered through a calculated level of neglect and abandonment. The world's first emancipation colony was a place, from the start, in which black people had to struggle against British rule to try to create their own nation. Only one other emancipation colony would ever officially be established.[19] Liberia was founded in 1821, this time by a group of white American philanthropists, members of the American Colonization Society, who wished to eradicate both slavery and the presence of emancipated black people from the United States. There, too, as we will later see, black emigrants used the space of the colony in ways unintended by the deportation patrons, to foster black solidarity and to reconstruct their lives.

The first settlement of black emigrants at Granville Town in Sierra Leone was followed by a second, more enduring experiment in 1791, when approximately fifteen hundred emigrants from among the emancipated black veterans in Nova Scotia arrived to establish a new encampment, Freetown. This time, the administration of the colony was transferred to a profit-making colonial enterprise, the Sierra Leone Company. British conquest, and conquest by European states more generally, came to rely on joint-stock "mercantile companies" to occupy the lands of other peoples across Asia and Africa and set up fledging systems of colonial rule. Once a colony was secured, large and successful British colonial mercantile companies could be formally transferred to the British Crown. The Sierra Leone Company was the first British colonial company-state in Africa. During the coming century, other enterprises such as the British Niger Company, Cecil Rhodes's South Africa Company, and the British East Africa Company, among many others, would follow the African precedent of Sierra Leone.

Unlike the first wave of Sierra Leonean emigrants, the Nova Scotians were deprived of representative government, and the colony was ruled from a distance by the London-based white board of directors, and the inaugural white governor on the spot, the twenty-eight-year-old John Clarkson. But the most influential governor in this period was a Scottish man, twenty-six years old, Zachary Macaulay. Macaulay had already served as an overseer on a Jamaica plantation at age sixteen. Now, as a young overseas captain of British antislavery, Macaulay instituted draconian colonial laws, including an extremely high land tax imposed on all the emigrants, protections for European slave-traffickers who passed through the colony, and the flat-out rejection of any form of representative government and of the emigrants' wish to name their own judges. The colonists, led by people such as Moses Wilkinson— forty-six years old, once enslaved in Virginia, veteran of the Revolutionary War, and a venerable preacher and community leader—established their own tithingman and hundreder system, nonetheless. Macaulay so aggravated the situation that an outright rebellion broke out in 1800, one year after he left his governorship and returned to London. Meanwhile, another 550 migrants, originally from Jamaica, arrived in the colony. They were members of a long-established stronghold of people who had fled slavery to forge their own Maroon community in the far west of the island. The colonial government began to divide and conquer, dangling benefits and favors to encourage the Jamaican Maroon people to take up arms against the insurrectionist Nova Scotians.[20]

EMANCIPATIONS BY SEA

Even though he returned to London, Zachary Macaulay continued to exercise great influence over developments in Sierra Leone. He led the push to make Sierra Leone a direct colony of the British Crown in 1806. With this, twenty years after its improvised creation, the emancipation colony became a formal possession of the British government and would be ruled exclusively by white governors sent from Britain until 1961.

Shortly thereafter, in 1807, the British parliament voted to abolish the slave trade. Zachary Macaulay, William Wilberforce, Thomas Clarkson, and other erstwhile members of the Sierra Leone Company's court of directors proposed using Sierra Leone not only as a colony for those few black people who had already been emancipated in 1783 but now also as a processing center where captive people intercepted on slave ships across the coasts of Africa could be legally transitioned from the category of ship cargo to that of person. In other words, Sierra Leone was to become the site of an international emancipation court for ships illegally transporting enslaved people, and a refugee colony for those people emancipated at sea.

The gradual emancipation in the United States, with its moral and legal epicenter in Quaker Philadelphia, informed the Sierra Leone endeavor. As we have seen, gradual emancipations involved a compensation payment to the people claiming to own property in African people, and the imposition of a debt burden on the persons nominally freed, either in ongoing servitude or a "redemption fee" paid to the slave-owner, or both. Philadelphia, in 1800, became the first place in the world where this legal formula of gradual emancipation took to the seas, targeting a ship trafficking in slaves, as opposed to the beneficiaries of slavery on land.

During the summer of 1800, the naval ship USS *Ganges* captured two American slave ships off the coast of Cuba, citing them for infringement of the largely ignored 1794 Slave Trade Act, which nominally prohibited American vessels from participating in slave-trafficking. The ships were brought to Philadelphia, where the twenty-year gradual emancipation had officially reached its completion in 1800. The 135 African captives on board, mostly young, aged five to seventeen, were emancipated and treated at the Lazaretto, a quarantine hospital at the port of Philadelphia. Those who survived the ordeal entered "indentureship," in which they were sentenced to time-bound servitude. The girls, approximately a third of the group, had to serve until they turned eighteen, and the boys until they turned twenty-one. The rescued captives were put into the service of Quaker families in Philadelphia County.[21]

A precedent had been set. For the first time, a slave ship had been intercepted *at sea*, and the captives on board put through an emancipation process and sentenced to servitude before becoming "free." The gradual emancipation procedures associated with the territorial North American states now took to the water. News of this Philadelphia test case circulated to London. Zachary Macaulay, in 1806, advocated transforming the new Crown Colony of Sierra Leone into a hub to adjudicate on a mass scale emancipations at sea. The British parliament passed the Abolition of the Slave Trade Act in 1807. Over the coming sixty years, some 66,600 African people, trapped in the holds of British, French, Portuguese, Spanish, Dutch, and other ships, destined for the slavery markets of the Americas, were diverted to Freetown, where they were legally emancipated and subjected to a variety of forms of reenslavement and neglect.[22] The majority of the captives arrived from African slave-trafficking ports within a one-day ship's journey from Freetown, especially from the ports of Lagos, Bonny, Ouidah, Old Calabar, Badagry, and Cabinda.

In emancipation in Freetown, enslaved people were counted and priced as property, then this price was paid as a bounty to their rescuers.[23] The rescuers received £13 for every man, £10 for every woman, and £3 for every child. To be emancipated at Sierra Leone, African captives on slave ships—people hauntingly called the "recaptured"—had to first be "condemned" as human cargo before the court could legally free them as emancipated people. The British state generated reports of the names of "captured negroes." It kept inventories of their nations of origin, their ages, their heights, and the distinguishing marks on their bodies.[24] In addition to the designations of "recaptured" and "captive negroes," the emancipated were also called "prize negroes." After

1821, the British government started calling intercepted captives "liberated Africans." Many terms were invented to separate postslavery freedom from true human freedom.

The theme of conquest, as the will and actions to rule, punish, and sequester other people, serves as a useful concept here. Colonial conquest targets people's lands, but also the coherence of their bodies and spirits. From 1807 to 1819, the "recaptured" were resold as "apprentices," and some were sold directly back into slavery. In the United States, prior to 1819, all Africans removed from slave ships were sold directly back into slavery in the Southern states. Despite the Philadelphia test case, the United States, until 1862, refused to participate in the emerging international court system for adjudicating emancipations at sea. Meanwhile, a small number of emancipated African people were delivered by American ships to the American colony of Liberia in the 1820s.[25]

Countercurrents of black diasporic solidarity created new wave patterns within this historical process of reinjury. Black emancipation communities worked in, through, and against the regime of European and American emancipation processes. Black people from overseas forged bonds of solidarity and mutual aid with the Sierra Leonians. Paul Cuffe was a black sailor and sea captain born in the Elizabeth Islands, Massachusetts. In 1811, he embarked on his own brig, manned entirely by his crew of black sailors, for Sierra Leone. Cuffe established the Friendly Society of Sierra Leone, a mutual aid organization. The founding document of the society expressed a concern for the experience of those coming out of slavery, and for their needs of restoration and redress. "We feel from an awfull Exsperience the distresses that many of our African Breatheren Groan Under," Cuffe wrote. He called for a time when "the Works of Regeneration may be more and more Exsperienced." Cuffe spoke of the need for love, care, and consolation. "We Could Receive all who are Disposed to come unto us With open arms our Dearly Beloved African Breathern we also salute you."[26]

Cuffe made the return sea voyage to Boston and organized a delivery of "agricultural and mechanical" tools, delivered on another forty-eight-day Atlantic Ocean journey. In 1815, he completed the transit of thirty-eight free black people from Boston and Philadelphia to Freetown, Sierra Leone, where they wished to settle. Cuffe put the African diaspora into practice by creating connections of solidarity and reciprocity between the emancipated African people in Sierra Leone and the American North. Within the vortex of postslavery, Cuffe, like many later black Pan-Africanist travelers of the mid and late nineteenth century, found ways to reconstruct long-distance interconnectedness.

Beginning in 1819, a new system of international courts was set up to adjudicate the sea emancipations. The Courts of Mixed Commission emerged, staffed by international panels of judges and clerks. The British government signed treaties with the Portuguese and Spanish respectively in 1817, the Dutch in 1818, and the French, much later in 1848, that gave British squadrons the right to board ships sailing under other flags that they suspected of slave-trafficking. In addition, the British government offered Spain £850,000 (£39.5 million today, calculated according to historical inflation rates) and Portugal £300,000 (£14 million today) as compensation for the expected losses due to slave-trade abolition. Once intercepted, vessels had to be escorted to one of the Courts of Mixed Commission at Sierra Leone, Rio de Janeiro, Havana, Suriname, or Luanda. The court at Sierra Leone was by far the most active. In certain cases, British Vice-Admiralty Courts, such as at St. Helena, also adjudicated sea emancipations.

The Courts of Mixed Commission delivered freedom in uneven and contradictory ways. They constituted not so much an international legal system as a loose network of improvisations, experiments, and corruptions. In the official terminology of the Sierra Leone administration, liberated Africans were subject to "disposal," which could mean conscription into the local militia or public works body, incorporation into the British army and navy, or forced migration to the West Indies, where they would work in servitude on plantations.[27] Some thirty thousand liberated Africans from the courts in Sierra Leone and St. Helena were trafficked onto the plantations of the West Indies. In some British colonies, such as the Bahamas and Tortola, the recaptured were required to serve fourteen-year indentureships. Even after the abolition of slavery in 1833 and the end of the apprenticeship in 1838, indentureship sentences continued to be imposed on liberated Africans sent to the Bahamas until 1860.[28]

In Cuba, the Court of Mixed Commission allowed the practice of *plagio*, or plagiarism. Here, slave-owners would appear at the court building with a doctored document, completed with the assistance of a local priest or village captain, indicating that a deceased slave was still alive and had run away. The slave-owner then pointed to one of the rescued African people in the court and committed "plagiarism" by presenting the document and claiming that he or she was a runaway. The person in question, only recently rescued from the terror of kidnapping and captivity in the ship hold, would be handed over to the new slave-owner on this ruse and given the name of the person who had already succumbed to slavery in Cuba. Think of it: the practice leveraged the law to overwrite death itself. The names of persons killed by slave-owners could be slapped onto new *emancipados*, who were then legally consigned to permanent enslavement.[29]

Even for those who made it alive into *emancipado* status in Cuba, the apprenticeship period lasted for eighteen years and did not grant the right of *coartación*, or manumission.[30] Meanwhile, in Brazil, the *libertos* were commonly traded back into slavery. Before 1831, the emancipated in Brazil served fourteen-year indentureships, mostly in public works. After 1831, *libertos* served lifetime indentureship sentences.[31]

As for the freed African captives in Sierra Leone, they were abandoned into bare freedom, left to fend for themselves in the environs of Freetown. The British colonial government set up "recapture villages," eventually twenty in all. The villages were ruled by a resident Christian missionary, often selected from among the black Nova Scotian inhabitants. The villages thus became sites of strict surveillance and Christian-settler control, especially onerous as the majority among the emancipated in Sierra Leone were either Muslim or practiced indigenous African religions.[32]

In Sierra Leone, emancipated people challenged the assignments and orders they received in a variety of ways. People who had experienced the holds of slave ships together tended to stay together when sent to the villages. These "shipmate families" demonstrate how friendship and succor formed in the space of terrorization and trauma. The friendships lasted, allowing kidnapped people to regain their bearings and reconstruct their lives. Villages were also places of ongoing resistance. The Cobolo War of 1832 threatened the colonial state, as emancipated Muslim Yoruba people who had been expelled from the colony returned to demand self-government. Finally, the emancipated people in Sierra Leone did not stay where assigned nor do as told. They challenged the boundaries of the village system and created spaces of seclusion from the state, sometimes through temporary or intermittent fugitivity. In Brazil, the *libertos* and the enslaved fled plantations in large numbers into the unsurveillable northwestern rain forests, establishing *quilombos*, or Maroon villages, together.[33]

INDIAN EMANCIPATION

Emancipation processes in Africa began as small, improvised endeavors to establish an emancipation colony and grew eventually into a large-scale, legal, and carceral system of emancipations by sea, adjudicated not just in Sierra Leone, but at specially designated courts across the rims of the Atlantic Ocean. The abolition of slavery across the British plantation colonies, 1833–1838, transformed Britain into a "conscience leader" of antislavery campaigns on the world stage. These campaigns brought a new kind of conquest to African shores and interior regions beginning in the 1840s.

In the 1830s, leading British antislavery campaigner and parliamentarian Thomas Fowell Buxton fought for the abolition of slavery and against the apprenticeship system that prolonged servitude after abolition. Already by 1839, in his famous tract *The African Slave Trade*, Buxton sought to redirect the target of mainstream antislavery in Britain from the West Indian planters and their counterparts in the American South to the state of "civilization" in Africa and the ongoing practice of enslavement. The problem, he insisted, was not with the European and American systems of racism and colonialism, but with the moral standing—with the hearts—of African people. In Africa, according to Buxton, "the parent—debased and brutalized as he is—barters his child."

"The African" trades in the enslaved to appease his "accustomed gratifications." And Africa, which he personified in the feminine, is "bound in the chains of the grossest ignorance, she is a party to the most savage superstition." The patriarchal and sexual innuendo at work in Buxton's fantasy of Africa, and his association of African societies with monstrosity and chaos, were common stock at the time, as they had been for centuries. Buxton worked from a well-establish racial repertoire, dating back to the 1500s, in which European male fantasies of sexual, political, and economic domination construed Africa as a monstrous feminine figure and an object of conquest.[34] Conquest, again, is the wish and effort to colonize, rule, and exploit other people's life forces. Buxton, in articulating a new vision for midcentury emancipation in Africa, drew on the same renderings of African peoples that once served to justify the practice of transoceanic slavery.

In his sequel volume, titled *The Remedy* (1840), Buxton paints a picture of conquest. "Africa can never be delivered, till we have called forth the rich productiveness of her soil, and [elevated] the minds of her people." Abolitionist Britons, Buxton prescribed, should expand the "legitimate trade" and "commercial intercourse" with African states and should promote Christian missionization. Only teaching the gospel, Buxton wrote, "can penetrate to the root of the evil, can teach [the African] to love and to befriend his neighbor, and cause him to act as a *candidate* for a higher and holier state of being."[35] For Buxton, the so-called *Pax Britannica*, the Peace of Britain, would use the alliance of Bible, plow, and purse to free African hearts.

Whereas a compensation had been paid to the slave-owners of Britain, Buxton maintained that the economic benefits of African participation in British trade and moral education would "furnish full compensation to that [African] country for the loss of the Slave Trade."[36] Ironically, British political leaders argued in the 1830s that a massive payout was needed to compensate British slave-owners for the losses they would incur in the shift from slavery-based trade to "free trade," involving wages for laborers and curbs on government barriers to international trade. Just five years later, British political leaders asserted that British "free trade" in new colonial domains of Africa and

Asia would be compensation enough for the African elites.[37] The gospel of free trade would come to serve as a powerful justification for European colonization of African people and the exploitation of their native lands.

In the 1840s, Buxton, a man of action, set to work with colleagues to open this new era of colonization. He foresaw the heightening of European "intercourse" and "penetration" in Africa under the aegis of antislavery. He helped found the Society for the Extinction of the Slave Trade and for the Cultivation of Africa (1839). In 1841, he sponsored a colonial expedition of three steamships and eventually 303 white and black travelers to the Niger Valley, West Africa. In May 1841, the expeditionary group disembarked near Lagos and entered the lands of the Aboh and Iddah peoples. They signed treaties for a small settlement colony.[38] Expedition members set up a farm to cultivate cash crops, including cotton. Ralph Moore, an emancipated Liberian man once enslaved in Mississippi, served as the overseer. In June 1842, the British government declared the end of the expedition, citing health risks specifically to the white expeditioners.[39]

Surprisingly, the most immediate outcome of this new period of triumphant British overseas antislavery activity manifested first in British India. In April 1843, the East India Company promulgated Act V, officially abolishing the "legal status" of slavery.[40] British India officials, some close to Thomas Buxton, argued that slavery in India would only be eradicated "naturally," over time and through the expansion of British "legitimate commerce." For its domains in Madras, Bombay, and Calcutta, the East India Company's Act V stipulated that "no public officer . . . [shall] sell or cause to be sold any person," that colonial courts would not enforce any "rights arising out of an alleged property in the person and services of another," and that people who were freed from slavery would be allowed to hold property. In other words, the law prescribes a fully passive stance toward the practice of slave owning and slave-trafficking in India. A later British imperial theorist could call this the doctrine of "permissive freedom," as opposed to regulated freedom—the British East India Company would permit enslaved people to be free, if they could find a way, but it would not take any actions to help them attain freedom.[41]

In diametrical contrast to the West Indian emancipation process of 1833–38, in which the state intervened to bring about universal emancipation across the British plantation colonies by appeasing British slave-owners, the East Indian emancipation process was pro forma and disengaged. The approach was justified by British-American ethnographers and missionaries, such as William Adam. Adam, who had lived in Calcutta for a time, proposed that slavery was a feature of Indian "custom." And respecting Indian customs through a gradual and noncommittal antislavery policy would be the mark of enlightened British overlordship.[42] Buxton praised Adam's work. During the same decade that the East India Company promulgated its toothless emancipation act, it also completed the conquest of many large and small Indian polities, including the Punjab and Sind, and sponsored experiments in cotton and sugar plantations, staffed by white overseers hired from the American South and the West Indies.[43]

The approach developed by the British East India Company came to be known, simply, as Indian Emancipation, which British colonial administrators from 1870s to 1915 explicitly applied to their programs of large-scale African conquest. It should not be a surprise that some of the military and governing personnel organizing the British conquest of Africa in the late nineteenth century had earlier participated in the conquest of India midcentury.[44]

HEARTS OF DARKNESS

In the 1840s, British colonial administration may have ruled over the "purse and plow" of their dark-skinned subjects in Sierra Leone, sections of the Ghana coast, and South Africa, but the Christian missions claimed to steward their hearts. The Church Mission Society, based in London, the German-language Basel Mission, and the French-language missionary orders of the Catholic Church all concentrated on African campaigns in the 1840s. David Livingstone, twenty-seven-year-old Scottish missionary traveler and publicist, had just arrived at a British colonial mission in South Africa. He soon emerged as a celebrity advocate for the union of church, commerce, and antislavery in Africa. According to Livingstone, Christian missions would save Africans from the Arab slave-traffickers and from the abominations of African indigenous spirituality.

Saharan and sub-Saharan slave-trafficking was indeed exploding in scale at the time Livingstone wrote. Omani networks of slavery, channeled through Zanzibar, were extending their reach across Central Africa and the Indian Ocean.[45] Yet, this development had to do with the interconnected gyre of increasing European demand for plantation productions, and the expansion of industrial agriculture across the Indian Ocean and the Pacific. Arab and African slave-trafficking and slave owning were certainly part of the problem, but the European imperial supremacist perspective saw the heart and soul of Arab and African people to be the root cause. In fact, Arab and African elites profited from world markets organized around the ruling economic classes of Europe and America.

When Livingstone traveled to South Africa to begin his missionary work, Europeans still had little geographical knowledge of the interior of the African continent. Livingstone became an inspiration for bands of European and American missionaries and explorers. His missionary letters from his travels up the Zambezi River, collected and widely published in the 1850s, emphasized what he perceived as the "savagery" and "primitiveness" of African cultures, as well as the urgent need for British militias to eradicate the internal African slave trade. "The slave trade seems pressed into the very center of the continent from both sides," he wrote.[46] His letters regularly communicated his sense of himself as an emancipator in Africa, a "crusader against slavery," and an apostle of Christ "among these poor savages," who lacked Britain's "civilization and commerce."[47] Livingstone in Africa, and the African Civilization Society in Britain, were committed to "civilizing [African] society" so as to rule its people and lands. Colonization was always part of the objective.

Missionaries established schools and prided themselves in the work of conversion. They mapped rivers and wrote travel logs. They published on their exploits in their international presses. Theirs was a conquest of ideas spreading across Africa, and their words symbolized and imposed a new imperial order. Christian missionaries, especially in the context of the series of universal-emancipation declarations in Britain in 1833, France in 1848, the Netherlands in 1862, and the United States of America in 1865, saw themselves as crusaders against Africa's inner enslavement.

In their effort to establish and extend their own order across parts of Africa, Christian missionaries actively sought, though not without important exceptions, to obliterate existing indigenous African symbols of social and spiritual order.[48] This work of destruction took on a material and physical manifestation through the missionary practice of "fetish" destruction. Ever since the time of European colonial interventions on the African coasts beginning in the 1400s, European merchants and travelers had remarked on the importance of plants, animals, and sculpted objects in African spiritual practices. The Portuguese on the Guinea coast used their own word, *feitiço*, meaning "relating to art or artifice," to record the sacred role of material objects in West African cultures. African philosophies saw the spiritual vibrancy of the material world. In African spiritualities, divinity was not separate from nature, and humans were not separate from the surrounding environment. Indigenous African worship took place in forms foreign to many colonizing European societies—through libations, dances, the sacramentalization of nonhuman entities, including animals and plants, and the offering of the human body as a ritual dwelling place for the gods.[49] European travelers viewed these ideas as "demonic" and "monstrous."[50] Today, these same ideas are embraced by New Age movements, and also by scientists and environmentalists because of their focus on multispecies interdependence. Early European travelers seeking control over the order of their own world were compelled to denigrate and destroy indigenous African ways of creating order, and to assert themselves, in superior distinction to all others, as Man.

During the great missionary awakening of the 1850s onward, missionaries committed themselves to destroying African "fetishes," or the materials and shrines of African spiritual practice. Robert Hamill Nassau's influential treatise *Fetishism in West Africa* (1904) detailed "sorcery" and "witchcraft" as key dangers of African spirituality. He cataloged a litany of purported monstrosities, including his particular fascination: cannibalism. Such missionary fantasies were reported through hearsay and rumor, allowing missionaries to make the case that African people's traditions had to be obliterated and replaced, for African people's hearts and souls to be emancipated.

Livingstone was later joined by younger European and American adventurers, who aped his style and gave European imperial audiences titillating and exoticized travel writing about Africa. The Welsh American Henry Morton Stanley, and the French Pierre de Brazza, were two major propagators of the "dark Africa" fantasy in the late nineteenth century. Their renditions helped to legitimate the exercise of extreme violence against African societies. Stanley filled his regular newspaper accounts in the *New York Herald* with lurid descriptions of the "African jungle," the "darkest continent," and the "lawlessness," "ferocity," and "horror" of a "myriad of dark nations."[51] This kind of fanatical writing reached such a high trill in the Victorian era that Joseph Conrad, in his 1899 *Heart of Darkness*, retrospectively reframed the extreme violence European missionaries and mercenaries committed against African peoples and their societies. In the novel, it is Kurtz, fashioned on the historical figure of David Livingstone, whose words are described as a "pulsating stream of light or the deceitful flow from the heart of an impenetrable darkness."[52]

Missionary emancipation involved attacks on the consciousness and psyche of African peoples. In the face of this forceful current, emancipated black people had little choice but to commit themselves to reconstruct new ideas of African dignity and sovereignty from out of the voids and debris that European conquest was leaving behind.

PAN-AFRICAN RECONSTRUCTION

During the 1850s and 1860s, the currents of emancipation organized by imperial governments and by mercantile and church institutions, including joint-stock companies and missionary societies, set out to destroy, whether in function or intent, the social, cultural, and political coherence of African societies. Historians call this the era of "informal empire," when a small number of powerful imperial states, foremost among them Britain, France, the Netherlands, the United States, Spain, Portugal, and Germany, sought to break down the existing societal order and interregional circulations of indigenous, African, Asian, and Pacific people worldwide, and to impose a new modular order. It was a time of major destruction in the name of the nebulous concept of "freedom": ideas about free trade and freeing hearts went along with talk about freeing the enslaved. The United States of America, itself an expanding and colonizing nation-state, sought out new frontiers for war in Indian country to the west, while also doubling down on its war against black people, enslaved and free.

Amid this era of destruction, black people across Africa and the African diaspora intended to make something new out of the compounding destruction of the postslavery era. This effort can be best described as "reconstruction," following W. E. B. Du Bois's term. Du Bois, in his book *Black Reconstruction* (1935), used the term with specific reference to two decades of US mid-nineteenth-century history, 1860–80. The idea behind the term has diasporic and global significance, however, and helps us understand the ways black people, scattered across the Americas, Europe, and Africa, participated in interconnected and assembled ways in the search for Pan-African coherence.

"Black reconstruction," for W. E. B. Du Bois, meant *combined action* by black people in motion to create new political and social coherence out of the chaos of America's ongoing war on black people's lives. During the American Civil War, Du Bois showed that black people did not stand still but were mightily on the move. They participated in the greatest general strike the United States has ever known as they fled plantations to cross Union lines during the Civil War. This great strike was the wartime culmination of the long-term marronage of the Underground Railroad. Black people spent eighty years before the outbreak of the war escaping the plantations through perilous northward passages. After the war, they organized themselves into new political parties through Union Leagues. They used their voting power to change the face of American legislatures at all levels of government during congressional Reconstruction. They wrote new constitutions that abolished imprisonment for debt. Black people, in collectivities, fought political battles to obtain land for the landless. They organized exodus and emigration movements to create new townships, both nearby and overseas, for sustainable societal reconstruction safe from the retribution and machinations of the planter classes and the impoverished white groups who did the bidding of the planter classes.[53] Du Bois's black reconstruction occurred through solidarity-based organizing, political mobilization, and the imagination of new itineraries of travel and movement.

Black agents across Africa and the diaspora, scattered by the winds of racial slavery and emancipation, conspired to rebond with alienated kin, and to make new meaning out of the fragments of black experience across vast distances of land and sea. As countercurrents in the gyre of separation and removal, the two emancipation colonies in Africa, Sierra Leone and Liberia, served as early epicenters for the reconstruction of international black solidarities.

The influential early black internationalist Edward Wilmot Blyden (1832–1912) was born to emancipated parents in St. Thomas, Danish West Indies. In 1850, he traveled to New Jersey in hopes of entering a theological college and becoming a Christian missionary. Three Northern theological colleges, including Rutgers, denied him admission on racial grounds. That same year, the US Congress passed the Fugitive Slave Act, endangering the security of black people everywhere in the United States. Blyden fled the United States for Africa. He used the networks of Christian missions and the emancipation settlement in Liberia to challenge ideas about white superiority, and to elevate the principle of unity among all black people worldwide rooted in their shared African descent. Already in 1857, at age twenty-five, Blyden published his essay *A Vindication of the African Race*, dedicated to the theme of the collective psychological and social perseverance of black people amid the onslaught of oppression.[54] Blyden spent the majority of his career working in the colonies of Liberia and Sierra Leone. He argued for the importance of solidarity among local African communities and the black migrants arriving from across the African Americas, and from other parts of Africa. He wrote about a collective "African personality" that drew from the richness of Christian, Muslim, and indigenous spiritualities and bridged diverse African ethnicities. Only the reconstruction of Pan-African unity would have the power to "move the world," he insisted.[55]

If figures such as Edward Blyden emphasized the cultural and intellectual aspects of Pan-Africanism, James Africanus Beale Horton (1835–83), born to emancipated parents in Sierra Leone, gave particular attention to the theory of building black political solidarity. He trained as a medical doctor in Edinburgh and returned to Sierra Leone to become a leading political figure. Horton believed that African polities across West Africa had to forge broad alliances to successfully contend with the European imperial presence and use it to their advantage. His *West African Countries and Peoples* (1868) called for the creation of a confederation of West African states. Indeed, the Fante Confederation (in today's Ghana) was founded in 1868. Horton hoped this confederation would work together to achieve full African self-governance. He envisioned confederated African collaborations to establish black internationalist universities, industrialization programs, banking systems, and railway infrastructures—groundwork for what we call today "the right to development." The Fante Confederation endured for a brief six years, disintegrating under the pressure of British imperial violence and the establishment of the Protectorate of the Gold Coast in 1874.

The American physician, social thinker, and novelist Martin Robison Delany (1812–85) helped expand the meaning of Pan-Africanism and black reconstruction. Born in Virginia and educated in Pittsburgh, he traveled across Louisiana and Texas in 1839, seeking to discover how a new political coherence might be forged among black people separated on plantations across Southern states.

Delany committed himself to the cause of collective emigration to Africa. He believed that the disarray and division among different African American diasporic communities could be transformed into a new solidarity through black-led emigration movements. Heavily critical of the white-run American Colonization Society with its deportation tendency, Delany did not so much envision a permanent departure of black people from their homes in the United

States as a new maritime regime of ongoing oceanic circulation of black people between their multiple homes, including the estranged ancestral homes that slave-trafficking and racial slavery had created. Delany moved to the town of Chatham, Canada West (Ontario), in 1856, a terminal stop on the Underground Railroad. In 1859, departing from his base in Canada, he traveled to New York City to lead the Niger Valley Exploring Party, which would ultimately comprise only him and a younger cotraveler, the Jamaican-born artist and writer Jacob Campbell. Delany sailed on a Liberian ship and stopped briefly in Monrovia, Liberia, before continuing to Lagos and then traveling eighty miles north to Abeokuta. There, Delany and Campbell signed a treaty with the chiefs in that town to allow a settlement of people from the African Americas. He explicitly cited the 1841 Niger Expedition as his touchstone. Now, Delany sought to reconstruct the project, but in ways that fostered Pan-African solidarity. Having finalized the treaty, Delany returned from the trip via a six-month stay in Britain. Due to the outbreak of the American Civil War, plans for the settlement did not materialize. Nevertheless, the trip provided the basis for Delany's novel *Blake*, in which he speculated with remarkable subtlety and complexity on the possibilities of his present moment as seen from the perspective of a truly free future.

Blake, published in serialized format between 1859 and 1862, on the eve of the American Civil War, is a novel about black reconstruction in motion, and the ways circuits of political interconnectedness form across Africa and the African Americas. According to Delany, Pan-Africanism need not be forged with negotiations and signed treaties. It might, instead, result from proper recognition of the relationships between seemingly disparate peoples—such as recognizing a star constellation or the circulatory patterns of ocean currents. Delany wrote that self-emancipation involved "head work," the mental work of deciphering the signs of social interconnectedness. Freedom is not a condition of pure individuality, but of getting one's bearings within a mobile historical and social system.

At the core of *Blake* are two intertwined plotlines. First, we learn of the forced separation of a black husband and wife when the wife, Maggie, is sold away from a plantation in Mississippi to a slave-owner in Cuba. The novel tells of the journey of the husband, Henry Blake, to reunite with her. The separation and reunion of family members entwines with a spiraling political narrative about "self-emancipation," and the journey to reconstruct a new "assembled" black political identity through insurrection in the Americas and travel to West Africa. *Blake* is about the Pan-African pursuit to reclaim the intimacies and alliances of a forcibly alienated people.

In the novel, Delany continually emphasizes the ways that Africans and the people of the African diaspora, despite the physical distance separating them, are always already part of a dynamic shared historical system. The same historical gyre gushes through their family lines. Therefore, according to the novel, Africa is already *in* the American South, and the American South is already *in* Cuba; Cuba is already *in* the West African coast, and the African slave-trading coast is already present in Cuba. The novel is less about the territorial locations traversed by the main character, Blake, than the signals of historical interconnection that Blake picks up in different locations and instantiations of the African Atlantic historical gyre. Delany suggests how centuries-long circulations of slave-trafficking and racial slavery have deposited histories of many distant places in black people's physical bodies and locales.[56] In the novel, Delany seems to be imploring his reader to learn how to read the signs of Pan-African interconnection. In this way, the novel dramatizes the idea that multiple locations across Africa and the African diaspora can together constitute one's identity, family, community, and political situation.

The main character, Henry Holland, renames himself Henry Blake after he joins the "runaways of the woods" and embarks on a circulating journey across the Southern states, then to Canada, then on to Cuba. In Cuba, he finds his wife, Maggie, and obtains her manumission from slavery. From Cuba, Blake then boards a slave ship, called the *Vulture*, chartered for West Africa and disguises himself as a member of the crew. After the crew takes on captives off the African coast and puts them into the "slave hole," Blake descends into the slave quarters, disguising himself now as one of the captives. He begins spreading plans for a midocean mutiny.[57] The plans for the mutiny are scuttled during a storm, and the slave ship reaches the Cuban coast. By the time the captives exit the ship, however, Blake has successfully convinced them of his revolutionary dictum: "Who would be free, themselves must strike the first blow." The enslaved thus combined with others in Cuba's multiethnic and multiracial society into an "army of emancipation," led by Blake, who turns out to have been born in Cuba. The Cuban army of emancipation, following the light from Haiti, successfully orchestrates insurrection and the destruction of all claims to slave property and secures democratic freedom for the people and protection of all laborers, for their work is the "real wealth of these places."[58]

Delany clearly lays out the purpose of his novel-length Pan-African meditation at its end. He has Blake speak these words at the outset of the insurrection: "We have been captured, torn from friends and home, sold and scattered among strangers in a strange land; yea, to and fro the earth. Sorely oppressed, mocked and ridiculed, refused and denied a common humanity, and not even permitted to serve the same God at the same time and place."[59] The remedy only comes, Delany concludes, through "assemblage," and the collective struggle for "self-emancipation." This reconstructed assemblage, this self-acknowledging transoceanic system of circulating interdependence among all black people, is what Delany calls the emigration to "Afraka"—not a place, but a state of mind. Afraka is of the future, but already has the power to transform the present, and redress the past.

Delany's writings and action, as well as that of figures such as Blyden and Horton, were among the early and influential midcentury expressions of Pan-African thought. This mode of thinking did more than help make sense of the unfolding destruction of emancipation and postslavery. It reconstructed coherence amid the chaos. Midcentury Pan-Africanists were part of a longer trajectory of black reconstruction, which included earlier expressions from the 1780s and 1790s, and later ones that emerged amid the coming era of the Global Jim Crow.

GLOBAL JIM CROW

The American Civil War concluded in 1865. By 1877, as Reconstruction ended, laws, policies, and extralegal pressures conspired to constitute the Jim Crow era—an era of tacit state approval for open-ended civic warfare against black communities in the United States across the South, North, and West. This period is best understood in a global framework, and with relation to the new phase of conquest emancipation underway in Africa, as both were part of the reconsolidation of a multinational war on black lives. Jim Crow oppression in the United States from the late 1870s onward coincided with the expansion of US imperialism across islands of the Pacific Ocean and Central America. European imperial states were pursuing large-scale violent conquests across Africa with implications that directly contributed to the outbreak of World War I. European imperialists increasingly conducted wars against African people under the headings of the civilizing mission, antislavery, and "good government," wars in which punishment would be the key practice of statecraft by the 1880s.

British imperial military heroes in Africa such as General Garnet Wolseley looked admiringly upon American Confederate war general Robert E. Lee. Wolseley, who led the British imperial war against the Asante in West Africa in 1874, and against the Mahdi in Sudan in 1884, saw the conquest of African people as essential to Britain's growing imperial grandeur. He identified with the Confederate general who also sought to create an empire based on white overlordship and black submission.[60] Henry Morton Stanley, the travel writer and political operator most associated with the European conquest of the Congo, even served in the Confederate Army for a brief time and afterward also wrote admiringly of General Lee.

Up until the 1870s, European territorial footholds in Africa were limited to slave forts and only a few permanent colonies, including the British Cape Colony and French Algeria. Over three decades, beginning in the 1870s, seven European powers divided West, South, Central, and East Africa—a continent of 11 million square miles and some three thousand different ethnic groups—into their own bulky and manufactured domains.[61] Imperialists vied to expand plantations and mines for their own economic benefit. What began with so-called conscience and clearing of souls ended with conquest and death and extraction of resources.

* * *

If the British had once proposed to free Africa from its internal slavery using merchants and missions, by the 1870s colonial planners relied heavily on guns and militaries. They justified the shift by flaunting the supposed benefits, such as good government and an end to slavery, that would come to African societies through "enlightened" European rule.[62] In 1874, as General Wolseley prepared for the British war against the Asante kingdom, he amassed a large reserve of British troops, eventually twenty-five hundred men in total, including black infantry from the West Indies, for the inland march to Kumasi, the royal city of the Asante empire. After completing the invasion in February 1874, British imperial troops plundered the king's palace, stole sacred objects from shrines, and confiscated materials, such as orbs and staffs that the Asante people saw as the embodiments of political sovereignty. Wolseley took the king's orb as his personal trophy. Soldiers auctioned off many of the objects to private collectors in London, and a significant portion was acquired by the Victoria and Albert Museum. All told, some five thousand Asante objects, embodying the people's sovereignty, were stolen and later sold for a price.

When the looting was over, British troops burned down the palace and set fire to the town. As the British troops left Kumasi and returned to the coast, King Kofi Karikari agreed to the peace terms, which included the payment of fifty thousand pounds of gold to Britain. Queen Victoria bestowed the Great Cross of St. Michael and St. George on General Wolseley and made him knight commander. The Lord Mayor of London presented Wolseley with a sword of honor. Oxford and Cambridge offered him honorary degrees. And parliament paid him a personal grant of £25,000.

Another war, against the people of Benin City, culminated in British soldiers looting bronzes and ivory masks. Forty percent of these exquisite pieces, or three thousand objects, ended up in the British Museum. The rest were sold to private collections and galleries. Today, 90 to 95 percent of Africa's cultural heritage is held outside the continent due to the war against African sovereignties in the late emancipation period. The British Museum in London holds at least 73,000 objects from sub-Saharan Africa. Belgium's Royal Museum for Central Africa holds more than 120,000 artifacts stolen from the Belgian

Congo during King Leopold II's rule.[63] More than 90,000 artifacts from Africa are in the French public collections. Germany's Humboldt Forum held, until recently, some 75,000 artifacts, including those looted after the German genocide in present-day Tanzania.[64]

In July 1874, the British established an official colony in present-day Ghana, the Gold Coast Protectorate. And in December, Governor George Strahan issued a proclamation to all African kings and chiefs now under British authority that the buying, selling, and pawning of persons was prohibited.[65] Strahan implemented the so-called Indian Emancipation. He wrote to the kings of the Gold Coast, "It is right that I should tell you distinctly that if you desire [the Queen's] protection you must do as she wishes—as she orders. . . . I will only say that, without the Queen's money and troops, you would have been Slaves of a bloodthirsty people. The Queen has paid a great price for your freedom."[66]

However, when it came to regulating the end of slave-trafficking and slave-owning, the British government introduced only "permissive freedom" for the enslaved. The number of children imported into the Gold Coast Protectorate onto Asante-owned palm plantations went up during the first years of British conquest. In 1876, Abina, an enslaved African girl in Salt Pond near Accra, ran away from her enslaver, Quamina Eddoo, a wealthy local notable. When Eddoo tried to reenslave Abina, she obtained assistance from a local lawyer to open a court case. The Indian Emancipation in the Gold Coast of 1874 made the case possible. However, during the trial, Magistrate William Melton accepted Eddoo's testimony that Abina had been purchased as one of his wives, not as one of the enslaved. Melton returned Abina to Eddoo and thereby consigned her back into slavery.[67] The example shows that British emancipation in its newly conquered African colonies both encouraged enslaved people to run away from their captors—as many thousands did from the Sokoto state (today's northern Nigeria), for example—and offered no effective protection to them if they were caught doing so. The British colonial state also made no intervention or regulation to aid those who did not or could not flee. Conquest emancipation went hand in hand with abandonment by the colonial state.

The clear connection between emancipation policies and conquest is evident in the writings and policies of Frederick Lugard, the most influential colonial administrator and colonial mercenary of British East Africa and, eventually, the governor of British Nigeria from 1912 to 1919. Lugard's *Rise of Our East African Empire* (1893) provides a theory of conquest emancipations across Africa. He argued that to abolish Arab and African slave-trafficking, "the application of the Indian Act to East Africa" was necessary.[68] This involved the abolition of the "legal status" of slavery, as British colonial administrators became the "protectors" of new colonies in Africa. At the same time, the administration had to remain hands-off in its implementation to prevent "friction" with and "dislocations" of the indigenous elites. "In a word, the non-recognition of the legal status [of slavery], unlike manumission, does not involve the overthrow of existing social institutions in the interior any more than on the coast [of Africa]. Its operation is only involved on appeal."[69] While refusing to regulate the abolition of slavery in colonial Africa, colonial administrations simultaneously pointed to slavery as their justification to extend wars of conquest across African society.

At the Berlin Conference of 1884–85, convened by German chancellor Otto von Bismarck, representatives from fourteen European and American states said they wished to collaborate in suppressing the slave trade in Africa. An antislavery report issued at the conference spoke of the "civilizing influence of the United European Powers" benefiting African societies.[70] A follow-up Anti-Slavery Conference in Brussels in 1889 declared the common interest of all European colonizers to stamp out slavery on the African continent, "for the benefits of peace and civilization." The actual purpose of the conference, however, was to divide up African territories among European imperial powers. Antislavery was little more than a cover.

Concessionary companies, such as Belgian king Leopold II's Free Congo Company and Cecil Rhodes's South Africa Company, carried out their worst abuses from 1890 to 1915. World demand for palm oil and rubber skyrocketed, and the veins of South African mines were bled of diamonds and gold. In the 1890s, during the Jim Crow backlash across the United States, as segregation policies spread across the US South and North restricting the use of public space by African Americans, expelling black people from the franchise, and subjecting them to lynching terror, European powers waged war to divide, control, and disenfranchise the peoples of Africa. Wherever the imperial militaries went with their steam, quinine, and repeating guns, they terrorized, ruled, and extracted. Global Jim Crow did not result in acquiescence, however, but resistance. The great Mahdi resistance of 1885, the Ethiopian victory over Italian forces in 1896, and the Malawi people's rising of 1915, to name just three examples, show us that where there is colonial force, there is also tireless and creative resistance to it.

PAN-AFRICANISM AND BLACK TRAVEL

During Global Jim Crow, black people across Africa and the African diaspora constructed new combinations of political affiliation and identity. In the 1890s, Bishop Henry McNeal Turner, a pastor in the American Methodist Episcopal Church in Atlanta, Georgia, pointed again to the Pan-African horizon and the work of constructing a new kind of black sovereignty. Turner traveled to Liberia four times between 1891 and 1898. In the 1890s, he insisted that true freedom was no longer possible in the United States for black people. "Yes, I would make Africa a place of refuge, because I see no other shelter from the stony blast, from the red tide of persecution, from the horrors of American prejudice."[71] Turner formed the International Migration Society in 1894. Although his movement only resulted in approximately a thousand African American migrants to Liberia, his broader influence was great. Turner inspired Callie House's program for reparations in the 1890s, the Ghanaian-born Alfred Sam's Back-to-African movement in Oklahoma in the 1900s, and Martin Mosiah Garvey's Black Star Line starting in 1919.

Pan-African movement building was not just men's work, as Callie House's example makes clear.[72] By the 1880s, many African American women participated in the construction of internationalist solidarity bonds with African peoples under the Global Jim Crow regime. The all-women's Spelman College, established in 1881 as the Atlanta Baptist Female Seminary, set out from its inception to promote black women as missionaries, educators, and social activists in West Central and East Africa. Spelman College also sponsored the study of African women in Atlanta.

Nora Antonia Gordon (1866–1901), who graduated from Spelman in 1888, traveled the following year to the American Baptist missions at Palabala and Lukunga in the Congo region.[73] Christian missions and black internationalism were heavily dominated by men and infused by paternalistic ideas about male preeminence and achievement. Figures such as Nora Gordon, and other African American women travelers to Africa, expressed a feminist countercurrent in the solidarity they fostered.

Gordon, twenty-three years old, traveled to Africa as a single black woman without the "headship" of a husband. She was displaced from social enfranchisement in two respects, by race and gender. Thus her travels into "darkest" Africa were very different from those of white men, such as Stanley and Brazza, who fantasized about Central Africa as a place of monstrosity and conquest. Her travels were also different from those of black men, who often styled themselves as stern father figures and leaders of long-lost families. Gordon joined another black woman, Louise Fleming, a graduate of Shaw University, and Gordon journeyed in the belief that she would find relationships, familiarity, and family in her African unknown.

The unknown, she suggests in her writings on her missionary work in Africa, was not a domain to be conquered, but rather one in which to create new bonds. "Such women are often unnoticed by the world in general, and do not receive the appreciation due them," she wrote, "yet we believe such may be called God's chosen agents."[74] Nora Gordon traveled the same path as the impetuous and self-aggrandizing Henry Stanley—a spinner of the darkest myths about the Congo that fed European imperial conquest. Gordon's work consisted mostly in running a school, and it included bringing the village girls to her home to cook together and to practice translation along the way. She called this "mother work."

In 1896, another African American missionary, Emma Beard Delaney (1871–1922), graduated from Spelman's Missionary Training Department. After six years of service in Florida, Delaney traveled to Nyasaland (today's Malawi) to begin work at the Providence Industrial Mission (PIM) in 1902. The PIM had a different mission from Nora Gordon's mission school, or perhaps an additional one. It taught basic education, but it also fostered labor unionism and anticolonial resistance to the British plantation and mining enterprises extending along the shores of Lake Malawi. The mission brought together Yao, Lomwe, Nguru, Mkolo, and African American people in political combination. Emma Delaney worked with John Chilembwe (1871–1915), a Malawi pastor who had studied in Virginia in 1897. She left the PIM in 1905, and ten years later, when she was running her own mission in Liberia, the news spread of the revolutionary uprising led by Chilembwe. The revolutionaries targeted the Bruce plantation estates in the foothills of Mount Chiradzulu, and the armory of the African Lakes Company in the capital of Blantyre. The British colonial authorities suppressed the uprising after two weeks and executed John Chilembwe on February 3, 1915.[75] But the revolutionary movement inspired labor union organizing among mining and plantation workers across Malawi and South Africa well into the 1920s.

The British empire, the self-proclaimed "conscience of antislavery" worldwide and a key proponent of various forms of African emancipation over the nineteenth century, killed black people on a global scale, especially those who resisted. Britain's imperialism, along with that of France, Belgium, Germany, the United States, Portugal, the Netherlands, Italy, and Spain, caused the tremendous excess death of African and African diasporic people during the late-nineteenth-century conquest emancipations beginning in the 1870s, to say nothing about the deadly emancipation processes implemented during the century preceding. In Africa alone, between the 1870s and 1950s, at least 50 million people perished as a direct consequence of the warfare and extreme oppression of European colonizers.[76] This level of destruction has been normalized in public discussion. Conquests result in genocide. The established order is happy to perpetuate the widespread silencing and ghostlining of this historical record.[77]

Countercurrents of black reconstruction developed amid currents of destruction. London, the heart of the British empire, served as a hub for international black people's assemblies, creative work, and social and political organizing in the time of Global Jim Crow. London had long been a site of liberation struggle for people such as Jonathan Strong, Ottobah Cugoano, the black Londoners who boarded the first two ships to Sierra Leone, Mary Prince, William Davidson, Robert Wedderburn, and others mentioned earlier. By late 1900, London was a world capital for African people from across the British empire's colonies. London, perhaps even more than Harlem, was the early-twentieth-century hub for the Pan-Africanist press, advocacy, and culture.[78]

In 1897, Alice Victoria Kinloch (1863–1961), a black South African woman and political activist who traveled to London in 1896, led the formation of the London African Association to promote Pan-African meetings in the city. Henry Sylvester Williams, a Trinidadian law student in London, cofounded the association with her. In July 1900, the African Association organized the first ever international Pan-African Conference. International supporters who helped conceive and organize the conference included the African American lodestar W. E. B. Du Bois, the Haitian philosopher and diplomat Benito Sylvain, and Mojola Agbebi, the influential Nigerian minister and Pan-Africanist.

The London Pan-African Conference of 1900 under Kinloch's leadership intentionally foregrounded the role of black women in forging international black solidarity. Anna Julia Cooper (1858–1964), a philosopher and organizer based in Washington, DC, and a founder of the Colored Women's League, attended. So, too, did Anna H. Jones (1855–1932), a Canadian-born educator and suffragist, and the principal of a school for black children in Kansas City, Missouri. Ella D. Barrier (1852–1945), an organizer from Washington, DC, and Fanny Barrier Williams (1855–1944), from Chicago, founder of the National Association of Colored Women, were all in attendance. Anna Julia Cooper and Anna H. Jones both delivered addresses at the conference, along with W. E. B. Du Bois.

In the context of the Global Jim Crow, this combination of black organizers and social philosophers, rather than proceeding as if to negotiate a new treaty between separate nations, sought to uncover their preexisting interdependence. They sought to understand what held them in relation to one another, and to reveal the historical and political systems that shaped their shared experience, even as they were all meeting for the first time. In this way, they met as a "nation," not in the statist sense of the term, but in the sense of a disparate people who nevertheless recognized in themselves a profound, shared historical and political relatedness and alignment. Their lives and struggles were all part of one great historical gyre, created by ancestral bonds, the winds of racial slavery, imperial conquest, and an ongoing global war on black lives. They met to ask what the mutual recognition of disparate black communities across Africa and the global diaspora could mean for social and political change in the future.

One of the outcomes of the 1900 Pan-African Conference in London was a public letter written to Queen Victoria, the eighty-one-year-old ultimate representative of the British imperial state:

> To Her Most Gracious Majesty . . . We, the undersigned representing the Pan-African Conference, lately assembled in your Majesty's City of London, comprising men and women of African blood and descent, being delegates to the conference from various of your Majesty's West and South African colonies, the West Indies, and other countries, viz., the United States, Liberia, etc., respectfully invite your august and energetic attention to the fact that the situation of the native races in South Africa is causing us and our friends alarm. The causes are described as follows:

> 1. The degrading and illegal compound system of native labour in vogue in Kimberley and Rhodesia.
> 2. The so-called indenture system, i.e. legalised bondage of native men and women and children to white colonists.
> 3. The system of compulsory labour on public works.
> 4. The "pass" or docket system used for people of colour.

5. Local byelaws tending to segregate and degrade the natives such as the curfew; the denial to the natives of the use of the footpaths; and the use of separate public conveyances.
6. Difficulties in acquiring real property.
7. Difficulties in obtaining the franchise.

Wherefore your Majesty's humble Memorialists pray your influence be used in order that these evils, to which we have respectfully called your attention, be remedied.[79]

At the end of the conference, the black Pan-African group in London stood in solidarity with the people of South Africa. The specific South African experience was fractal, in that it contained identifying glints of other, geographically distant, black social experiences that nevertheless belonged to the same global system of forced migration, oppression, and resistance.[80] The compound system forced South African mine workers to live on plantation-like enclosures. The indenture system sentenced black workers to periods of servitude, like the apprenticeship and convict-leasing regimes in the Americas. The pass system kept black South Africans under permanent surveillance, as in the postslavery Caribbean, in Brazil and Cuba, and in the American South. The apartheid policies were related to Jim Crow segregation across the United States and its empire, including in Guam, Hawaii, the Philippines, and Puerto Rico. Because the delegates worked from an understanding of their circulating interconnectedness, their choice to foreground a particular local set of political demands, and to escalate these demands to the attention of Britain's queen, carried the weight, and the truth, of an impassioned and interrelated global choir. This choir spoke back to the system of oppression, embodied in the seat of the monarch herself, with the demand that the ongoing "evils" be "remedied."

The same message, articulated in a different register, appears in W. E. B. Du Bois's closing address at the conference. He called for the decisive shift from a conquest mindset to a reparative-justice mindset, in which the world would have to "bend itself," transforming its structures, to ensure the "largest and broadest opportunity for education and self-development" for all people oppressed by racial slavery and colonialism. He said that the coming century would pose "the problem of the color line." Those words continue to move across time to our present with the momentum of oceans.

CONCLUSION

THE INSURGENT PRESENCE OF
REPARATIONS

The idea of reparations has an ancient history. The principle that wrongs give rise to remedies underpins systems of law around the world. In law, remedies might involve apologies and commitments not to repeat, restitutions of stolen things and damaged conditions, payments of compensation, and the satisfaction of the wronged parties. In European law, questions of reparations have largely been limited to property damage, and the principle that wrongs committed against property rights require a remedy. Over the centuries, this has guided compensation for property in land, in livestock, in buildings and institutions, but also property in enslaved African people. Limiting reparations to property has justified centuries of compensation to slave-owners for the loss of their "rights" to ownership over African people.

Even European legal frameworks, however, recognize that much more stands to be damaged than property rights when wrongs are committed against other human beings. The committing of wrongs within a society destroys interrelations and interrupts reciprocity, and the safeguarding of reciprocity is the purest essence of all ideas of justice. A whole domain of reparations practices across many different legal systems around the world, especially indigenous systems of law, focuses on restoring the *relationships* between persons after wrongdoing.

With mass violence, the problem is immensely complicated since the wrongs are not only committed against persons but against the concept of personhood itself. It is one thing to try to repair relationships when persons have been targeted by aggression. It's a whole other thing to undertake reparations when the personhood of a vast group of people has been denied. The work of reparations and remaking good relationships then requires nothing less than the transformation of the world.[1]

In the twentieth century, the problem of reparations for genocide emerged as a central focus of human rights legal debate after World War II. The postwar German government paid reparations to Jewish survivor communities and the newly established Israeli state of more than $89 billion over six decades. Commemorative programs including museums, memorials, and other institutions in Germany are devoted to reckoning with the Nazi past. More recently, the truth and reconciliation processes in Argentina in the 1980s, in South Africa in the 1990s, and in Rwanda in the 2000s developed new frameworks to address the haunting continuities of denial and silence in postgenocide societies in ways that engage victims, perpetrators, and bystanders in dealing with collective trauma.[2]

Reparations for slavery, however, stand out from this spectrum of post–World War II reparations and reconciliation processes in at least three ways. First, antiblack racism, as a crime against humanity, is still not recognized under international law, despite the ongoing efforts of advocates in the international arena. Second, in the case of slavery, European and American governments maintain that the problem of slavery has already been solved and ended because of the state-run emancipation processes of the nineteenth century. However, this end was just a new beginning, as the emancipations of the nineteenth century only aggravated state-sanctioned antiblack racist policies, domestically and internationally. Finally, unlike other programs for reparations, the pursuit of reparative justice for slavery is rooted in a specific lineage of liberation struggle and the centuries-long resistance of black people themselves to slavery and emancipations.[3] The struggle for reparative justice belongs to the history of slavery and emancipation itself. Reparative justice for racial slavery and its cascading future is one of the oldest ongoing political movements of our world.[4]

Ottobah Cugoano, in 1791, articulated the need not just for the end of enslavement, but for "deliverance" and "protections" of the survivors, and their "adequate reparation and restitution." Paul Cuffe, the black American sailor, in 1815 called for "the work of regeneration" to benefit the abducted and captured. Robert Wedderburn, a black British organizer, in 1817 called for immediate abolition and the redistribution of plantation lands to the victimized and assaulted, so that they could construct a new freedom independent of the perpetrators. David Walker, in 1829, writing from Boston, demanded more than slavery's extinguishment. He asked for a change of the power structure through new laws, voting rights, and for black people to be represented among the political leaders of the state. Caribbean Liberian reparationist Edward Blyden, in 1857, envisioned justice as the development of a black solidarity movement between Africa and the African Americas to uplift and vindicate African sovereignties in the international order.

Anna Julia Cooper, born into slavery in North Carolina, wrote in 1892 about reparative justice as "a general amnesty and universal reciprocity" and called for new civic relationships based in mutual respect. Callie House, in 1896, formed a large reparative justice organization demanding the redistribution of wealth and security in the form of pensions to black people born under slavery. Marcus Mosiah Garvey, the Jamaican activist and scholar, in 1913 demanded the "privileges and opportunities" of sovereignty for all black people on earth, and the immediate cessation and nonrepetition of the imperial wars of plunder.

Audley Moore, daughter of sharecroppers in Louisiana, grew up with the inspiration of Garvey's Universal Negro Improvement Association (UNIA) movement and rose to become the most visible reparationist of the twentieth century. She demanded wealth redistribution by postslavery governments to black people, to redress the plundered wealth as well as the ensuing trap of arrested socioeconomic development. Moore spent her life as an itinerant national and international traveler in pursuit of international black solidarity. In 1963, she published her demand for $500 trillion over four generations from the American government as a partial payment of what was owed.

Imari Obadele established the Republic of New Africa movement in 1968 to create a homeland of security and political friendship for black people within the United States. "[We] see the brutality of the police all against us, and the fact that jobs are denied our people, housing is denied us," he wrote. In the United States, where the vast number of imprisoned black people could itself constitute a whole nation, it is still considered a radical thought by the white mainstream to insist on the absolute nonrepetition of violence against black people in everyday life.

In 1969, James Forman, born in Chicago, and a member of the Student Nonviolent Coordinating Committee, published the Black Manifesto. He demanded new state institutions devoted to atoning for and remedying the historical harm suffered by black communities. The measures he envisioned included a land bank to stop the eviction of black families from farmlands, the establishment of new media groups and publishing enterprises to end the alternating hypervisibility and invisibility of antiblack media representation, new agencies to ensure access to education, and the protection of black workers' rights. He demanded the contribution of funds from white churches to support solidarity-based economic collaborations between African Americans and people across Africa.[5]

Senegalese diplomat Kéba M'Baye, in 1972, framed reparations as the demand for the international community to ensure African people's sovereign "right to development" and self-determination. This would require the elimination of all ongoing imperial bonds, including the legacies of indebtedness and economic extraction encumbering African nations' rights. In the United States, the reparations movement coalesced again in 1987 with the formation of the National Coalition of Blacks for Reparations in America (N'COBRA). Many members of this organization were black lawyers deeply involved in decades of Civil Rights struggle. They organized around House Resolution 40 championed by US congressman John Conyers to establish a House commission to study the impact of enslavement, and the de jure and de facto discrimination against freed slaves and their descendants from the end of the Civil War to the present. Conyers introduced the bill at every congressional session from 1989 until 2017.[6]

In 1989, Bernie Grant, a black British parliamentarian, established the African Reparations Movement in the United Kingdom. The organization demanded official apologies from all governments involved in Atlantic slave-trafficking, and an international agreement on nonrepetition and reparations. In 1993, Grant worked with the Nigerian reparations leader, Chief M. K. O. Abiola, and the Organisation of African Unity to hold a Pan-African conference in Abuja, Nigeria, on reparations. Attendees published a proclamation stating, "The damage sustained by the African peoples is not a 'thing of the past,' but is painfully manifest in the damaged lives of contemporary Africans from Harlem to Harare, in the damaged economies of the Black World from Guinea to Guyana, from Somalia to Surinam." The statement concluded with the demand that the international community "recognize that there is a unique and unprecedented moral debt owed to the African peoples which has yet to be paid."

Meanwhile, the Caribbean has continued its role as a hub of reparative justice. In June 2003, President Jean-Bertrand Aristide of Haiti demanded $21 billion in reparations from the French government, and the French state responded by working to destabilize Aristide's government. Joint French-US military forces invaded Haiti and removed Aristide from office in early 2004. Five years later, the Caribbean Community of nation-states (CARICOM) established a Reparations Commission, drawing on the scholarship and advocacy of historians and social leaders Hilary Beckles and Verene Shepherd. The Caribbean Reparations Commission, established in 2013, included a ten-point plan for reparative justice. The plan, drawing on decades of international organizing and Pan-African collaborations, including at the Abuja conference of 1993 and the Durban conference of 2001, demanded formal apologies from states whose economies are built on wealth from slavery, arrangements for reparations payments to indigenous peoples and to the worldwide diaspora of Africans, and policies that promote and sustain self-determination across the continent of Africa and the Caribbean.[7]

Since the moment emancipation processes commenced, an unbroken succession of new generations has demanded reparations for slavery. Black liberationists have protested the terms and outcomes of emancipation for the past 250 years. And the struggle will continue. As Hilary Beckles has said, "The reparations movement is going to be the great political movement of the twenty-first century. And there is nothing that can stop it because it is embedded in the search for justice, equality, and democracy."[8]

EMANCIPATION DAYS

For black communities, Emancipation Day celebrations are times of festival, when people share large-scale gatherings, jubilantly take up public space, parade in the streets, and picnic. During the nineteenth century, in the period of the recurring wave of emancipations across the shores of the Atlantic, black communities celebrated Emancipation Day on varying calendar dates. In New York City, after the end of gradual emancipation in 1827, communities convened every year on July 4 for street processions, speeches, and afternoon meals.[9] The formal abolition of slavery in the British empire, on August 1, 1838, occasioned yearly commemorations among Caribbean people and black Britons, continuing to this day. Rooted in the long-standing migration links between African communities in New England and the British Caribbean, black people across New England adopted August 1 as the date for their own Emancipation Day celebration well into the 1880s.

Black communities in Washington, DC, commemorated Emancipation Day on May 12, after Lincoln's compensated general manumission of 1862. And New Year's Day became a black holiday for decades after the Emancipation Proclamation of January 1, 1863.[10] In 1865, the enslaved people in Galveston, Texas, started the Juneteenth celebration on June 19, the date on which the enslaved received news of their freedom from Union troops. The two-year delay between the time of the Emancipation Proclamation and the announcement to the enslaved in Galveston is symbolic of emancipation's deferral of freedom for black people. Indeed, not until December 1865 was the Thirteenth Amendment, outlawing slavery in the United States, ratified.

Even then, the amendment specifically kept enslavement "legal" in the case of the incarcerated, and the coming years and decades saw a continuation of state-abetted warfare on black people's lives. The first Juneteenth celebration emerged amid slavery's long death.

Living amid this long death, black communities find significance in the celebration of Emancipation Day. The occasion provides a moment to reflect on the sheer power of black communities to create joy together. In the hold of slave ships, in the enclosures of plantations, in the midst of state-sanctioned dirty wars against black personhood, the enslaved and their descendants have survived and persisted. Black people continue creating despite the emancipationist attempts to ghostline their creativity. The Jamaican Rastafarian term *livity*, or "vibrant aliveness," refers to a capacity to create, and to hold on to being, when faced with the imperative to be nothingness.[11] Celebrating the vibrancy of black life has been and remains the theme of Emancipation Day celebrations, regardless of the date or the location.

Erna Brodber, the Jamaican novelist and sociologist, observed in her oral histories from the 1970s with elderly rural people in the island's parish of Saint Catherine, "It was what happened during slavery and the celebration of the end of slavery that was most consistently real to them," even at the remove of many generations.[12] Emancipation, what the Jamaican village people call "getting the free," was an object of historical memory. It symbolized the reclaiming of black personhood from the gulf of slavery's annihilation.

It also symbolized the need for continued watchfulness and vigilance. People remembered their ancestors' "keep[ing] vigils on the emancipation eve, the thirty-first of July, waiting for the day of their freedom." This observation of the annual Emancipation Day in Woodside, Jamaica, takes place as a night vigil, as a practice of staying awake and watchful in postslavery. As Brodber observed, "Who could follow the lead of a state which announces the end of slavery but requires the freed to give forty hours per week to the old Massa; a state which gives you freedom but takes away the necessities of life . . . a state which sees you as the enemy."[13] Those whom society makes into its ghosts return to trouble, unsettle, and haunt the systems of their oppression. But they also exert another kind of power: the power to witness and to watch.

Ralph Ellison, in 1963, when describing the historical imagination of African Americans, wrote, "The Negro American consciousness is not a product (as so often seems true of so many American groups) of a will to historical forgetfulness. It is a product of our memory, sustained and constantly reinforced by events, *by our watchful waiting, and by our hopeful suspension of final judgement as to the meaning of our grievance*" [my italics].[14] It is the nature of those held in the void by the forces of slavery and emancipation to see, as if from outside, the recurring nature of broken relationships and withheld reciprocity. The reparative historical memory of black communities arises not from an inability to move on from the past,[15] but from a "hopeful suspension of final judgement"—a vibrant belief that our civic, national, and international future will be new, and not just the repetition of postslavery remains.

Ralph Ellison's posthumous philosophical novel *Juneteenth* begins with the story of forty-four black Texans who travel to Washington, DC. They seek a "more human" relationship with the political entities that had long engineered the system of their social evisceration. The question at the center of the novel, which in a certain way is the question of reparative justice after slavery and emancipation, is framed in the language of a poet:

HOW THE HELL DO YOU GET LOVE INTO POLITICS OR COMPASSION INTO HISTORY? *And if you can't get here from there, that too is truth.*[16]

The novel's conundrum is never solved. It hangs in hopeful suspension. *Juneteenth* becomes the watchword for the ongoing ingenuous black insurgency to try to "end the old brutal dispensation" by any means necessary, including by the balm of historical recognition for shared social trauma that afflicts victims, perpetrators, and bystanders in postslavery societies.

One of the reasons to remain vigilant in "hopeful suspension of final judgement" is to create space for the possibility of a societal softening, to see if "you can't get here from there." Resonating with Martin Delany's futuristic reconstruction of *Afraka* from a century earlier, Ellison ends his novel with a scene of new departures for a transnational community of black reparative justice organizers and activists. They construct a futuristic vehicle together, "an arbitrary assemblage of chassis, wheels, engine, hood, horns, none of which had ever been part of a single car!" They take the "junk" of history to design and engineer a new machine, which "in their violation of the rigidities of mechanical tolerances and in their defiance of the laws of physics, property rights, patents—everything—they've forced part after part to mesh and made it run!" The novel leaves us wondering what would happen if the representatives of postslavery states would get in for the ride to an Afrofuturistic horizon, as opposed to seeing black reconstruction and self-determination as a source of terror. European and American governments spent so much thought and effort trying to stick black communities back into emancipationist voids because of a lurking fear—indeed, an obscure understanding—that to truly embrace black futurism would necessarily require the demise of white supremacist ends.

The centuries-long commitment to reparations on the part of generations of the enslaved and their descendants may indeed boil down, at its simplest level, to the search for love in politics and compassion in history. Put differently, it is the search to re-create sovereignties and social reciprocities that hundreds of years of bondage, emancipation, racist property rights, imperial myths, and postslavery have destroyed.

Each year in the Jamaican village of Woodside, high up in the Cockpit mountains, Erna Brodber organizes a reenactment of Emancipation Day with her community. Woodside is on the site of an eighteenth-century coffee plantation, and many people in the village trace their families back to the enslaved and emancipated on this ground. On July 31, the village stays up all night. At daybreak, community members parade to the hill where the enslaved had once erected their own small church. Those gathered perform a play and someone reads aloud the Emancipation Proclamation of 1838. In the performance, the community talks back to the proclamation. People ask, for example, "Why should God save the queen and not the people?" "How come there was no apology for our enslavement?" "How can there be freedom without access to the materials to enable and protect freedom?" Villagers speak to those who never stopped to heed the voice of the oppressed. Then comes a five-mile procession, with drumming and singing, around the perimeter of the old coffee estates. The day ends with a common meal of food brought from homes. The reenactment, the celebration, and the rituals of redress, all serve to create space around forgotten history. This "black space," as Brodber calls it, is the needed psychic and political space, even on the scale of a village, to offer safe harbor to our ghosts and to imagine how the future of the whole world can be radically different from the trajectory of the past.

History's unendings demand that we linger with the voids and not look past them. And history requires that individuals, institutions, states, and international organizations participate in reckoning with reparations for slavery. Emancipation processes saw the future after slavery through the eyes of perpetrators. Justice requires the proper readjustment of the relationship between all of us affected by the legacies of slavery to something more human—something more than human—so that we may make something shared and new together from all the plundered parts.

ACKNOWLEDGMENTS

For all the magic, thank you Lucia Volk, Portia Williams, Klaus Steinhaus, Jennifer Brown, Betty Burkes, Melony Swasey, Melissa Bartholomew, Bo Forbes, Zooey Wilkinson, Bunny Asher, and Nana Erna Brodber. For our friendship, thank you Zeenat Potia, Dan Cross, Hammad Ahmed, Josh Smith, Daniel Schönpflug, Joyce Bell, Ayesha Chaudhury, Ross Gay, Alyssa Mt. Pleasant, Laurence Ralph, Tiana Kahakauwila, Alice von Bieberstein, Zeynep Kivilcim, Barbara Hobson, Sonia Faleiro, Malik Al Nasir, and Kareem Khubchandani. For your generosity of mind, thank you Hilary Beckles, Verene Shepherd, Toyin Falola, Carina Ray, Craig Wilder, Zachariah Mampilly, Paul Haney, Patricia Lott, Jake Richards, Yesenia Barragan, Kelly Foster, Niambi Hall, Joyce Boggess, Darrell Fielder, Margaret Burnham, Tyler Winkler, Anne Gardulski, and Christina Sharpe. For the inspiration of your work, thank you Esther Sanford-Xosei, Kofi Klu, Emery Wright, Rachel Mayes, Malcolm Byrd, Mawuse Agorkor, Ned and Kit Eccles, Jean Appolon, Bayyinah Bello, Fatimah Jackson, Robin Rue Simmons, Don Rojas, Pat Barrow, Earl Bousquet, Kiara Boone, Kenneth Stewart, Kamau Sadaki, Dinizulu Gene Tinnie, and Ron Daniels. For your editorial brilliance and keen eye, and for helping me on this journey, thank you Kathryn Belden and Laura Stickney. For guiding me and rooting for me, thank you Ed Wilson and Markus Hoffman. For our love that makes this possible, thank you Saugato Datta. For giving me a beginning, a past, and a flight path, thank you Jeanile Patrice and Amma Laurenna.

NOTES

INTRODUCTION
EMANCIPATION AND THE VOID

1. Howard Johnson, *The Bahamas from Slavery to Servitude: 1783–1933* (Gainsville: University Press of Florida, 1996), 4–11; Gail Saunders, *Bahamian Society after Emancipation* (Kingston, Jamaica: Ian Randle, 2003).
2. Katherine Dunham, *Island Possessed* (Chicago: University of Chicago Press, 1969), 127, discusses her encounter with "assorted unknowns" during her participation in a Vodou initiation ceremony; Cathy Caruth, *Unclaimed Experience: Trauma, Narrative, and History* (Baltimore: Johns Hopkins University Press, 1996), 11–25.
3. W. E. B. Du Bois, *The Souls of Black Folk* (1903; repr., New York: W. W. Norton, 1999), 17.
4. Michel-Rolph Trouillot, *Silencing the Past: Power and the Production of History* (Boston: Beacon Press, 1995), 141; Fred Moten, *Stolen Life* (Durham, NC: Duke University Press, 2018), 242.
5. Nicholas Mirzoeff, *The Right to Look: A Counterhistory of Visuality* (Durham, NC: Duke University Press, 2011); Christopher Bollas, *Forces of Destiny: Psychoanalysis and Human Idiom* (New York: Routledge, 2018), 87.
6. Toni Morrison, *Playing in the Dark* (New York: Vintage, 2007), 5–7; Hilary Beckles introduces the term *reparative justice* in Hilary McD. Beckles, *Britain's Black Debt: Reparations for Caribbean Slavery and Native Genocide* (Kingston, Jamaica: University of the West Indies, 2013), 13.
7. Avery Gordon, *Ghostly Matters: Haunting and the Sociological Imagination* (London: University of Minnesota Press, 2008), 8.
8. Ralph Ellison, *Invisible Man* (New York: Vintage International, 1995), 3.
9. Ibid., 94.
10. "[Antislavery] destroyed or sharply restricted an institution, which had devastated and abbreviated the lives of tens of millions of human beings in two hemispheres": Seymour Drescher, *Abolition: A History of Slavery and Antislavery* (Cambridge: Cambridge University Press, 2009), 459. Recent historians are rewriting the history of abolitionism and antislavery with particular attention to the contributions of black peoples. See Christopher Leslie Brown, *Moral Capital: Foundations of British Abolitionism* (Chapel Hill: University of North Carolina Press, 2006).
11. See important recent work: Rinaldo Walcott, *The Long Emancipation: Moving toward Black Freedom* (Durham, NC: Duke University Press, 2021); Yesenia Barragan, *Freedom's Captives: Slavery and Gradual Emancipation on the Columbian Black Pacific* (Cambridge: Cambridge University Press, 2021); Thomas E. Smith, *Emancipation*

without Equality: Pan-African Activism and the Global Color Line (Amherst: University of Massachusetts Press, 2018). Other foundational texts include Stanley Engerman, *Slavery, Emancipation & Freedom* (Baton Rouge: Louisiana State University Press, 2007); Frederick Cooper, Thomas C. Holt, and Rebecca J. Scott, *Beyond Slavery: Explorations of Race, Labor, and Citizenship in Postemancipation Societies* (Berkeley: University of California Press, 2000); David Brion Davis, *The Problem of Slavery in the Age of Emancipation* (New York: Alfred A. Knopf, 2014); Hilary McD. Beckles, *Great House Rules: Landless Emancipation and Workers' Protest in Barbados, 1838–1938* (Oxford: James Currey, 2004); Robin Blackburn, *The American Crucible: Slavery, Emancipation and Human Rights* (London: Verso, 2011); Eric Foner, *Nothing but Freedom: Emancipation and Its Legacy* (Baton Rouge: Louisiana State University Press, 1983); Howard Temperley, *After Slavery: Emancipation and Its Discontents* (London: Frank Cass, 2000).

12. William Smith, William Wayte, and G. E. Marindin, *A Dictionary of Greek and Roman Antiquities* (London: John Murray, 1890), 276.

13. Patricia Williams, *Alchemy of Race and Rights* (Cambridge, MA: Harvard University Press, 1992).

14. Katherine McKittrick, *Demonic Grounds: Black Women and the Cartographies of Struggle* (Minneapolis: University of Minnesota Press, 2006).

15. Christina Sharpe, *In the Wake: On Blackness and Being* (Durham, NC: Duke University Press, 2016), 130–34.

16. "History that hurts" is an expression in Saidiya V. Hartman, *Scenes of Subjection: Terror, Slavery, and Self-Making in Nineteenth-Century America* (New York: Oxford University Press, 1997), 51.

CHAPTER 1
MAKING AFRICANS PAY, GRADUALLY, IN THE AMERICAN NORTH

1. Lorenzo Johnson Greene, *The Negro in Colonial New England, 1620–1776* (New York: Kennikat Press, 1942), 290–315.

2. Karwan Fatah-Black, "Urban Slavery in the Age of Abolition: Introduction," *International Review of Social History* 65 (2020): 1–14.

3. Craig Steven Wilder, *In the Company of Black Men: The African Influence on African American Culture in New York City* (New York: New York University, 2001), 14.

4. "An Act for Preventing, Suppressing, and Punishing the Conspiracy and Insurrection of Negroes and Other Slaves," 1712, New York Public Library, http://digitalcollections .nypl.org/items/510d47db-bd0f-a3d9-e040-e00a18064a99.

5. Greene, *Negro in Colonial New England*, 24.

6. Joseph Inikori, "Caribbean Slavery in the Atlantic World," in *Caribbean Slavery in the Atlantic World*, ed. Verene A. Shepherd and Hilary McD. Beckles (Princeton, NJ: Markus Wiener, 2000), 290–308.

7. Greene, *Negro in Colonial New England*, 317; Royall's endowment founded Harvard Law School, and his land became the site of Tufts University. The 2006 Brown University "Slavery and Justice Report" established that not only were the Browns a slave-trading

New England family but also that a multitude of other early benefactors of the university derived wealth from slave-owning or slave-trading, and that the university's first structures were, in part, built using the labor of enslaved people. Moses Brown, a scion of the mercantile family, became an important antislavery activist. The report is available at https://www.brown.edu/Research/Slavery_Justice/documents /SlaveryAndJustice.pdf.

8. David Gellman, *Emancipating New York: The Politics of Slavery and Freedom, 1777–1827* (Baton Rouge: Louisiana State University Press, 2006), 21–25; Shane White, "Slavery in New York State in the Early Republic," *Australasian Journal of American Studies* 14, no. 2 (1995): 1–29.

9. Bernard Bailyn, *The Ideological Origins of the American Revolution* (Cambridge, MA: Belknap Press, 1967), 55–93.

10. Herbert Aptheker, "Maroons within the Present Limits of the United States," *Journal of Negro History* 24 (1939): 167.

11. Petition by Peter Bestes, Sambo Freeman, Felix Holbrook, and Chester Joie, April 20, 1773, in Herbert Aptheker, ed., *A Documentary History of the Negro People in the United States* (New York: Citadel Press, 1951), 5.

12. "To the Honorable Counsel & House of Representatives for the State of Massachusetts Bay," January 13, 1777, ibid., 9.

13. "Negroes Protest against Taxation," ibid., 14–16.

14. The "Germantown protest of 1688" testified against the "traffick in men's-body": see Arthur Zilversmit, *The First Emancipation: The Abolition of Slavery in the North* (Chicago: University of Chicago Press, 1967), 55.

15. Christopher Schmidt-Nowara, *Slavery, Freedom, and Abolition in Latin America and the Atlantic World* (Albuquerque: University of New Mexico Press, 2011), 115; Alejandro de la Fuente, *Becoming Free, Becoming Black: Race, Freedom, and Law in Cuba, Virginia, and Louisiana* (Cambridge: Cambridge University Press, 2020), 39.

16. Elsa Goveia, *The West Indian Slave Laws of the 18th Century* (London: Caribbean Universities Press, 1970), 9.

17. Harry Yoshpe, "Record of Slave Manumissions in New York during the Colonial and Early National Periods," *Journal of Negro History* 26, no. 1 (1941): 78–107.

18. Ibid., 92.

19. Ruth Wallis Herndon and John Murray, *Children Bound to Labor: The Pauper Apprentice System in Early America* (Ithaca, NY: Cornell University Press, 2009), 19–37.

20. Harvey Amani Whitfield, *The Problem of Slavery in Early Vermont, 1777–1810* (Barre: Vermont Historical Society, 2014), 44.

21. Jared Ross Hardesty, *Black Lives, Native Lands, White Lords: A History of Slavery in New England* (Amherst, MA: Bright Leaf, 2019), 143–54.

22. Isabel Wilkerson, *Caste: The Origins of Our Discontents* (New York: Random House, 2020).

23. James Mars, *Life of James Mars, a Slave Born and Sold in Connecticut* (Philadelphia: Historic Publications, 1969), 1–36.

24. Joanne Pope Melish, *Disowning Slavery: Gradual Emancipation and "Race" in New England, 1780–1860* (Ithaca, NY: Cornell University Press, 1998); Margot Minardi, *Making Slavery History: Abolitionism and the Politics of Memory in Massachusetts* (Oxford: Oxford University Press, 2010).

25. Yoshpe, "Record of Slave Manumissions."

26. "An Act for the Gradual Abolition of Slavery," 1799, http://www.archives.nysed.gov/education/act-gradual-abolition-slavery-1799.

27. Jonathan Daniel Wells, *The Kidnapping Club: Wall Street, Slavery, and Resistance on the Eve of the Civil War* (New York: Bold Type Books, 2020), 135.

28. Anne C. Bailey, "They Sold Human Beings Here," *New York Times Magazine*, February 12, 2020, https://www.nytimes.com/interactive/2020/02/12/magazine/1619-project-slave-auction-sites.html.

29. Barragan, *Freedom's Captives*, 19, notes that José Félix Restrepo, architect of Gran Colombia's gradual emancipation law, took Pennsylvania's emancipation as his model.

30. Schmidt-Nowara, *Slavery, Freedom, and Abolition*, 152.

31. Barragan, *Freedom's Captives*, 107–59.

32. Wilder, *In the Company of Black Men*, 52.

33. Evelyn Brooks Higginbotham, *Righteous Discontent: The Women's Movement in the Black Baptist Church, 1880–1920* (Cambridge, MA: Harvard University Press, 1993), 150–84.

34. Michael Blakey, "Archaeology under the Blinding Light of Race," *Current Anthropology* 61, supp. 22 (2020): 186.

35. Henry Sipkins, *An Oration on the Abolition of the Slave Trade* (New York: Samuel Wood, 1808), 18.

36. *New York American* (newspaper), July 6, 1827.

37. William Hamilton, "In the African Zion Church," in *Early Negro Writing, 1760–1837*, ed. Dorothy Porter Wesley (Boston: Beacon Press, 1971), 96.

38. Peter Williams, "This Is Our Country," in *African American Theological Ethics: A Reader*, ed. Paris J. Peter and Julius Crump (Louisville, KY: Presbyterian Publishing Corporation, July 4, 1830).

39. *Free Negroes and Mulattoes*, January 16, 1822.

40. Leslie M. Harris, *In the Shadow of Slavery: African Americans in New York City, 1626–1863* (Chicago: University of Chicago Press, 2003), 76.

41. Ronald Bailey, "The Other Side of Slavery: Black Labor, Cotton, and Textile Industrialization in Great Britain and the United States," *Agricultural History* 68 (1994): 44.

42. Wells, *Kidnapping Club*, 38–42.

43. Shane White, *Stories of Freedom in Black New York* (Cambridge, MA: Harvard University Press, 2002), 21.

44. Wells, *Kidnapping Club*, 23.

45. William Lloyd Garrison, "Editorial," *Liberator* (Boston), February 5, 1831.

46. Melish, *Disowning Slavery*, 165.

47. Eric Lott, *Love and Theft: Blackface Minstrelsy and the American Working Class* (New York: Oxford University Press, 2013), 66–91; David R. Roediger, *The Wages of Whiteness: Race and the Making of the American Working Class* (London: Verso, 1991), 115–32.

48. Harris, *In the Shadow of Slavery*, 198.

49. David Walker, *Appeal, in Four Articles* (1829; repr., New York: Hill and Wang, 1965), 11.

50. The process is described in Hosea Easton, *A Treatise on the Intellectual Character, and Civil and Political Condition of the Colored People of the United States and the Prejudice Exercised Towards Them* (Boston: I. Knapp, 1837), 51.

51. Larry Reynolds, *Devils and Rebels: The Making of Hawthorne's Damned Politics* (Ann Arbor: University of Michigan Press, 2008), 196.

52. Yuko Miki, "In the Trial of the Ship," *Social Text* 37, no. 1 (2019): 87.

53. Ibid., 89; Dale T. Graden, *Disease, Resistance, and Lies: The Demise of the Transatlantic Slave Trade to Brazil and Cuba* (Baton Rouge: Louisiana State University Press, 2014), 189.

54. Harriet E. Wilson, *Our Nig, or, Sketches from the Life of a Free Black, in a Two-Story White House, North, Showing That Slavery's Shadows Fall Even There* (Boston: Rand and Avery, 1859).

55. Anderson, introduction to W. E. B. Du Bois, *The Philadelphia Negro: A Social Study* (1899; repr., Philadelphia: University of Pennsylvania Press, 1996), xv.

56. Du Bois, *Philadelphia Negro*.

CHAPTER 2

PUNISHING THE BLACK NATION IN HAITI

1. Michael Paiewonsky, *Conquest of Eden: 1493–1515. Other Voyages of Columbus to Guadeloupe, Puerto Rico, Hispaniola and the Virgin Islands* (Chicago: Academy Chicago, 1993).

2. Michel-Rolph Trouillot, "Motion in the System: Coffee, Color, and Slavery in Eighteenth-Century Saint-Domingue," *Review Fernand Braudel Center* 4, no. 3 (1982): 337.

3. Antonio Barros de Castro, *As mãos e os pés do senhor de engenho* (Campinas, Brazil: Departamento de Ciências Sociais, 1975), 50.

4. Jason Daniels, "Recovering the Fugitive History of Marronage in Saint Domingue, 1770–1791," *Journal of Caribbean History* 46, no. 2 (2012): 121; Robin Blackburn, *The Overthrow of Colonial Slavery, 1776–1848* (London: Verso, 1988), 213; Carolyn Fick, *The Making of Haiti: The Saint Domingue Revolution from Below* (Knoxville: University of Tennessee Press, 1990), 25.

5. Pompée-Valentin de Vastey, *The Colonial System Unveiled* (1814; repr., Oxford: Liverpool University Press, 2014), 108.

6. P. J. Laborie, *The Coffee Planter of Saint Domingo* (London: T. Cadell and W. Davies, 1798).

7. Sylvia Wynter, "Black Metamorphosis" (unpublished, 1978–8?), Schomburg Center, New York Public Library.

8. Jean Fouchard, *The Haitian Maroons: Liberty or Death* (New York: E. W. Blyden, 1981).

9. Ibid., 152; Jean Casimir, *La culture opprimée* (Delmas, Haiti: Communication Plus, 1981), 61.

10. Hérard Dumesle, *Voyage dans le nord d'Haiti* (Berlin: Les Cayes, 1824); Marlene Daut, "'Nothing in Nature Is Mute': Reading Revolutionary Romanticism in *L'Haïtiade* and Hérard Dumesle's *Voyages dans le nord D'Hayti* (1824)," *New Literary History* 49, no. 4 (2018): 501.

11. David Patrick Geggus, "The Bois Caïman Ceremony," in *Haitian Revolutionary Studies* (Bloomington: Indiana University Press, 2002), 81–92.

12. C. L. R. James, *The Black Jacobins: Toussaint L'Ouverture and the San Domingo Revolution* (New York: Vintage Books, 1963), 128–29.

13. Casimir, *La culture opprimée*, 101.

NOTES

14. Marlene Daut, "The Wrongful Death of Toussaint Louverture," *History Today* 70, no. 6 (2020), https://www.historytoday.com/archive/feature/wrongful-death-toussaint -louverture.

15. "The 1805 Constitution of Haiti: Second Constitution of Haiti (Hayti)," May 20, 1805, article 1, http://faculty.webster.edu/corbetre/haiti/history/earlyhaiti/1805-const.htm.

16. Restorationist nostalgia for bygone times followed the French and Haitian revolutions, as discussed by Peter Fritzsche, "Chateaubriand's Ruins: Loss and Memory after the French Revolution," *History and Memory* 10, no. 2 (1998): 105.

17. Mary Dewhurst Lewis, "Legacies of French Slave-Ownership, or the Long Decolonization of Saint-Domingue," *History Workshop Journal* 83, no. 1 (2017): 151–75.

18. Jean-François Brière, *Haïti et la France, 1804–1848: Le rêve brisé* (Paris: Karthala, 2008).

19. *Project d'accommodement avec Saint-Domingue*, March 25, 1820, P10360, Foreign Ministry of France Archive, Paris, 24.

20. Collective letter by colonists to the Secretary of States, March 1, 1831, Foreign Ministry of France Archive, Paris.

21. Correspondence from the Consulat Général de la Republique d'Haiti, B0066894, Finance Ministry of France Archive, Paris.

22. David Armitage, *The Declaration of Independence: A Global History* (Cambridge, MA: Harvard University Press, 2007), 107–8.

23. Jean Casimir, *The Haitians: A Decolonial History*, trans. Laurent Dubois (Chapel Hill: University of North Carolina Press, 2020), 22.

24. Bolívar would travel twice to Haiti seeking military support, and he viewed Haiti as a model for the national revolutions of Gran Colombia (present-day Venezuela, Colombia, Panama, and Ecuador): Ada Ferrer, *Freedom's Mirror: Cuba and Haiti in the Age of Revolution* (Cambridge: Cambridge University Press, 2014), 333; Julius Scott, *The Common Wind: Afro-American Currents in the Age of the Haitian Revolution* (London: Verso, 2018), 209.

25. Pierre-Victor Malouet, *Collection de mémoires sur les colonies* (Paris: Baudouin, 1802), 46. Quoted in Marlene Daut, *Baron de Vastey and the Origins of Black Atlantic Humanism* (New York: Palgrave Macmillan, 2017), xxiii.

26. Westenley Alcenat, "The Case for Haitian Reparations," *Jacobin*, January 14, 2017, https://www.jacobinmag.com/2017/01/haiti-reparations-france-slavery-colonialism -debt/.

27. Julia Gaffield, *Haitan Connections in the Atlantic World: Recognition after Revolution* (Chapel Hill: University of North Carolina Press, 2015), 93–152.

28. James Franklin, *The Present State of Hayti* (London: J. Murray, 1828), 282.

29. Thomas Carlyle, "Occasional Discourse on the Negro Question," *Fraser's Magazine for Town and Country* 40 (February 1849): 675.

30. Spencer St. John, *Hayti or the Black Republic* (New York: Schribner and Welford, 1889).

31. James Anthony Froude, *The English in the West Indies* (1888; repr., Cambridge: Cambridge University Press, 2010), 8.

32. Cristian Cantir, "'Savages in the Midst': Revolutionary Haiti in International Society," *Journal of International Relations and Development* 20, no. 1 (2017): 251; David Patrick Geggus, "Haiti and the Abolitionists: Opinion, Propaganda and International Politics in Britain and France, 1804–1838," in *Abolition and Its Aftermath: The Historical Context, 1790–1916* (London: Frank Cass, 1985), 113–40.

33. Earl Leslie Griggs and Clifford H. Prator, eds., *Henry Christophe & Thomas Clarkson: A Correspondence* (Berkeley: University of California Press, 1952); Cantir, "'Savages in the Midst,'" 253.

34. Trouillot, *Silencing the Past*, 70.

35. D. Nicholls, "Haiti: Race, Slavery and Independence," in *Slavery and Other Forms of Unfree Labor*, ed. L. J. Archer (New York: Routledge, 1988), 62.

36. Haiti 33ADP, 1826, Foreign Ministry of France Archive, Paris.

37. Brière, *Haïti et la France*, 103.

38. Michel-Rolph Trouillot, *Haiti: State Against Nation* (Boston: Beacon Press, 1990), 57.

39. David Patrick Geggus, *The Impact of the Haitian Revolution in the Atlantic World* (Columbia: University of South Carolina, 2001), 93–192; Ferrer, *Freedom's Mirror*; David Barry Gaspar and David Patrick Geggus, eds., *A Turbulent Time: The French Revolution and the Greater Caribbean* (Bloomington: Indiana University Press, 1997); Scott, *Common Wind*.

40. Ferrer, *Freedom's Mirror*, 83–145.

41. Brandon Byrd, *The Black Republic: African Americans and the Fate of Haiti* (Philadelphia: University of Pennsylvania Press, 2020), 2–4; Du Bois, *Souls of Black Folk*, 38, made these connections.

42. Johnhenry Gonzalez, *Maroon Nation: A History of Revolutionary Haiti* (New Haven, CT: Yale University Press, 2019), 95; Segun Shabaka, "An Afrocentric Analysis of the 19th Century African-American Migration to Haiti" (PhD diss., Temple University, 2001), 249, ProQuest.

43. Scott, *Common Wind*, 210.

44. "Hayti, no. V," *Freedom's Journal*, June 29, 1827.

45. Casimir, *La culture opprimée*, 110–51.

46. Gonzalez, *Maroon Nation*, 229–49.

47. Peter James Hudson, *Bankers and Empire: How Wall Street Colonized the Caribbean* (Chicago: University of Chicago Press, 2017), 98–104.

48. Mary Renda, *Taking Haiti: Military Occupation and the Culture of U.S. Imperialism, 1915–1940* (Chapel Hill: University of North Carolina Press, 2001), 183.

49. Frederick Hickling, "Owning Our Madness: Contributions of Jamaica Psychiatry to Decolonizing Global Mental Health," *Transcultural Psychiatry* 57, no. 1 (2020): 19–31.

CHAPTER 3

BRITISH ANTISLAVERY AND THE EMANCIPATION OF PROPERTY

1. P. J. Marshall, *The Cambridge Illustrated History of the British Empire* (Cambridge: Cambridge University Press, 1996); C. A. Bayly, *Imperial Meridian: The British Empire and the World, 1780–1833* (London: Longman, 1989).

2. Brown, *Moral Capital*, 105–54.

3. Davis, *Problem of Slavery*, 256, 261.

4. Eric Williams, *Capitalism and Slavery* (New York: Russell and Russell, 1944).

5. Seymour Drescher, *Econocide: British Slavery in the Era of Abolition* (Chapel Hill: University of North Carolina Press, 2010).

6. Dale Tomich, ed., *New Frontier of Slavery* (New York: State University of New York Press, 2016).

7. James Harrington, *The Commonwealth of Oceana* (1656; repr., Cambridge: Cambridge University Press, 1992), 100.

8. David Eltis, *The Rise of African Slavery in the Americas* (West Nyack, NY: Cambridge University Press, 1999), 223.

9. William Pettigrew, *Freedom's Debt: The Royal African Company and the Politics of the Atlantic Slave Trade, 1672–1752* (Chapel Hill: University of North Carolina Press, 2013).

10. Postlethwayt cited in Davis, *Problem of Slavery*, 150.

11. Julia n Hoppit, "Compulsion, Compensation, Property Rights in Britain, 1688–1833," *Past & Present* 210, no. 1 (February 2011), 96; Richard A. Posner, *Economic Analysis of Law* (Boston: Little, Brown, 1986), 29.

12. Sylvia Wynter, "Unparalleled Catastrophe for Our Species? Or, To Give Humanness a Different Future: Conversations," in *Sylvia Wynter: On Being Human as Praxis*, ed. Katherine McKittrick (Durham, NC: Duke University Press, 2015), 9–69.

13. Michael Craton, "Property and Propriety: Land Tenure and Slave Property in the Creation of a British West Indian Plantocracy, 1612–1740," in *Early Modern Conceptions of Property*, ed. John Brewer and Susan Staves (London: Routledge, 1995), 515.

14. Inikori, "Caribbean Slavery," 295.

15. "Maritime Tales—Slave Traders," accessed August 20, 2021, https://www.liverpool museums.org.uk/stories/maritime-tales-slave-traders.

16. Greenwood Great House Museum still operates today as a plantation museum in the vicinity of Montego Bay. On Elizabeth Barrett Browning, see Elizabeth Berridge, *The Barretts at Hope End* (London: J. Murray, 1974).

17. Barbara Bush, "'Sable Venus,' 'She Devil,' and 'Drudge'? British Slavery and the 'Fabulous Fiction' of Black Women's Identities, c. 1650–1838," *Women's History Review* 9, no. 4 (2000): 761–89.

18. Trevor Burnard, *Mastery, Tyranny, and Desire: Thomas Thistlewood and His Slaves in the Anglo-Jamaican World* (Chapel Hill: University of North Carolina Press, 2004), 79.

19. Ray Costello, *Black Salt: Seafarers of African Descent on British Ships* (Liverpool: Liverpool University Press, 2012).

20. Blackburn, *Overthrow of Colonial Slavery*, 96.

21. The Jamaican amelioration act was passed in 1788, and others followed in the 1790s: The Code of Laws for the Government of the Negro Slaves in the Island of Jamaica, 1789, British Archives, London; B. W. Higman, *Slave Populations of the British Caribbean, 1807–1834* (Baltimore: Johns Hopkins University Press, 1984), 109–11, 140.

22. House of Commons, April 2, 1792, *Parliamentary Debates* 29:1055–158, ProQuest UK Parliamentary Papers.

23. Gretchen Gerzina, *Black London Life before Emancipation* (New Brunswick, NJ: Rutgers University Press, 1995), 6; Cassandra Pybus, *Epic Journeys of Freedom: Runaway Slaves of the American Revolution and Their Global Quest for Liberty* (Boston: Beacon Press, 2006), 75–88.

24. Granville Sharp, *Memoirs of Granville Sharp* (1820; repr., London: Henry Colburn, 1828), 61–72.

25. See the case *Rex v. Stapylton* (February 20, 1771), discussed in James Oldham, "New Light on Mansfield and Slavery," *Journal of British Studies* 27, no. 1 (1988).

26. Trevor Burnard, *Jamaica in the Age of Revolution* (Philadelphia: University of Pennsylvania Press, 2020), 175.

27. James Walvin, *Crossings: Africa, the Americas and the Atlantic Slave Trade* (London: Reaktion Books, 2013), 79.

28. "Trans-Atlantic Slave Trade Estimates," Slave Voyages, accessed August 19, 2021, https://www.slavevoyages.org/assessment/estimates?selected_tab=timeline.

29. Granville Sharp, *A Representation of the Injustice and Dangerous Tendency of Tolerating Slavery* (London, 1769), 103.

30. Douglas Hay and Paul Craven, eds., *Masters, Servants, and Magistrates in Britain and the Empire, 1562–1955* (Chapel Hill: University of North Carolina Press, 2004), 7.

31. Granville Sharp, *"The System of Colonial Law" Compared With the Eternal Laws of God; And with the Indispensable Principles of the English Constitution* (London: R. Edwards, 1807), 16.

32. Thomas Clarkson, *An Essay on the Impolicy of the African Slave Trade* (London: J. Phillips, 1788), 100, 115.

33. Thomas Clarkson, *The History of the Rise, Progress, and Accomplishment of the Abolition of the African Slave-Trade by the British Parliament* (London: Longman, Hurst, Rees, and Orme, 1808), 1:146.

34. Verene A. Shepherd, "Past Imperfect, Future Perfect? Reparations, Rehabilitation, Reconciliation," *Journal of African American History* 13, no. 12 (2018): 23; David Barclay, *An Account of the Emancipation of the Slaves of Unity Valley Pen, in Jamaica* (Cornhill, London: J. and A. Arch, 1825), 9.

35. Quobana Ottobah Cugoano, *Thoughts and Sentiments on the Evil of Slavery* (1787; repr., New York: Penguin, 1999), 64.

36. Ibid., 112.

37. Ibid., 73.

38. Ibid., 113.

39. Ibid., 138.

40. David Patrick Geggus, "British Opinion and the Emergence of Haiti, 1791–1805," in *Slavery and British Society, 1776–1846*, ed. James Walvin (Baton Rouge: Louisiana State University Press, 1982), 126.

41. Robert Isaac Wilberforce and Samuel Wilberforce, eds., *The Life of William Wilberforce* (London: John Murray, 1838), 4:286–307.

42. Robert Myers, *Archaeological Materials from Dominica in North American and European Museums*, http://ufdcimages.uflib.ufl.edu/AA/00/06/19/61/00240/8-39.pdf.

43. The remains are held at the North Devon Museum. After more than twenty years the museum has failed to publish a definitive report on the provenance of the bones, thought to be from the wreck of the ship *London*, in 1796. See Pat Barrow, *Slaves of Rapparree: The Wreck of the* London (Devon, UK: Edward Gaskell, 1998).

44. "An Account of All Sums of Money Granted by Parliament since the 6th October 1796, and Expended before 5th April 1797; with a Statement of the Services to Which the Same Was Applied," 1797, ProQuest UK Parliamentary Papers.

45. K. J. Kesselring, "'Negroes of the Crown': The Management of Slaves Forfeited by Grenadian Rebels, 1796–1831," *Journal of the Canadian Historical Association* 22, no. 2 (2011): 1–29.

46. E. P. Thompson, *The Making of the English Working Class* (London: V. Gollancz, 1963), 213–68.

47. Hoppit, "Compulsion, Compensation, Property Rights," 93–128.

48. Jake Richards, "Anti-Slave-Trade Law, 'Liberated Africans' and the State in the South Atlantic World, c. 1839–1852," *Past & Present* 241, no. 1 (2018): 241.

49. Brown, *Moral Capital*, 259–330.

50. *King v. Wedderburn* in Robert Wedderburn, *The Horrors of Slavery, and Other Writings*, ed. Iain McCalman (1824; repr., Princeton, NJ: Markus Wiener Publishers, 2017), 125; Peter Linebaugh and Marcus Rediker, *The Many-Headed Hydra: Sailors, Slaves, Commoners, and the Hidden History of the Revolutionary Atlantic* (Boston: Beacon Press, 2000), 287–326.

51. Clare Midgley, "Dissenting Voice of Elizabeth Heyrick: An Exploration of the Links between Gender, Religious Dissent, and Anti-Slavery Radicalism," in *Women, Dissent, and Anti-Slavery in Britain and America, 1790–1865*, ed. Elizabeth Clapp and Julie Roy Jeffrey (Oxford: Oxford University Press, 2011), 100.

52. Elizabeth Heyrick, *Immediate, Not Gradual Abolition* (London: F. Westley and S. Burton, 1824), 184.

53. Ibid., 186, 192.

54. Clare Midgley, *Women Against Slavery: The British Campaigns, 1780–1870* (London: Routledge, 1992), 62.

55. Ibid., 63.

CHAPTER 4
REWARDING PERPETRATORS AND ABANDONING VICTIMS ACROSS THE CARIBBEAN

1. Michael Craton, *Testing the Chains: Resistance to Slavery in the British West Indies* (Ithaca, NY: Cornell University Press, 1982), 275.

2. Sidney Mintz, "Panglosses and Pollyannas; or, Whose Reality Are We Talking About?," in *The Meaning of Freedom: Economics, Politics, and Culture after Slavery*, ed. Frank McGlynn and Seymour Drescher (Pittsburgh: University of Pittsburgh Press, 1992), 245–56.

3. Thomas C. Holt, *The Problem of Freedom: Race, Labor, and Politics in Jamaica and Britain, 1832–1938* (Baltimore: Johns Hopkins University Press, 1992), 14.

4. "Newspaper Article," *Watchman and Jamaica Free Press*, January 4, 1832; Tom Zoellner, *Island on Fire: The Revolt That Ended Slavery in the British Empire* (Cambridge, MA: Harvard University Press, 2020), 127.

5. Quoted in Zoellner, *Island on Fire*, 177.

6. Aaron Graham, "The Colonial Sinews of Imperial Power: The Political Economy of Jamaican Taxation, 1768–1838," *Journal of Imperial and Commonwealth History* 45 (2017): 195.

7. The House of Common Select Committee on the State of the West India Colonies, and the House of Common Select Committee on the Extinction of Slavery throughout the British Dominions, 1832, Proquest UK Parliamentary Papers.

8. Quoted in Nicholas Draper, *The Price of Emancipation: Slave-Ownership, Compensation and British Society at the End of Slavery* (Cambridge: Cambridge University Press, 2010), 82; Hoppit, "Compulsion, Compensation, Property Rights," 117.

NOTES

9. Frédérique Beauvois, *Between Blood & Gold: The Debates over Compensation for Slavery in the Americas* (New York: Berghahn Books, 2017), 1–11.
10. Beckles, *Britain's Black Debt*.
11. Ibid., 131.
12. On women and children apprentices: Colleen Vasconcellos, *Slavery, Childhood, and Abolition in Jamaica, 1788–1838* (Athens: University of Georgia Press, 2015), 81–91.
13. "From Governor Sligo of Jamaica," *Jamaica Royal Gazette* (Kingston), August 1, 1834.
14. Miranda Joseph, *Debt to Society: Accounting for Life under Capitalism* (Minneapolis: University of Minnesota Press, 2014), 18.
15. James Williams, "A Narrative of Events, since the First of August 1834," ed. Diana Paton (1837; repr., Durham, NC: Duke University Press, 2001), 15–25.
16. Demetrius L. Eudell, *The Political Languages of Emancipation in the British Caribbean and the U.S. South* (Chapel Hill: University of North Carolina Press, 2002), 41–66.
17. William Green, *British Slave Emancipation: The Sugar Colonies and the Great Experiment, 1830–1865* (Oxford: Clarendon Press, 1976), 51; Holt, *Problem of Freedom*, 37.
18. Thomas Tyson, David Oldroyd, and Richard Fleischman, "Accounting, Coercion and Social Control during Apprenticeship: Converting Slave Workers to Wage Workers in the British West Indies, c. 1834–1838," *Accounting Historians Journal* 32, no. 2 (2005): 209.
19. The colonies were Bahamas, Barbados, British Guiana, Dominica, Grenada, Jamaica, Nevis, Antigua, St. Kitts, St. Lucia, Tobago, St. Vincent, Tortola, Trinidad, Bermuda, St. Christopher's, Honduras, Virgin Islands, Mauritius, Cape Coast.
20. R. E. P. Wastell, "The History of Slave Compensation, 1833 to 1845" (master's thesis, University of London, 1932), 56.
21. See, for example, "Slave Owner Compensation Records," 1833–42, T71/757 Guiana, no. 2061, National Archives of Great Britain.
22. Ibid., T71/697, no. 251.
23. Ibid., T71/701, no. 145.
24. Ibid., T71/701, no. 698.
25. Ibid., T71/712, no. 1004.
26. John Finlaison, "Slave Compensation Fund. Return to an Order of the Honourable the House of Commons, 17 August 1836," *UK Parliamentary Papers*, 4.
27. 1835 Consol Bond Index, AC2000, R index, Bank of England Archives.
28. My last of six written attempts, ranging over a year, to obtain comment from the Rothschilds' bank was dated January 28, 2021.
29. Freedom of Information Act request FOI2017/19045 submitted to HM Treasury by the author, response on November 24, 2017.
30. Alexander Sack, *Les effets des transformations des états sur leurs dettes publiques et autres obligations financièrs* (Paris; Receuil Sirey, 1927), 157; Odette Lienau, *Rethinking Sovereign Debt* (Cambridge: Harvard University Press, 2014), 58.
31. From 2017 to 2020, I filed a series of Freedom of Information Act requests with the Exchequer of the United Kingdom (HM Treasury) and the Debt Management Office of the United Kingdom to get to the bottom of the Abolition of Slavery Act Loan: FOI2017/19045, FOI2017/24209, FOI2018/01699, FOI2018/03351, FOI2019/15774, FOI2019/17743, FOI2020/0206.
32. Williams, *Capitalism and Slavery*, 136, 169.
33. Nicholas Draper, "Helping to Make Britain Great: The Commercial Legacies of Slave-

NOTES

Ownership in Britain," in *Legacies of British Slave-Ownership: Colonial Slavery and the Formation of Victorian Britain*, ed. Catherine Hall, Nicholas Draper, and Keith McClelland (Cambridge: Cambridge University Press, 2014), 78–126.

34. Draper, *Price of Emancipation*, 168.

35. Stephanie Jones, *Merchants of the Raj: British Managing Agency Houses in Calcutta Yesterday and Today* (London: Palgrave Macmillan, 1992).

36. Sally-Anne Huxtable et al., *Interim Report on the Connections between Colonialism and Properties Now in the Care of the National Trust* (Swindon, UK: National Trust, 2020).

37. Lowell Ragatz, *The Decline of the British West Indies, 1763–1833: A Study in the Fall of the Planter Class* (New York: Century, 1928), 10, 243, 361; Draper, *Price of Emancipation*, 232–69.

38. A number of historical banks received compensation funds and were later incorporated by present-day banking firms: Bosanquet, Anderson & Co is part of Lloyds Bank. Barclays, Bevan & Tritton, and Cocks, Biddulph & Co., are part of Barclays. Hankeys & Co., Martin's Bank, Coutts & Co., Robarts, Curtis & Co., and Smith, Payne & Smiths are part of the Royal Bank of Scotland.

39. Jean Besson, *Transformations of Freedom in the Land of the Maroons: Creolization in the Cockpits, Jamaica* (Kingston, Jamaica: Ian Randle, 2015), 189. See, for example, the relationship between Annette, a white woman presiding over a dying plantation and her black domestic servant Christophine in Jean Rhys, *Wide Sargasso Sea* (New York: Norton, 1966). On the historical accuracy of this kind of depiction, see Jean Besson, "Freedom and Community," in *Meaning of Freedom*, ed. McGlynn and Drescher, 191–210.

40. Douglas Hall, *Free Jamaica, 1838–1865: An Economic History* (New Haven, CT: Yale University Press), 163.

41. Holt, *Problem of Freedom*, 185.

42. Carl Campbell, "Early Post-Emancipation Jamaica: The Historiography of Plantation Culture, 1834–1865," in *Jamaica in Slavery and Freedom*, ed. Kathleen Monteith and Glen Richards (Mona, Jamaica: University of the West Indies Press), 57.

43. Besson, *Transformations of Freedom*, 192.

44. Alan Adamson, *Sugar without Slaves* (New Haven, CT: Yale University Press, 1972), 61.

45. Natasha Lightfoot, *Troubling Freedom: Antigua and the Aftermath of British Emancipation* (Durham, NC: Duke University Press, 2015), 124.

46. Ibid., 128.

47. Hilary McD. Beckles, *Black Rebellion in Barbados: The Struggle against Slavery, 1627–1838* (Bridgetown, Barbados: Carib Reseaerch and Publications, 1987), 50.

48. Johnson, *Bahamas from Slavery to Servitude*, 84; Samuel Prescod, "Letter," *British Emancipator* (London), July 8, 1838; Beckles, *Britain's Black Debt*, 87.

49. Holt, *Problem of Freedom*, 190.

50. Martha W. Beckwith, *Black Roadways: A Study of Jamaican Folk Life* (Chapel Hill: University of North Carolina Press, 1929), 97.

51. Erna Brodber, foreword in *Obeah and Other Powers: The Politics of Caribbean Religion and Healing*, ed. Diana Paton and Maarti Forde (Durham, NC: Duke University Press, 2012), xi.

52. Martha Beckwith, an American anthropologist who traveled through Jamaica in the 1920s, took notes on the healing practices of Mammy Forbes in western Jamaica: Beckwith, *Black Roadways*, 104–82.

53. Erna Brodber, *The Second Generation of Freemen in Jamaica, 1907–1944* (Gainesville: University Press of Florida, 2004), 14.

54. Wedderburn, "Horrors of Slavery," 43.

55. Stefano Harney and Fred Moten, *The Undercommons: Fugitive Planning & Black Study* (New York: Minor Compositions, 2013), 50.

56. Marcus Garvey, "The British West Indies in the Mirror of Civilization," *African Times and Orient Review* (London), October 1913, reproduced in Robert A. Hill ed., *The Marcus Garvey and Universal Negro Improvement Association Papers*, vol. 1 (Berkeley: UC Press, 1983), 27.

57. Marcus Garvey, "Meeting, New Orleans," *Negro World* (Harlem, NY), July 14, 1921.

CHAPTER 5

FROM CIVIL WAR TO THE DIRTY WAR AGAINST BLACK LIVES

1. Alexander Hamilton, James Madison, and John Jay, *The Federalist Papers* (1788; repr., Harmondsworth, UK: Penguin, 1987), no. 9.

2. Ibid., no. 10.

3. Ibid., no. 17.

4. Thomas Jefferson, ed., *Notes on the State of Virginia* (London: John Stockdale, 1785), 214.

5. Walter Johnson, *River of Dark Dreams: Slavery and Empire in the Cotton Kingdom* (Cambridge, MA: Belknap Press of Harvard University Press, 2013).

6. Adam Rothman, *Slave Country: American Expansion and the Origins of the Deep South* (Cambridge, MA: Harvard University Press, 2005), 221.

7. Eltis, *Rise of African Slavery*, 13; Joseph E. Inikori, "The Slave Trade and the Atlantic Economies, 1451–1870," reprinted in: Verene A. Shepherd and Hilary McD. Beckles eds., *Caribbean Slavery in the Atlantic World* (Kingston: Ian Randle Publishers, 2000), 192.

8. Johnson, *River of Dark Dreams*, 176.

9. Michael Gomez, *Exchanging Our Country Marks: The Transformation of African Identities in the Colonial and Antebellum South* (Chapel Hill: University of North Carolina Press, 1998), 1–4.

10. Jefferson, *Notes on the State of Virginia*, 147.

11. Fred Moten, "Resistance of the Object: Aunt Hester's Scream," in *In the Break: The Aesthetics of the Black Radical Tradition* (Minneapolis: University of Minnesota Press, 2003), 1–24, discusses the long tradition of interpreting this passage in Douglass's autobiography, especially in terms of black motherhood and childhood in a social world seeking to "pulverize" the generational wealth of black people.

12. Frederick Douglass, *Narrative of the Life of Frederick Douglass* (1845; repr., New York: Penguin, 2014), 50.

13. Hamilton, Madison, and Jay, *Federalist Papers*.

14. Michael Blakey, "On the Biodeterministic Imagination," *Archaeological Dialogues* 27, no. 1 (2020): 1–16.

15. Roediger, *Wages of Whiteness*, 3–19.

16. Gomez, *Exchanging Our Country Marks*, 3; Sterling Stuckey, *Slave Culture: Nationalist Theory and the Foundations of Black America* (New York: Oxford University Press,

NOTES

1987), 29, 30. On the rise of the blues out of the tradition of black spirituals and jeremiads, see Amiri Baraka, *Blues People: Negro Music in White America* (1963; repr., New York: Harper, 2002), 60–80; Clyde Woods, *Development Arrested: The Blues and Plantation Power in the Mississippi Delta* (London: Verso, 1998), 25–39.

17. Stuart Hall, "'Encoding/Decoding,'" in *Culture, Media, Language: Working Papers in Cultural Studies, 1972–79*, ed. Centre for Cultural Studies (1973; repr., London: Hutchinson, 1980), 128–38.

18. I draw inspiration for this paragraph from Chandra Manning, *Troubled Refuge: Struggling for Freedom in the Civil War* (New York: Penguin, 2016), 2–4.

19. Estimates for current-day equivalents of historical payouts are notoriously imprecise. In most cases, I calculate the payout as a percentage of the country's gross national income (GNI) at the time, and then determine its equivalent based on present-day GNI. On the patronato system, see Rebecca Scott, "Gradual Abolition and the Dynamics of Slave Emancipation in Cuba, 1868–86," *Hispanic American Historical Review* 63:3, 1993, 447–77. On the planned compensation to Cuban slave-owners see Yesenia Barragan, *Freedom's Captives: Slavery and Gradual Emancipations on the Colombian Black Pacific* (Cambridge: Cambridge University Press, 2021), 251. On the compensation amount in the case of Puerto Rico, see Frédérique Beauvois, *Between Blood and Gold*, translated by Andrene Everson (New York: Berghahn, 2017), 5.

20. Dale Tomich, *Slavery in the Circuit of Sugar: Martinique and the World Economy, 1830–1848* (Baltimore: Johns Hopkins University Press, 1990).

21. W. E. B. Du Bois, *Black Reconstruction in America* (1935; repr., New York: Free Press, 1998), 83.

22. Frederick Douglass, "What the Black Man Wants" (1865), in Frederick Douglass, *The Frederick Douglass Papers: 1864–80* (New Haven, CT: Yale University Press, 1985), 4:59.

23. Abraham Lincoln, "Address on Colonization to a Deputation of Negroes," August 14, 1862, in *The Collected Works of Abraham Lincoln*, ed. Roy Basler (New York: Wolff Book Manufacturing, 1955), 5:371–73; Eric Foner, *The Fiery Trial: Abraham Lincoln and American Slavery* (New York: W. W. Norton, 2010), 224.

24. Foner, *Fiery Trial*, 42, 57.

25. Oliver Otis Howard, *Autobiography* (New York: Baker and Taylor, 1908), 165.

26. John Eaton, *Grant, Lincoln, and the Freedmen: Reminiscences of the Civil War* (New York: Longmans, Green, 1907), 2.

27. Cam Walker, *Corinth: The Story of a Contraband Camp* (Kent, OH: Kent State University Press, 1974), 18; Manning, *Troubled Refuge*, 163.

28. Hartman, *Scenes of Subjection*, 125–40.

29. Frederick Douglass, "Declaration of Wrongs and Rights, National Convention of Colored Men, Syracuse, New York" (1864), in *Frederick Douglass Papers*.

30. Howard, *Autobiography*, 2:234.

31. Ibid., 2:244.

32. Woods, *Development Arrested*, 64.

33. Philip Foner, *The Life and Writings of Frederick Douglass*, 4 vols. (New York: International Publishers, 1955), 4:184.

34. John T. Trowbridge, *The Desolate South, 1865–66: A Picture of the Battlefields and of the Devastated Confederacy* (New York: Duell, Sloan and Pearce, 1956), 159.

35. Carl Schurz, *Report on the Condition of the Defeated South* (1865), 39th Congress, Senate. Ex. Doc. 1st Session. No. 2, 18.

36. Tera Hunter, *To 'Joy My Freedom: Southern Black Women's Lives and Labors after the Civil War* (Cambridge, MA: Harvard University Press, 1997).

37. David Oshinsky, *"Worse than Slavery": Parchman Farm and the Ordeal of Jim Crow Justice* (New York: Free Press, 1996), 12.

38. Foner, *Nothing but Freedom*, 49.

39. Ibid., 203.

40. "Reconstruction in America: Racial Violence after the Civil War, 1865–1876," accessed August 20, 2021, https://eji.org/report/reconstruction-in-america/.

41. Mary Frances Berry, *My Face Is Black Is True: Callie House and the Struggle for Ex-Slave Reparations* (New York: Alfred A. Knopf, 2005).

42. Anna Julia Cooper, *A Voice from the South* (Xenia, OH: Aldine Printing House, 1892), 20.

CHAPTER 6

GLOBAL JIM CROW AND EMANCIPATION IN AFRICA

1. Thanks to my gracious colleague at Tufts University Anne Gardulski, sedimentologist, for explaining these patterns to me.

2. Stephanie Smallwood, *Saltwater Slavery: A Middle Passage from Africa to American Diaspora* (Cambridge, MA: Harvard University Press, 2007), 45.

3. Walter Rodney, "African Slavery and Other Forms of Social Oppression on the Upper Guinea Coast in the Context of the Atlantic Slave-Trade," *Journal of African History* 7, no. 3 (1966): 434.

4. Paul Lovejoy, *Transformations in Slavery: A History of Slavery in Africa* (Cambridge: Cambridge University Press, 1983), 1–23; Patrick Manning, *Slavery and African Life: Occidental, Oriental, and African Slave Trades* (Cambridge: Cambridge University Press, 1990).

5. Claude Meillassoux, *The Anthropology of Slavery: The Womb of Iron and Gold*, trans. Alide Dasnois (Chicago: University of Chicago Press, 1991).

6. Stanley Engerman and Stanley Fogel, *Time on the Cross: The Economics of American Negro Slavery* (Boston: Little, Brown, 1974), 13.

7. G. Ugo Nwokeji, *The Slave Trade and Culture in the Bight of Biafra* (Cambridge: Cambridge University Press, 2010), 117.

8. Manning, *Slavery and African Life*, 18, 19.

9. Madhavi Kale, *Fragments of Empire: Capital, Slavery, and Indian Indentured Labor Migration in the British Caribbean* (Philadelphia: University of Pennsylvania Press, 1998).

10. Dale Tomich, *Through the Prism of Slavery: Labor, Capital, and World Economy* (Lanham, MD: Rowman and Littlefield, 2003).

11. Philip Curtin, *The Rise and Fall of the Plantation Complex* (Cambridge: Cambridge University Press, 1998); Adam McKeown, *Melancholy Order: Asian Migration and the Globalization of Borders* (New York: Columbia University Press, 2008). On blackbirding, see Gerald Horne, *The White Pacific: U.S. Imperialism and Black Slavery in the South Seas after the Civil War* (Honolulu: University of Hawai'i Press, 2007), 33.

12. Pybus, *Epic Journeys of Freedom*, 98–102.

13. Alexander Byrd, *Captives and Voyagers: Black Migrants across the Eighteenth-Century British Atlantic World* (Baton Rouge: Louisiana State University Press, 2008), 125.

14. Granville Sharp, *A Short Sketch of Temporary Regulations (Until Better Shall Be Proposed) for the Intended Settlement on the Grain Coast of Africa, near Sierra Leone* (London: H. Baldwin, 1788), chap. 3, xx.

15. Byrd, *Captives and Voyagers*, 407.

16. Henry Smeathman, *Plan of Settlement to Be Made Near Sierra Leona, on the Grain Coast of Africa* (London: T. Stockdale, 1786).

17. Richard Anderson, *Abolition in Sierra Leone: Re-building Lives and Identities in Nineteenth-Century West Africa* (Cambridge: Cambridge University Press, 2020), 17; Byrd, *Captives and Voyagers*, 126.

18. Olaudah Equiano, *The Interesting Narrative and Other Writings*, rev. ed. (New York: Penguin Books, 2003), chap. 9.

19. The island of Fernando Po is a third example, but different from Sierra Leone and Liberia in that it was not an official emancipation colony.

20. Anderson, *Abolition in Sierra Leone*, 23–28.

21. V. Chapman-Smith, "Philadelphia and the Slave Trade: The *Ganges* Africans," *Pennsylvania Legacies* 5, no. 2 (2005); Daniel Domingues da Silva et al., "The Diaspora of Africans Liberated from Slave Ships in the Nineteenth Century," *Journal of African History* 55, no. 3 (2014): 348.

22. Domingues da Silva et al., "Diaspora of Africans Liberated," 347–89.

23. Once the naval squadron system was set up, these bounty payments ended.

24. Richards, "Anti-Slave-Trade Law," 241.

25. Karen Virginia Fischer Younger, "'African Stretches Forth Her Hands unto You': Female Colonization Supporters in the Antebellum United States" (PhD diss., Pennsylvania State University, 2006); Karen Fischer Younger, "Liberia and the Last Slave Ships," *Civil War History* 54, no. 4 (2008): 424–44.

26. Paul Cuffe, "An Epistle of the Society of Sierra Leone in Africa," in *Captain Paul Cuffe's Logs and Letters, 1808–1817: A Black Quaker's "Voice from within the Veil"* (Washington, DC: Howard University Press, 1996), 117.

27. James St. G. Walker, *The Black Loyalists: The Search for a Promised Land in Nova Scotia and Sierra Leone, 1783–1870* (Toronto: Toronto University Press, 1992), 278.

28. Domingues da Silva et al., "Diaspora of Africans Liberated," 347–69.

29. Inés Roldán de Montaud, "On the Blurred Boundaries of Freedom: Liberated Africans in Cuba, 1817–1870," in *New Frontiers of Slavery*, ed. Dale Tomich (New York: State University of New York Press, 2016), 136.

30. Jan Hogendorn and Paul Lovejoy, "Keeping Slaves in Place: The Secret Debate on the Slavery Question in Northern Nigeria, 1900–1904," in *The Atlantic Slave Trade: Effects on Economies, Societies, and Peoples in Africa, the Americas, and Europe*, ed. Joseph E. Inikori and Stanley L. Engerman (Durham, NC: Duke University Press, 1992), 5.

31. Richards, "Anti-Slave-Trade Law," 201–2. da Silva et al., "Diaspora of Africans Liberated," 357.

32. Padraic X. Scanlan, *Freedom's Debtors: British Anti-Slavery in Sierra Leone in the Age of Revolution* (New Haven, CT: Yale University Press, 2017); Anderson, *Abolition in Sierra Leone*; Gibril Raschid Cole, *The Krio of West Africa: Islam, Culture, Creolization, and Colonialism in the Nineteenth Century* (Athens: Ohio University Press, 2013).

33. Cole, *Krio of West Africa*; Jonathan Abreu, "Fugitive Slave Communities in Northern

Brazil between 1880 and 1900: Territoriality, Resistance, and the Struggle for Autonomy," *Journal of Latin American Geography* 17, no. 1 (2018): 195–221.

34. Willem Bosman, *A New and Accurate Description of the Coast of Guinea: Divided into the Gold, the Slave, and the Ivory Coasts* (London: James Knapton, 1705); Jennifer Morgan, "'Some Could Suckle over Their Shoulder': Male Travelers, Female Bodies, and the Gendering of Radical Ideology, 1500–1770," *William and Mary Quarterly* 54, no. 1 (1997): 170; Jennifer Morgan, *Laboring Women: Reproduction and Gender in New World Slavery* (Philadelphia: University of Pennsylvania Press, 2004), 27.

35. Thomas Fowell Buxton, *The African Slave-Trade* (London: J. Murray, 1840), 229.

36. Thomas Fowell Buxton, *The Remedy: Being a Sequel to the African Slave Trade* (London: J. Murray, 1840), xv.

37. Firoze Manji and Carl O'Coill, "The Missionary Position: NGOs and Development in Africa," *International Affairs* 78, no. 3 (2002): 586–83.

38. K. Onwuka Dike, *Trade and Politics in the Niger Delta, 1830–1885* (Oxford: Oxford University Press, 1956), 203.

39. C. C. Ifemesia, "The 'Civilizing' Mission of 1841," *Journal of the Historical Society of Nigeria* 2 (1962): 291.

40. East India Company Act no. V of 1843: Indrani Chatterjee, "Abolition by Denial: The South Asian Example," in *Abolition and Its Aftermath in Indian Ocean Africa and Asia,* ed. Gwyn Campbell (London: Routledge, 2005), 150–68.

41. Frederick Lugard, *The Rise of Our East African Empire: Early Efforts in Nyasaland and Uganda* (Edinburgh: William Blackwood and Sons, 1893), 179; Edmund Sturge, *West India "Compensation" to the Owners of Slaves* (Gloucester, UK: J. Bellows, 1893).

42. William Adam, *The Law and Custom of Slavery in British India: In a Series of Letters to Thomas Fowell Buxton, Esq.* (Boston: Weeks, Jordan, 1840).

43. Zach Sell, *Trouble the World: Slavery and Empire in the Age of Capital* (Chapel Hill: University of North Carolina Press, 2021).

44. For example, Garnet Wolesley, who led the British offensive in West Africa, had first served as an imperial army officer in Burma. Frederick Lugard, leader in the British conquest of East and West Africa, was born in India to missionary parents and first served as an officer of the British Indian army.

45. Richard Allen, *Europe Slave Trading in the Indian Ocean, 1500–1850* (Athens: Ohio University Press, 2014), 168–70; Frederick Cooper, *Plantation Slavery on the East Coast of Africa* (New Haven, CT: Yale University Press, 1977), 116–19.

46. I. Schapera, ed., *Livingstone's Private Journal, 1851–1853* (London: Chatto and Windus, 1960), 228.

47. David Livingstone, *Missionary Travels and Researches in South Africa* (London: J. Murray, 1899).

48. The missionary Joseph Booth wrote the book *Africa for the African* (1897) and collaborated with African revolutionary John Chilembwe. Some missionaries used their positions to anticolonial ends: George Shepperson, *Independent African: John Chilembwe and the Origins, Setting and Significance of the Nyasaland Native Rising of 1915* (Edinburgh: Edinburgh University Press, 1969).

49. David Chidester, *Empire and Religion: Imperialism and Comparative Religion* (Chicago: University of Chicago Press, 2014), 206.

50. William Pietz, "The Problem of the Fetish, II: The Origin of the Fetish," *RES* 13, no. 13 (1987): 99.

51. Henry Stanley, *Stanley's Despatches to the* New York Herald (Boston: Boston University Press, 1970), 5.

52. Joseph Conrad, *Heart of Darkness* (1899; repr., New York: Heritage Press, 1969), 47.

53. Nell Irvin Painter, *Exodusters: Black Migration to Kansas after Reconstruction* (New York: Knopf, 1976), 108.

54. Edward Wilmot Blyden, *A Vindication of the African Race: Being a Brief Examination of the Arguments in Favor of African Inferiority* (Monrovia, Liberia: G. Killian, 1857), 22.

55. Teshale Tibebu, *Edward Wilmot Blyden and the Racial Nationalist Imagination* (Rochester, NY: University of Rochester Press, 2012). Blyden first used the term *African personality* in an article in the *Sierra Leone Times*, May 27, 1893.

56. Martin Delany, *Blake, or, The Huts of America* (London: Harvard University Press, 2017), 132.

57. Maggie Montesinos Sale, *The Slumbering Volcano: American Slave Ship Revolts and the Production of Rebellious Masculinity* (Durham, NC: Duke University Press, 1997).

58. Delany, *Blake*, 288.

59. Ibid., 284.

60. Garnet Wolseley, *The America Civil War: An English View* (Charlottesville: University of Virginia, 1964).

61. The seven powers that divided up African polities in the 1880s are: Great Britain, France, Germany, Portugal, Belgium, Italy, and Spain.

62. These claims are best encapsulated in Lugard, *Rise of Our East African Empire*.

63. Suzanne Preston Blier, *African Vodun: Art, Psychology, and Power* (Chicago: University of Chivago Press, 1995).

64. Felwine Sarr and Bénédicte Savoy, *The Restitution of African Cultural Heritage: Toward a New Relational Ethics*, trans. Drew Burk (Paris: Ministry of Culture of France, 2018), http://restitutionreport2018.com/sarr_savoy_en.pdf.

65. Strahan's proclamation: PRO Co 96/115, G.C. no. 1310, National Archives of the United Kingdom.

66. Strahan's report appears in *Accounts and Papers of the House of Commons* 52 (1875): 29.

67. Trevor R. Getz and Clarke Liz, *Abina and the Important Men: A Graphic History* (New York: Oxford University Press, 2016), 32.

68. Lugard, *Rise of Our East African Empire*, 182.

69. Ibid., 184.

70. The conference was held between November 15, 1884, and February 26, 1885, to discuss problems connected with West Africa. Every major power in Europe (except Switzerland) and the United States attended. The five main powers among the fourteen in attendance were France, Germany, Great Britain, Portugal, and the International Association of the Congo (Belgium). The British, Germans, French, Americans, and Belgians envisioned Africa as a geopolitical terrain upon which to compete for imperial prowess.

71. Edwin Redkey, *Black Exodus: Black Nationalist and Back-to-Africa Movements, 1890–1910* (New Haven, CT: Yale University Press, 1969), 33.

72. Return to chapter 5 for more discussion of Callie House.

73. Brandi Suzanne Hughes, "Middle Passages: The Redemption of African America through the African Mission Field, 1862–1905" (PhD diss., Yale University, 2009).

74. "Annual Report of the Principals of Spelman Seminar," *Spelman Messenger*, May 1896.

75. Shepperson, *Independent African*.

76. Rudolph J. Rummel, *Statistics of Democide: Genocide and Mass Murder since 1900*

(Münster, Germany: Rutgers University Press, 1998). See Rummel's updated estimates at https://www.hawaii.edu/powerkills/COMM.7.1.03.HTM.

77. Dirk Moses, *The Problems of Genocide: Permanent Security and the Language of Transgression* (Cambridge: Cambridge University Press, 2021); Dominik Schaller, "Genocide and Mass Violence in the 'Heart of Darkness': Africa in the Colonial Period," in *Genocide Studies and Prevention: An International Journal*, ed. Dirk Moses and Donald Bloxham (Oxford: Oxford University Press, 2012).

78. Peter Fryer, *Staying Power: The History of Black People in Britain* (London: Pluto Press, 1984); Paul Gilroy, *The Black Atlantic: Modernity and Double Consciousness* (Cambridge, MA: Harvard University Press, 1993).

79. J. R. Hooker, "The Pan-African Conference 1900," *Transition* 46 (1974): 20–24.

80. Erna Brodber, *Nothing's Mat* (Mona, Jamaica: University of West Indies Press, 2014), explores the fractals of African experience after slavery.

CONCLUSION
THE INSURGENT PRESENCE OF REPARATIONS

1. Robin D. G. Kelley, "'A Day of Reckoning': Dreams of Reparations," in *Freedom Dreams: The Black Radical Imagination* (Boston: Beacon Press, 2002), 110–34.

2. Elazar Barkan, *The Guilt of Nations: Restitution and Negotiating Historical Injustices* (New York: W. W. Norton, 2000).

3. Beckles, *Britain's Black Debt*, uses the term *reparative justice* to refer to this long-standing tradition.

4. Beckles, speech on May 21, 2021, at the Reparations under International Law Conference, https://www.youtube.com/watch?v=7fYe6WQg2x8.

5. James Forman, "The Black Manifesto," *Accounting Historians Journal* 1, no. 1 (1969), https://episcopalarchives.org/church-awakens/exhibits/show/specialgc/item/202.

6. Adjoa Aiyetoro, "N'COBRA and the Reparations Movement," *Guild Practitioner* 40 (2003): 40–45.

7. "Declaration of the Conference against Racism, Racial Discrimination, Xenophobia and Related Intolerance," 2001, https://www.un.org/WCAR/durban.pdf.

8. Speech to the House of Lords, UK, 2015, https://caricom.org/address-delivered-by -professor-sir-hilary-beckles-chairman-of-the-caricom-reparations-commission-house -of-commons-parliament-of-great-britain-committee-room-14-thursday-july-16-20.

9. Ethan Kytle and Blain Roberts, *Denmark Vesey's Garden: Slavery and Memory in the Cradle of the Confederacy* (New York: New Press, 2019).

10. David Blight, *Race and Reunion: The Civil War in American Memory* (Cambridge: Cambridge University Press, 2011), 300.

11. John Homiak, "Dub History: Soundings on Rastafari Livity and Language," in *Rastafari and Other African-Caribbean Worldviews*, ed. Barry Chevannes (New Brunswick, NJ: Rutgers University Press), 127.

12. Erna Brodber, "On Blackspace," transcript of a lecture on November 11, 2019, at Tufts University.

13. Ibid.

14. Ralph Ellison, "The World and the Jug," in *Shadow and Act* (New York: Random House, 1964), 124.
15. John Torpey, *Making Whole What Has Been Smashed: On Reparations Politics* (New Brunswick, NJ: Rutgers University Press, 2017).
16. Ralph Ellison, *Juneteenth: A Novel* (New York: Vintage, 2000), 264.

SELECTED BIBLIOGRAPHY

For researching readers, this list brings together the most essential primary and secondary sources from among this book's references.

"An Act for the Gradual Abolition of Slavery." 1799. http://www.archives.nysed.gov/edu cation/act-gradual-abolition-slavery-1799.

Adamson, Alan. *Sugar without Slaves.* New Haven, CT: Yale University Press, 1972.

Aiyetoro, Adjoa. "N'COBRA and the Reparations Movement." *Guild Practitioner* 40 (2003): 40–45.

Allen, Richard. *Europe Slave Trading in the Indian Ocean, 1500–1850.* Athens: Ohio University Press, 2014.

Anderson, Richard. *Abolition in Sierra Leone: Re-building Lives and Identities in Nineteenth-Century West Africa.* Cambridge: Cambridge University Press, 2020.

Aptheker, Herbert, ed. *A Documentary History of the Negro People in the United States.* New York: Citadel Press, 1951.

———. "Maroons within the Present Limits of the United States." *Journal of Negro History* 24 (1939): 167–84.

Baraka, Amiri. *Blues People: Negro Music in White America.* 1963. Reprint, New York: Harper, 2002.

Barkan, Elazar. *The Guilt of Nations: Restitution and Negotiating Historical Injustices.* New York: W. W. Norton, 2000.

Barragan, Yesenia. *Freedom's Captives: Slavery and Gradual Emancipation on the Columbian Black Pacific.* Cambridge: Cambridge University Press, 2021.

Bayly, C. A. *Imperial Meridian: The British Empire and the World, 1780–1833.* London: Longman, 1989.

Beauvois, Frédérique. *Between Blood & Gold: The Debates over Compensation for Slavery in the Americas.* New York: Berghahn Books, 2017.

Beckles, Hilary McD. *Britain's Black Debt: Reparations for Caribbean Slavery and Native Genocide.* Kingston, Jamaica: University of the West Indies, 2013.

Beckwith, Martha W. *Black Roadways: A Study of Jamaican Folk Life.* Chapel Hill: University of North Carolina Press, 1929.

Berry, Mary Frances. *My Face Is Black Is True: Callie House and the Struggle for Ex-slave Reparations.* New York: Alfred A. Knopf, 2005.

SELECTED BIBLIOGRAPHY

Besson, Jean. *Transformations of Freedom in the Land of the Maroons: Creolization in the Cockpits, Jamaica.* Kingston, Jamaica: Ian Randle, 2015.

Blackburn, Robin. *The Overthrow of Colonial Slavery, 1776–1848.* London: Verso, 1988.

Blakey, Michael. "Archaeology under the Blinding Light of Race." *Current Anthropology* 61, supp. 22 (2020).

Blight, David. *Race and Reunion: The Civil War in American Memory.* Cambridge: Cambridge University Press, 2011.

Brodber, Erna. *The Second Generation of Freemen in Jamaica, 1907–1944.* Gainesville: University Press of Florida, 2004.

Brown, Christopher Leslie. *Moral Capital: Foundations of British Abolitionism.* Chapel Hill: University of North Carolina Press, 2006.

Burnard, Trevor. *Mastery, Tyranny, and Desire: Thomas Thistlewood and His Slaves in the Anglo-Jamaica World.* Chapel Hill: University of North Carolina Press, 2004.

Byrd, Alexander. *Captives and Voyagers: Black Migrants across the Eighteenth-Century British Atlantic World.* Baton Rouge: Louisiana State University Press, 2008.

Cantir, Cristian. "'Savages in the Midst': Revolutionary Haiti in International Society." *Journal of International Relations and Development* 20, no. 1 (2017): 238–61.

Caruth, Cathy. *Unclaimed Experience: Trauma, Narrative, and History.* Baltimore: Johns Hopkins University Press, 1996.

Casimir, Jean. *The Haitians: A Decolonial History.* Translated by Laurent Dubois. Chapel Hill: University of North Carolina Press, 2020.

———. *La culture opprimée.* Delmas, Haiti: Communication Plus, 1981.

Chatterjee, Indrani. "Abolition by Denial: The South Asian Example." In *Abolition and Its Aftermath in Indian Ocean Africa and Asia,* edited by Gwyn Campbell. London: Routledge, 2005.

Chidester, David. *Empire and Religion: Imperialism and Comparative Religion.* Chicago: University of Chicago Press, 2014.

Conrad, Joseph. *Heart of Darkness.* 1899. Reprint, New York: Heritage Press, 1969.

Cooper, Anna Julia. *A Voice from the South.* Xenia, OH: Aldine Printing House, 1892.

Cooper, Frederick. *Plantation Slavery on the East Coast of Africa.* New Haven, CT: Yale University Press, 1977.

Cooper, Frederick, Thomas C. Holt, and Rebecca J. Scott. *Beyond Slavery: Explorations of Race, Labor, and Citizenship in Postemancipation Societies.* Berkeley: University of California Press, 2000.

Craton, Michael. *Testing the Chains: Resistance to Slavery in the British West Indies.* Ithaca, NY: Cornell University Press, 1982.

Cuffe, Paul. *Captain Paul Cuffe's Logs and Letters, 1808–1817: A Black Quaker's "Voice from within the Veil."* Washington, DC: Howard University Press, 1996.

Cugoano, Quobana Ottobah. *Thoughts and Sentiments on the Evil of Slavery.* 1787. Reprint, New York: Penguin, 1999.

Curtin, Philip. *The Rise and Fall of the Plantation Complex.* Cambridge: Cambridge University Press, 1998.

Daut, Marlene. *Baron De Vastey and the Origins of Black Atlantic Humanism.* New York: Palgrave Macmillan, 2017.

Davis, David Brion. *The Problem of Slavery in the Age of Emancipation.* New York: Alfred A. Knopf, 2014.

de la Fuente, Alejandro. *Becoming Free, Becoming Black: Race, Freedom, and Law in Cuba, Virginia, and Louisiana.* Cambridge: Cambridge University Press, 2020.

Delany, Martin. *Blake, or, the Huts of America.* London: Harvard University Press, 2017.

Dike, K. Onwuka. *Trade and Politics in the Niger Delta, 1830–1885.* Oxford: Oxford University Press, 1956.

Domingues da Silva, Daniel, David Eltis, Philip Misevich, and Olantunji Ojo. "The Diaspora of Africans Liberated from Slave Ships in the Nineteenth Century." *Journal of African History* 55, no. 3 (2014): 347–69.

Douglass, Frederick. *Narrative of the Life of Frederick Douglass.* 1845. Reprint, New York: Penguin, 2014.

Draper, Nicholas. *The Price of Emancipation: Slave-Ownership, Compensation and British Society at the End of Slavery.* Cambridge: Cambridge University Press, 2010.

Drescher, Seymour. *Abolition: A History of Slavery and Antislavery.* Cambridge: Cambridge University Press, 2009.

Du Bois, W. E. B. *Black Reconstruction in America.* 1935. Reprint, New York: Free Press, 1998.

———. *The Philadelphia Negro: A Social Study.* 1899. Reprint, Philadelphia: University of Pennsylvania Press, 1996.

———. *The Souls of Black Folk.* 1903. Reprint, New York: W. W. Norton, 1999.

Dunham, Katherine. *Island Possessed.* Chicago: University of Chicago Press, 1969.

Easton, Hosea. *A Treatise on the Intellectual Character, and Civil and Political Condition of the Colored People of the United States and the Prejudice Exercised Towards Them.* Boston: I. Knapp, 1837.

Ellison, Ralph. *Invisible Man.* New York: Vintage International, 1995.

———. *Juneteenth: A Novel.* New York: Vintage, 2000.

———. *Shadow and Act.* New York: Random House, 1964.

Eltis, David. *The Rise of African Slavery in the Americas.* West Nyack, NY: Cambridge University Press, 1999.

Engerman, Stanley. *Slavery, Emancipation & Freedom.* Baton Rouge: Louisiana State University Press, 2007.

Equiano, Olaudah. *The Interesting Narrative and Other Writings.* Rev. ed. New York: Penguin Books, 2003.

Eudell, Demetrius L. *The Political Languages of Emancipation in the British Caribbean and the U.S. South.* Chapel Hill: University of North Carolina Press, 2002.

Fatah-Black, Karwan. "Urban Slavery in the Age of Abolition: Introduction." *International Review of Social History* 65 (2020): 1–14.

Ferrer, Ada. *Freedom's Mirror: Cuba and Haiti in the Age of Revolution.* Cambridge: Cambridge University Press, 2014.

Fick, Carolyn. *The Making of Haiti: The Saint Domingue Revolution from Below.* Knoxville: University of Tennessee Press, 1990.

Foner, Eric. *The Fiery Trial: Abraham Lincoln and American Slavery.* New York: W. W. Norton, 2010.

———. *Nothing but Freedom: Emancipation and Its Legacy.* Baton Rouge: Louisiana State University Press, 1983.

Forman, James. "The Black Manifesto." *Accounting Historians Journal* 1, no. 1 (1969): 36–44. https://episcopalarchives.org/church-awakens/exhibits/show/specialgc/item/202.

Fouchard, Jean. *The Haitian Maroons: Liberty or Death.* New York: E. W. Blyden Press, 1981.

Fryer, Peter. *Staying Power: The History of Black People in Britain.* London: Pluto Press, 1984.

Gaffield, Julia. *Haitian Connections in the Atlantic World: Recognition after Revolution.* Chapel Hill: University of North Carolina Press, 2015.

Garvey, Marcus. "Jubilee of UNIA." *Negro World* (Harlem), October 30, 1919.

Gaspar, David Barry, and David Patrick Geggus, eds. *A Turbulent Time: The French Revolution and the Greater Caribbean.* Bloomington: Indiana University Press, 1997.

Geggus, David Patrick. *The Impact of the Haitian Revolution in the Atlantic World.* Columbia: University of South Carolina, 2001.

Gellman, David. *Emancipating New York: The Politics of Slavery and Freedom, 1777–1827.* Baton Rouge: Louisiana State University Press, 2006.

Gerzina, Gretchen. *Black London Life before Emancipation.* New Brunswick, NJ: Rutgers University Press, 1995.

Getz, Trevor R., and Clarke Liz. *Abina and the Important Men: A Graphic History.* New York: Oxford University Press, 2016.

Gilroy, Paul. *The Black Atlantic: Modernity and Double Consciousness.* Cambridge, MA: Harvard University Press, 1993.

Gomez, Michael. *Exchanging Our Country Marks: The Transformation of African Identities in the Colonial and Antebellum South.* Chapel Hill: University of North Carolina Press, 1998.

Gonzalez, Johnhenry. *Maroon Nation: A History of Revolutionary Haiti.* New Haven, CT: Yale University Press, 2019.

Gordon, Avery. *Ghostly Matters: Haunting and the Sociological Imagination.* London: University of Minnesota Press, 2008.

Goveia, Elsa. *The West Indian Slave Laws of the 18th Century.* London: Caribbean Universities Press, 1970.

Graden, Dale T. *Disease, Resistance, and Lies: The Demise of the Transatlantic Slave Trade to Brazil and Cuba.* Baton Rouge: Louisiana State University Press, 2014.

Green, William. *British Slave Emancipation: The Sugar Colonies and the Great Experiment, 1830–1865.* Oxford: Clarendon Press, 1976.

Greene, Lorenzo Johnson. *The Negro in Colonial New England, 1620–1776.* New York: Kennikat Press, 1942.

Griggs, Earl Leslie, and Clifford H. Prator, eds. *Henry Christophe & Thomas Clarkson: A Correspondence.* Berkeley: University of California Press, 1952.

Hahn, Steven. *A Nation under Our Feet: Black Political Struggles in the Rural South from Slavery to the Great Migration.* Cambridge: Belknap Press, 2003.

Hall, Stuart. "'Encoding/Decoding.'" In *Culture, Media, Language: Working Papers in Cultural Studies, 1972–79,* edited by the Centre for Cultural Studies, 128–38. 1973. Reprint, London: Hutchinson, 1980.

Hamilton, Alexander, James Madison, and John Jay. *The Federalist Papers.* 1788. Harmondsworth, UK: Penguin, 1987.

Hardesty, Jared Ross. *Black Lives, Native Lands, White Lords: A History of Slavery in New England.* Amherst, MA: Bright Leaf, 2019.

Harney, Stefano, and Fred Moten. *The Undercommons: Fugitive Planning & Black Study.* New York: Minor Compositions, 2013.

Harrington, James. *The Commonwealth of Oceana.* 1656, Reprint, Cambridge: Cambridge University Press, 1992.

Harris, Leslie M. *In the Shadow of Slavery: African Americans in New York City, 1626–1863.* Chicago: University of Chicago Press, 2003.

Hartman, Saidiya V. *Scenes of Subjection: Terror, Slavery, and Self-Making in Nineteenth-Century America.* New York: Oxford University Press, 1997.

Hay, Douglas, and Paul Craven, eds. *Masters, Servants, and Magistrates in Britain and the Empire, 1562–1955.* Chapel Hill: University of North Carolina Press, 2004.

Herndon, Ruth Wallis, and John Murray. *Children Bound to Labor: The Pauper Apprentice System in Early America.* Ithaca, NY: Cornell University Press, 2009.

Heyrick, Elizabeth. *Immediate, Not Gradual Abolition.* London: F. Westley and S. Burton, 1824.

Hickling, Frederick. "Owning Our Madness: Contributions of Jamaica Psychiatry to Decolonizing Global Mental Health." *Transcultural Psychiatry* 57, no. 1 (2020): 19–31.

Higginbotham, Evelyn Brooks. *Righteous Discontent: The Women's Movement in the Black Baptist Church, 1880–1920.* Cambridge, MA: Harvard University Press, 1993.

Higman, B. W. *Slave Populations of the British Caribbean, 1807–1834.* Baltimore: Johns Hopkins University Press, 1984.

Holt, Thomas C. *The Problem of Freedom: Race, Labor, and Politics in Jamaica and Britain, 1832–1938.* Baltimore: Johns Hopkins University Press, 1992.

Hoppit, Julian. "Compulsion, Compensation and Property Rights in Britain, 1688–1833." *Past & Present* 210, no. 1 (2011): 93–128.

Horne, Gerald. *The White Pacific: U.S. Imperialism and Black Slavery in the South Seas after the Civil War.* Honolulu: University of Hawai'i Press, 2007.

Howard, Oliver Otis. *Autobiography.* New York: Baker and Taylor, 1908.

Hudson, Peter James. *Bankers and Empire: How Wall Street Colonized the Caribbean.* Chicago: University of Chicago Press, 2017.

Hughes, Brandi Suzanne. "Middle Passages: The Redemption of African America through the African Mission Field, 1862–1905." Phd diss., Yale University, 2010.

Hunter, Tera W. *To 'Joy My Freedom: Southern Black Women's Lives and Labors after the Civil War.* Cambridge, MA: Harvard University Press, 1997.

Huxtable, Sally-Anne, Corinne Fowler, Christo Kefalas, and Emma Slocombe. *Interim Report on the Connections between Colonialism and Properties Now in the Care of the National Trust.* Swindon, UK: National Trust, 2020.

Ifemesia, C. C. "The 'Civilizing' Mission of 1841." *Journal of the Historical Society of Nigeria* 2 (1962): 291–310.

Inikori, Joseph. "Caribbean Slavery in the Atlantic World." In *Caribbean Slavery in the Atlantic World,* edited by Verene A. Shepherd and Hilary McD. Beckles, 290–308. Princeton, NJ: Markus Wiener, 2000.

James, C. L. R. *The Black Jacobins: Toussaint L'Ouverture and the San Domingo Revolution.* 2d ed., rev. ed. New York: Vintage Books, 1963.

Johnson, Howard. *The Bahamas from Slavery to Servitude: 1783–1933.* Gainesville: University Press of Florida, 1996.

Johnson, Walter. *River of Dark Dreams: Slavery and Empire in the Cotton Kingdom.* Cambridge: Belknap Press of Harvard University Press, 2013.

Jones, Stephanie. *Merchants of the Raj: British Managing Agency Houses in Calcutta Yesterday and Today.* London: Palgrave Macmillan, 1992.

Joseph, Miranda. *Debt to Society: Accounting for Life under Capitalism.* Minneapolis: University of Minnesota Press, 2014.

Kale, Madhavi. *Fragments of Empire: Capital, Slavery, and Indian Indentured Labor Migration in the British Caribbean.* Philadelphia: University of Pennsylvania Press, 1998.

Kelley, Robin D. G. "'A Day of Reckoning': Dreams of Reparations." In *Freedom Dreams: The Black Radical Imagination*, 110–35. Boston: Beacon Press, 2002.

Kytle, Ethan, and Blain Roberts. *Denmark Vesey's Garden: Slavery and Memory in the Cradle of the Confederacy.* New York. New Press, 2019.

Lewis, Mary Dewhurst. "Legacies of French Slave-Ownership, or the Long Decolonization of Saint-Domingue." *History Workshop Journal* 83, no. 1 (2017): 151–75.

Lightfoot, Natasha. *Troubling Freedom: Antigua and the Aftermath of British Emancipation.* Durham, NC: Duke University Press, 2015.

Linebaugh, Peter, and Marcus Rediker. *The Many-Headed Hydra: Sailors, Slaves, Commoners, and the Hidden History of the Revolutionary Atlantic.* Boston: Beacon Press, 2000.

Lott, Eric. *Love and Theft: Blackface Minstrelsy and the American Working Class.* New York: Oxford University Press, 2013.

Lovejoy, Paul. *Transformations in Slavery: A History of Slavery in Africa.* Cambridge: Cambridge University Press, 1983.

Manji, Firoze, and Carl O'Coill. "The Missionary Position: NGOs and Development in Africa." *International Affairs* 78, no. 3 (2002): 567–83.

Manning, Chandra. *Troubled Refuge: Struggling for Freedom in the Civil War.* New York: Penguin, 2016.

Manning, Patrick. *Slavery and African Life: Occidental, Oriental, and African Slave Trades.* Cambridge: Cambridge University Press, 1990.

Marshall, P. J. *The Cambridge Illustrated History of the British Empire.* Cambridge: Cambridge University Press, 1996.

McKeown, Adam. *Melancholy Order: Asian Migration and the Globalization of Borders.* New York: Columbia University Press, 2008.

McKittrick, Katherine. *Demonic Grounds: Black Women and the Cartographies of Struggle.* Minneapolis: University of Minnesota Press, 2006.

Meillassoux, Claude. *The Anthropology of Slavery: The Womb of Iron and Gold.* Translated by Alide Dasnois. Chicago: University of Chicago Press, 1991.

Melish, Joanne Pope. *Disowning Slavery: Gradual Emancipation and "Race" in New England, 1780–1860.* Ithaca, NY: Cornell University Press, 1998.

Midgley, Clare. *Women Against Slavery: The British Campaigns, 1780–1870.* London: Routledge, 1992.

Miki, Yuko. "In the Trial of the Ship." *Social Text* 37, no. 1 (2019): 87–105.

Minardi, Margot. *Making Slavery History: Abolitionism and the Politics of Memory in Massachusetts.* Oxford: Oxford University Press, 2010.

Mintz, Sidney. "Panglosses and Pollyannas; or, Whose Reality Are We Talking About?" In *The Meaning of Freedom: Economics, Politics, and Culture after Slavery*, edited by Frank McGlynn and Seymour Drescher, 245–56. Pittsburgh: University of Pittsburgh Press, 1992.

Mirzoeff, Nicholas. *The Right to Look: A Counterhistory of Visuality.* Durham, NC: Duke University Press, 2011.

Morgan, Jennifer. "'Some Could Suckle over Their Shoulder': Male Travelers, Female Bodies, and the Gendering of Radical Ideology, 1500–1770." *William and Mary Quarterly* 54, no. 1 (1997): 167–92.

Morrison, Toni. *Playing in the Dark.* New York: Vintage, 2007.

Moses, Dirk. *The Problems of Genocide: Permanent Security and the Language of Transgression.* Cambridge: Cambridge University Press, 2021.

Moten, Fred. "Resistance of the Object: Aunt Hester's Scream." In *In the Break: The Aesthetics of the Black Radical Tradition*, 1–24. Minneapolis: University of Minnesota Press, 2003.

Nwokeji, G. Ugo. *The Slave Trade and Culture in the Bight of Biafra*. Cambridge: Cambridge University Press, 2010.

Oshinsky, David. *"Worse Than Slavery": Parchman Farm and the Ordeal of Jim Crow Justice*. New York: Free Press, 1996.

Paiewonsky, Michael. *Conquest of Eden: 1493–1515. Other Voyages of Columbus to Guadeloupe, Puerto Rico, Hispaniola and the Virgin Islands*. Chicago: Academy Chicago, 1993.

Painter, Nell Irvin. *Exodusters: Black Migration to Kansas after Reconstruction*. New York: Knopf, 1976.

Pettigrew, William. *Freedom's Debt: The Royal African Company and the Politics of the Atlantic Slave Trade, 1672–1752*. Chapel Hill: University of North Carolina Press, 2013.

Posner, Richard A. *Economic Analysis of Law*. Boston: Little, Brown, 1986.

Pybus, Cassandra. *Epic Journeys of Freedom: Runaway Slaves of the American Revolution and Their Global Quest for Liberty*. Boston: Beacon Press, 2006.

Ragatz, Lowell. *The Decline of the British West Indies, 1763–1833: A Study in the Fall of the Planter Class*. New York: Century, 1928.

Redkey, Edwin. *Black Exodus: Black Nationalist and Back-to-Africa Movements, 1890–1910*. New Haven, CT: Yale University Press, 1969.

Renda, Mary. *Taking Haiti: Military Occupation and the Culture of U.S. Imperialism, 1915–1940*. Chapel Hill: University of North Carolina Press, 2001.

Rhys, Jean. *Wide Sargasso Sea*. New York: Norton, 1966.

Richards, Jake. "Anti-Slave-Trade Law, 'Liberated Africans' and the State in the South Atlantic World, c. 1839–1852." *Past & Present* 241, no. 1 (2018): 179–219.

Rodney, Walter. "African Slavery and Other Forms of Social Oppression on the Upper Guinea Coast in the Context of the Atlantic Slave-Trade." *Journal of African History* 7, no. 3 (1966): 431–43.

Roediger, David R. *The Wages of Whiteness: Race and the Making of the American Working Class*. London and New York: Verso, 1991.

Rothman, Adam. *Slave Country: American Expansion and the Origins of the Deep South*. Cambridge, MA: Harvard University Press, 2005.

Sale, Maggie Montesinos. *The Slumbering Volcano: American Slave Ship Revolts and the Production of Rebellious Masculinity*. Durham, NC: Duke University Press, 1997.

Scanlan, Padraic X. *Freedom's Debtors: British Anti-Slavery in Sierra Leone in the Age of Revolution*. New Haven, CT: Yale University Press, 2017.

Schaller, Dominik. "Genocide and Mass Violence in the 'Heart of Darkness': Africa in the Colonial Period." In *Genocide Studies and Prevention: An International Journal*, edited by Dirk Moses and Donald Bloxham. Oxford: Oxford University Press, 2012.

Schmidt-Nowara, Christopher. *Slavery, Freedom, and Abolition in Latin America and the Atlantic World*. Albuquerque: University of New Mexico Press, 2011.

Scott, Julius. *The Common Wind: Afro-American Currents in the Age of the Haitian Revolution*. London: Verso, 2018.

Scott, Rebecca J. "Gradual Abolition and the Dynamics of Slave Emancipation in Cuba, 1868–86." *Hispanic American Historical Review* 63: 3, 1993, 447–77.

Sharp, Granville. *Memoirs of Granville Sharp*. 1820. Reprint, London: Henry Colburn, 1828.

———. *A Representation of the Injustice and Dangerous Tendency of Tolerating Slavery.* London, 1769.

———. *A Short Sketch of Temporary Regulations (until Better Shall Be Proposed) for the Intended Settlement on the Grain Coast of Africa, near Sierra Leone.* London: H. Baldwin, 1788.

———. *"The System of Colonial Law" Compared with the Eternal Laws of God.* London: R. Edwards, 1807.

Sharpe, Christina. *In the Wake: On Blackness and Being.* Durham, NC: Duke University Press, 2016.

Shepherd, Verene A. "Past Imperfect, Future Perfect? Reparations, Rehabilitation, Reconciliation." *Journal of African American History* 13, no. 12 (2018): 19–43.

Shepperson, George. *Independent African: John Chilembwe and the Origins, Setting and Significance of the Nyasaland Native Rising of 1915.* Edinburgh: Edinburgh University Press, 1969.

Smallwood, Stephanie. *Saltwater Slavery: A Middle Passage from Africa to American Diaspora.* Cambridge, MA: Harvard University Press, 2007.

Smith, Thomas E. *Emancipation without Equality: Pan-African Activism and the Global Color Line.* Amherst: University of Massachusetts Press, 2018.

Stuckey, Sterling. *Slave Culture: Nationalist Theory and the Foundations of Black America.* New York: Oxford University Press, 1987.

Temperley, Howard. *After Slavery: Emancipation and Its Discontents.* London: Frank Cass, 2000.

Thompson, E. P. *The Making of the English Working Class.* London: V. Gollancz, 1963.

Tomich, Dale. *Through the Prism of Slavery: Labor, Capital, and World Economy.* Lanham, MD: Rowman and Littlefield, 2003.

Trouillot, Michel-Rolph. *Haiti: State Against Nation.* Boston: Beacon Press, 1990.

———. *Silencing the Past: Power and the Production of History.* Boston: Beacon Press, 1995.

Tyson, Thomas, David Oldroyd, and Richard Fleischman. "Accounting, Coercion and Social Control during Apprenticeship: Converting Slave Workers to Wage Workers in the British West Indies, c. 1834–1838." *Accounting Historians Journal* 32, no. 2 (2005): 201–31.

Vasconcellos, Colleen. *Slavery, Childhood, and Abolition in Jamaica, 1788–1838.* Athens: University of Georgia Press, 2015.

Walcott, Rinaldo. *The Long Emancipation: Moving toward Black Freedom.* Durham, NC: Duke University Press, 2021.

Walker, Cam. *Corinth: The Story of a Contrband Camp.* Kent, OH: Kent State University Press, 1974.

Walker, David. *Appeal, in Four Articles.* 1829. Reprint, New York: Hill and Wang, 1965.

Walker, James W. St. G. *The Black Loyalists: The Search for a Promised Land in Nova Scotia and Sierra Leonne. 1783–1870.* Toronto: Toronto University Press, 1992.

Walvin, James. *Crossings: Africa, the Americas and the Atlantic Slave Trade.* London: Reaktion Books, 2013.

Wastell, R. E. P. "The History of Slave Compensation, 1833 to 1845." M.A. thesis, University of London, 1932.

Wedderburn, Robert. "The Horrors of Slavery, and Other Writings." Edited by Iain McCalman. 1824. Reprint, Princeton, NJ: Markus Wiener, 2017.

Wells, Jonathan Daniel. *The Kidnapping Club: Wall Street, Slavery, and Resistance on the Eve of the Civil War.* New York: Bold Type Books, 2020.

Wesley, Dorothy Porter, ed. *Early Negro Writing, 1760–1837.* Boston: Beacon Press, 1971.

White, Shane. *Stories of Freedom in Black New York.* Cambridge, MA: Harvard University Press, 2002.

Whitfield, Harvey Amani. *The Problem of Slavery in Early Vermont, 1777–1810.* Barre: Vermont Historical Society, 2014.

Wilder, Craig Steven. *In the Company of Black Men: The African Influence on African American Culture in New York City.* New York: New York University, 2001.

Wilkerson, Isabel. *Caste: The Origins of Our Discontents.* New York: Random House, 2020.

Williams, Eric. *Capitalism and Slavery.* New York: Russell and Russell, 1944.

Williams, James. "A Narrative of Events, since the First of August 1834." Edited by Diana Paton. 1837. Reprint, Durham, NC: Duke University Press, 2001.

Williams, Patricia. *The Alchemy of Race and Rights.* Cambridge, MA: Harvard University Press, 1992.

Wilson, Harriet E. *Our Nig, or, Sketches from the Life of a Free Black, in a Two-Story White House, North, Showing That Slavery's Shadows Fall Even There.* Boston: Rand and Avery, 1859.

Wolesley, Garnet. *The America Civil War: An English View.* Charlottesville: University of Virginia, 1964.

Woods, Clyde. *Development Arrested: The Blues and Plantation Power in the Mississippi Delta.* London: Verso, 1998.

Wynter, Sylvia. "Black Metamorphosis." Unpublished. Schomburg Center for Research in Black Culture, New York Public Library.

Yoshpe, Harry. "Record of Slave Manumissions in New York during the Colonial and Early National Periods." *Journal of Negro History* 26, no. 1 (1941): 78–107.

Younger, Karen Virginia Fischer. "'African Stretches Forth Her Hands unto You': Female Colonization Supporters in the Antebellum United States," PhD diss. Pennsylvania State University, 2006.

Zilversmit, Arthur. *The First Emancipation: The Abolition of Slavery in the North.* Chicago: University of Chicago Press, 1967.

PHOTO CREDITS

1. Oil portrait by unidentified artist held by the Royal Albert Museum in Exeter, UK.
2. European magazine of 1816. Obtained from the Charles Sumner Scrapbook, MS Am 108. Houghton Library, Harvard University.
3. Courtesy of the John Carter Brown Library.
4. From Amelia Opie, *The Black Man's Lament, or, How to Make Sugar* (London: Harvey and Darnton, 1826).
7. T51/285, National Archives of the United Kingdom.
8. *Jaw-Bone, or House John-Canoe,* From Isaac Mendes Belisario, *Sketches of Character in the Island of Jamaica: Drawn After Nature, and in Lithography* (1837–38). *Slavery Images: A Visual Record of the African Slave Trade and Slave Life in the Early African Diaspora.* http://www.slaveryimages.org/s/slaveryimages/item/2311.
9. *Treadmill, Jamaica, 1837.* This engraving first appeared in James Williams's *A Narrative of Events Since the First of August 1834* (London, 1837). *Slavery Images: A Visual Record of the African Slave Trade and Slave Life in the Early African Diaspora.* http://www.slaveryimages.org/s/slaveryimages/item/1297.
10. *La rebellion d'un escalve sur un navire négrier.* Musée du Nouveau Monde, La Rochelle, France.
11. National Archives of the United States (M433:1).
12. Library of Congress, LC-DIG-pga-03898.
13. Engraving from Ernst von Hesse-Wartegg's *Mississippi-Fahrten* (1881).
14. David and Charles Livingstone, *Narrative of an Expedition to the Zambesi* (1866).

15. David and Charles Livingstone, *Narrative of an Expedition to the Zambesi* (1866).
16. Courtesy of Spelman College Archives.
17. Courtesy of Spelman College Archives.
18. W. E. B. Du Bois Papers (MS 312). Special Collections and University Archives, University of Massachusetts Amherst Libraries.

INDEX

INDEX

INDEX

Cugoano, Ottobah, 83–84, 89, 91, 181, 187

Cunliffe family, 73

Dartmouth, Mass., 16

Davidson, William (Black Davidson), 87–88, 90, 181

Davis Bend, Miss., 135

Dawkins family, 74

Dawkins-Pennant, George Hay, 108

Delaney, Emma Beard, 180

Delany, Martin Robison, 170–73, 193

Delaware, 24, 25, 119, 131

Delmé, Peter, 72

Dessalines, Jean-Jacques ("the African"), 55–56, 60, 65, 66

Dominica, 107, 110

Douglass, Frederick, 122–23, 128, 131, 134, 137–38, 209

Dred Scott v. Sandford, 27, 39

Drescher, Seymour, 5

Du Bois, W. E. B., 2, 43–44, 123, 127, 168–69, 181, 183–84

Dundas, Henry, 84–85

Dunmore, Lord, 15

Dunn, Oscar, 140

Dutch colonies, 18

Dutch Mennonitism, 17

East Africa, British, 177

East Africa, slave trade in, 150

East India Company, British, 107, 163

Easton, Hosea, 37–38

Eaton, John, 132–33

Ecuador, 26

Eddoo, Quamina, 176

Edisto Island, S.C., 135

Elgin, James Bruce, Earl of, 111

Ellison, Ralph, 4, 192–93

emancipation:

  etymology of word, 6

  insistence on indebtedness of freed people in, 6, 8, 18, 19–20, 45, 57–58, 61–64, 66, 81, 99–100, 111, 133, 140–41, 144, 156, 188

manumission vs., 18; *see also* manumission

as pretext for colonial conquest and occupation, 9, 70–72, 97, 99–100, 147–49, 151–55, 158, 161–64, 167–68, 173–78, 180

by revolution, *see* Haitian Revolution

by sea, 156–61

slave-owner compensation in, *see* compensated emancipation

as systematic extension of war against African peoples, 1, 5–6, 8, 81–82, 97, 99, 126, 140–41, 142, 148–49, 151–52, 186

see also gradual emancipation; retroactive emancipation; war emancipation

Emancipation Day celebrations, 190–91

Emancipation Proclamation, U.S. (1863), 125, 132, 190, 193

  preliminary, 131

Emmanuel Appadocca (Philip), 112–13

Enclosure Acts, British, 86

English in the West Indies, The (Froude), 59–60

Equiano, Olaudah, 87, 89, 154

Essay on Slavery, An (Clarkson), 82

Europe, imperial, 8, 25, 45, 53, 60, 66, 69, 70, 72, 74, 86, 97, 174, 187, 188

  emancipation as pretext for conquest and occupation by, 70–72, 97, 99, 107–9, 151–55, 161–68, 174–77, 180

  slavery system of, *see* black people, enslaved; plantations, plantation economies; slavery; slave trade

  staggering death toll of blacks in, 180

  see also British Empire

Faneuil family, 14

Fante Confederation, 170

Fatiman, Cécile, 51

Federalist Papers, 118

Female Anti-Slavery Society, British, 92–93

Fetishism in West Africa (Nassau), 166

Fifteenth Amendment, 125

Fisk University, 43

Fleming, Louise, 179

Foote, Julia, 27

Forman, James, 188

"forty acres and a mule," 136, 143

INDEX

INDEX

INDEX

INDEX

ABOUT THE AUTHOR

Kris Manjapra was born in the Caribbean of African and Indian parentage. He grew up in Canada and completed his undergraduate and graduate degrees at Harvard. He is a professor of history at Tufts University and a recipient of the 2015 Emerging Scholar Award from *Diverse* magazine. He has held fellowships at the Berlin Institute for Advanced Study, at the Radcliffe Institute for Advanced Study, and at UCLA. He lives in Boston.